Politics, Planning and Homes in a World City

This is an insightful study of spatial planning and housing strategy in London, focusing on the period 2000–2008 and the mayoralty of Ken Livingstone. Duncan Bowie presents a detailed analysis of the development of Livingstone's policies and their consequences.

Examining the theory and practice of spatial planning at a metropolitan level, Bowie explores the relationships between:

- planning, the residential development market and affordable housing;
- environmental, economic and equity objectives;
- national, regional and local planning agencies and their policies.

The book places Livingstone's mayoralty within its historical context and looks forward to the different challenges faced by Livingstone's successors in a radically changed political and economic climate.

Clear and engaging, this critical analysis provides a valuable resource for academics and their students as well as planning, housing and development professionals. It is essential reading for anyone interested in politics and social change in a leading 'world city' and provides a base for parallel studies of other major metropolitan regions.

Duncan Bowie is Reader in Urban Planning and Regeneration at London Metropolitan University. He has worked in London for thirty years as a professional housing strategist and planner, most recently developing the housing policies for the Mayor's London Plan and also as analyst of its implementation.

Housing, Planning and Design Series

Editors: Nick Gallent and Mark Tewdwr-Jones
UCL Bartlett School of Planning

This series of books explores the interface between housing policy and practice, and spatial planning, including the role of planning in supporting housing policies in the countryside, the pivotal role that planning plays in raising housing supply, affordability and quality, and the link between planning/housing policies and broader areas of concern including homelessness, the use of private dwellings, regeneration, market renewal and environmental impact. The series positions housing and planning debates within the broader built environment agenda, engaging in a critical analysis of different issues at a time when many planning systems are being modernized and prepared for the challenges facing twenty-first-century society.

Housing Market Renewal and Social Class
Chris Allen

Decent Homes for All
Nick Gallent and Mark Tewdwr-Jones

Planning and Housing in the Rapidly Urbanising World
Paul Jenkins, Harry Smith and Ya Ping Wang

International Perspectives on Rural Homelessness
Edited by Paul Cloke and Paul Milbourne

Housing in the European Countryside
Rural pressure and policy in Western Europe
Edited by Nick Gallent, Mark Shucksmith and Mark Tewdwr-Jones

Private Dwelling
Contemplating the use of housing
Peter King

Housing Development
Andrew Golland and Ron Blake

Politics, Planning and Homes in a World City
Duncan Bowie

Politics, Planning and Homes in a World City

Duncan Bowie

Routledge
Taylor & Francis Group

LONDON AND NEW YORK

First published 2010
by Routledge
2 Park Square, Milton Park, Abingdon, Oxon OX14 4RN

Simultaneously published in the USA and Canada
by Routledge
270 Madison Avenue, New York, NY 10016, USA

Routledge is an imprint of the Taylor & Francis Group, an informa business

© 2010 Duncan Bowie

Typeset in Galliard by Prepress Projects Ltd, Perth, UK
Printed and bound in Great Britain by TJ International Ltd, Padstow,
Cornwall

British Library Cataloguing in Publication Data
A catalogue record for this book is available from the British Library

Library of Congress Cataloging in Publication Data
A catalog record for this book has been requested

ISBN10: 0-415-48636-X (hbk)
ISBN10: 0-415-48637-8 (pbk)
ISBN10: 0-203-85557-4 (ebk)

ISBN13: 978-0-415-48636-1 (hbk)
ISBN13: 978-0-415-48637-8 (pbk)
ISBN13: 978-0-203-85557-7 (ebk)

Contents

Foreword

Anyone who is seriously interested in the subject of London's governance – and that should include any serious Londoner – ought to look inside Duncan Bowie's book and try to distil its lessons. For, despite many excellent previous contributions from academic political scientists, this is the first time that any researcher has examined in such depth and such detail the story which began with the Greater London Act of 1999 and the election of Ken Livingstone as London's first Mayor a year later. Not only did this give London a completely new system of strategic planning through the mechanism of a single elected mayor; it was the first time that such a system, based on American models, had ever been attempted in this country. And the new mayor was not only given very wide responsibilities, later enlarged, to prepare and regularly revise an overall spatial strategic plan for London; he was also charged with overall responsibility for very major agencies – for London's transport, its development, and (through an uneasy shared arrangement with central government) its policing.

Many openly doubted at the time whether such a bold and unprecedented reform could work in practice. As many previous studies have shown, London has never proved a very governable entity. That it did prove to work, that it did survive multifarious political pressures and political crises, finally to result in a smooth transition from London's first Mayor to his political opponent, is testimony to the fact that a decade later the experiment has worked.

Duncan Bowie's book tells the story in rich detail, culminating in the mayoral election and handover of 2008. It is essential reading for students of government and planning, not only in London and more widely in the United Kingdom but in other great cities across the world. But it should find a wider audience among those curious to understand a great and finally successful innovation in democratic urban governance.

Sir Peter Hall
Bartlett Professor of Planning and Regeneration, UCL
October 2009

Preface

This work draws on some thirty years' experience working for public sector agencies on housing strategy and spatial planning in London. I must, however, first acknowledge the work of my colleagues in the Mayor's London Plan team between 2002 and 2007, especially Debbie McMullen, John Lett, David Taylor-Valiant, Eleanor Young and Alex Bax. I am also appreciative of comments on drafts from, or more informal discussions with, a number of professional and academic colleagues, including Christine Whitehead, Michael Edwards, Michael Bach and Peter Eversden. The work draws on the writings of a number of scholars of London planning, including Andrew Thornley, Mike Hebbert, Peter Newman, Michael Collins, Yvonne Rydin and Sir Peter Hall. I would also wish to record my thanks to London Metropolitan University for appointing me to a post which allowed me the time and space to write this book.

My special thanks go to Julia Atkins, my colleague at London Metropolitan University and collaborator for nearly thirty years as we have moved between various agencies within the London governance structure, both for her contribution to planning and housing practice and for her help on the book. My thanks to the series editors, Mark Tewdwr-Jones and Nick Gallent, for accepting into their series a book which is more of a case study than a thematic text book. I of course take responsibility both for the opinions expressed as well as any remaining errors in the book. I hope that the former Mayor, Ken Livingstone, and his deputy, Nicky Gavron, both accept this book as the politically neutral and at least semi-independent analysis intended. I learned much from working with them and appreciate the opportunity I was given to work for five years at the centre of such an important innovation in spatial planning.

I also acknowledge permission by the Greater London Authority and the Government Office for London to reprint images from the London Plan and related documents. My appreciation also of the contribution made by Catherine Lynn and colleagues at Routledge to getting the work through the publication process.

I should also thank my family, Jackie, Jenny and Chris, for putting up with my hogging of the computer and covering the floor with books and papers.

Duncan Bowie
London, June 2009

Introduction

The main purpose of this book is to examine the impact of the Mayor of London's spatial planning powers on housing in London between 2000 and 2008. The book is a case study of a new form of regional governance and of the inter-relationship between spatial planning and housing strategy at regional level. It is also a study of how spatial planning in a world city responds to the pressures of population and economic growth.

The Greater London Authority (GLA) was created in 2000 as a new form of strategic citywide government for London. It consists of an elected Mayor and a separately elected Assembly. The Mayor of London between May 2000 and April 2008 was Ken Livingstone, elected initially as an Independent and then re-elected as a Labour candidate in 2004. On 1 May 2008, he was succeeded by Boris Johnson, the Conservative candidate.

This book will examine both the outputs and outcomes of spatial planning and housing strategy during this period and will draw lessons which may be applicable to other world cities, which face similar challenges of economic and demographic change.

The structure of the book is as follows.

Chapter 1 contextualizes the study by setting out London's position as a world city at the beginning of the twenty-first century, reviewing the existing academic literature on theory and practice of spatial planning, and considering previous studies of planning in London and other world cities.

Chapter 2 reviews the development of strategic planning arrangements for London before the establishment of the mayoralty and the Greater London Authority in 2000.

Chapter 3 sets out the framework for the new structure of regional governance in London as it impacts on housing policy and considers some of the early initiatives of the Mayor and the London Assembly to consider housing policy issues.

Chapter 4 sets out the process for developing the spatial planning policies within the London Plan, focusing on policies relating to housing. This covers the inheritance from the predecessor bodies, including the London Planning Advisory Committee, the initial research undertaken by the GLA and the process of taking the Plan from draft through public consultation, public inquiry and adoption.

Chapter 5 reviews the process from adoption to implementation, reviewing the process of preparing and the content of the detailed planning guidance on housing and the mechanisms for ensuring that borough plans and strategic planning applications were in conformity with the Mayor's policies.

Chapter 6 considers the effectiveness of the Mayor's policies in achieving his housing policy objectives. It analyses trends before and after the adoption of the London Plan in terms of housing and affordable housing outputs, the geographical distribution of residential development, its density and built form.

Chapter 7 examines the process of policy review. It considers the process of the new housing capacity study as a basis for setting increased housing targets and the reviews of density policy and residential space standards. It considers the debates over housing needs assessment, the threshold for application of affordable housing requirements and the impact of the government's new planning policy statement on housing and subsequent technical guidance and considers their application in the London context. The chapter reviews the implications for housing policies and outputs of new policies relating to climate change.

Chapter 8 focuses on the relationship between developing government policy at national level and the specific requirements of London. This includes consideration of government thinking as set out in the reviews of housing supply and planning led by the economist Kate Barker; government policies on the Thames Gateway and growth areas; the nature of sustainable communities; and the importance of transport and social infrastructure. The chapter also considers funding issues, including the level and form of public housing investment and the role of planning obligations.

Chapter 9 considers the role of the Mayor in seeking to plan for significant population growth, which relates in part to increased migration. This includes consideration of the relationship of London to other world cities as well as the debate about residential and employment dispersal within the UK. This looks at both the rationale for the Mayor's positive response to growth and his rejection of the arguments for constraint. This will also consider the conflicts between the Mayor's growth and environmental agendas.

Chapter 10 reviews the experience of the Mayor in using his planning powers to both support and manage the private market. This will include consideration of the extent to which the Mayor has used his planning powers to support market investment and whether this has been consistent with promoting other policy objectives. This will also examine the contrast between the Mayor's approach to market demands within and adjacent to the Central Activities Zone (CAZ) and the approach operated by the Greater London Council under his leadership twenty years earlier.

Chapter 11 considers the impact of spatial planning on the allocation of land and spaces for specific purposes. It considers the relationship between spatial planning and development control, including the extent to which the Mayor's use of his development control powers has been consistent with published spatial planning policies. This will consider the extent to which, in London, the spatial plan, through its status as part of each local planning authority's development plan documentation, has in fact become a development control document in contrast with previous regional planning documents.

Chapter 12 considers the implications of the Mayor's policies on housing and planning for the competing needs of different social and ethnic groups within the increasingly diverse London populations. This includes consideration of the spatial effects of the Mayor's policies in terms of impacting on the geographical distribution of different social groups within London and will assess the extent to which the use of spatial planning powers has reduced or increased social polarization.

Chapter 13 reviews the changing relationships between the Mayor, central government and the local planning authorities within London, including the impact of the 1999 Greater London Act on the balance of power and the significant changes brought into effect by the 2007 Greater London Act. It will review the role of the London Assembly in spatial planning and consider the issue of democratic deficit in the relationship between strategic intervention and local decision making. The chapter will also contrast the position in London with the position in other regions in terms of the strengthening of regional governance in London in relation to the weakening of regional governance in other English regions.

Chapter 14 will relate the practice of spatial planning in London in the period 2000 to 2008 to the different characterisations of spatial planning set out in the theoretical studies considered in the first chapter.

The chapter then assesses the evidence examined in relation to:

- the role and limitations of spatial planning in delivering housing and affordable housing;
- London as a case study for the new approach of combining spatial planning and strategic intervention in development control;
- the practice of combining spatial planning and strategic housing policy.

The chapter considers whether on the evidence of the first two terms of the London mayoralty the overall outputs of the new structures and powers have been positive or negative, and the lessons this may provide for other world cities.

Chapter 1

London and the planning of a world city

London: a 'world city' at the beginning of the twenty-first century

As the new century started, London was generally perceived as being one of a group of six leading world cities, the other members of the elite group being New York, Tokyo, Paris, Moscow and Beijing. Of the two Western European cities, it was widely accepted that London had the more prominent role in the world economy (Sassen 2001). By 2007, there was a lively debate as to whether or not London had overtaken New York in the world ranking, with a report in the *New York Times* in March 2007 (Mcgeehan 2007). London's success in winning the 2012 Olympic Games bid against its French rival was seen as the culmination of London's return to the world stage. This success reflected well on the role of Ken Livingstone, the London Mayor who had campaigned so strongly for the Olympics, bringing on board the country's initially reluctant Prime Minister, Tony Blair.

London's status derived from its role as a European and world financial centre, a role which in effect recreated the nineteenth-century role of imperial capital for an age in which economic control superseded territorial dominance. London's world city status, however, also derived from the extent to which London had become an international city in terms of both its residential and business population. Within its population of 7 million, every nationality and nearly every language in the world was represented. The 2001 census showed that nearly a third of London's population had been born abroad. Thirty-one per cent of London's population belonged to non-white ethnic groups (GLA 2008a). As a metropolitan city, London is diverse but has a reputation for both racial and religious tolerance. This was demonstrated by the response of the Mayor and the population as a whole to the terrorist bombings of July 2005, with the anti-Muslim backlash limited – the diversity of London being apparent in the diverse national, racial and religious affiliations of the bombs' victims (BBC 2005).

London is nevertheless an unequal and divided city (Hamnett 2003, Fainstein *et al.* 1992, Buck *et al.* 2002, Massey 2007). Spatial divisions between rich and poor have changed little from the Victorian period – the map of the most deprived areas in the Mayor's London Plan shares similarities with the maps prepared by Charles Booth for his study of *Life and Labour of the People in London* at the end of the nineteenth century (GLA 2004a, Booth 1886–1903). The extent of social polarization is also reflected in the variations in household income across London. This is mirrored in the spatial distribution of housing tenure and the distribution of property values.

The main challenge faced by the Mayor in 2000 was significant population growth. Although not matching the growth rates of cities in the developing world such as Mumbai, Jakarta or Mexico City, the projected population growth in London from 7.3 million to 8.7 million people between 2003 and 2026, an increase of 1.4 million, nevertheless generated a requirement for a considerable increase in both housing and social infrastructure. The geographical boundary of London is tightly drawn, with the sprawl of London protected by restrictive planning policies including the 'Green Belt'. As will be discussed below, the Mayor was to support and in fact seek to respond positively to this growth agenda, while asserting that the growing needs of London could and would be met within the existing London boundary. Although the Mayor was to have difficulty providing sufficient evidence to demonstrate that this was achievable, this response, following from the perspective adopted by both the central government and predecessor bodies such as the London Planning Advisory Committee (LPAC), was not subject to a comprehensive critique. The relationship between London and the wider metropolitan region is, however, an issue which requires fuller consideration.

The re-establishment of a regional authority for London in 2000 was based on an ongoing recognition that strategic governance arrangements were necessary for a world city. The debate over governance arrangements for London has been lengthy and the subject of a number of academic studies (Davis 1988, Rhodes 1970, Forrester *et al.* 1985). There has always been a tension between local borough-level governance, a regional tier and central government. Although a Metropolitan Board of Works (MBW) had operated since 1855, the establishment of the London County Council (LCC) in 1889 can be seen as the first significant advance for the principle of regional government, with the establishment of the Greater London Council (GLC) in 1964 extending the geographical remit of this strategic body to the whole Greater London area. The abolition of the GLC in 1986 by Margaret Thatcher's Conservative government was a party political decision rather than one supported by logic or analysis. The abolition of the Labour-controlled GLC was accompanied by the winding up of the six midlands and northern Metropolitan County Councils, which were also Labour controlled. Margaret Thatcher did not need a Royal Commission to consider governance options before reaching her decision. She combined a belief in strong central government at a national level with an advocacy of local decision making, supporting localism and the protection

Map 1.1 London boroughs map. Source: Government Office for London. Crown Copyright. Crown Copyright material reproduced under the terms of the Click-use Licence by permission of the Office of Public Sector Information (OPSI).

of the suburban, mainly conservative (if not all Conservative party-controlled) boroughs and districts against the demands of the mainly Labour-controlled and more deprived inner city areas.

The re-establishment of a new Londonwide authority in 2000 was primarily in response to representations from London business, represented through London First, that a world city required some form of regional advocacy. New York, Berlin, Paris, Tokyo and Moscow had their Mayors. Why not London (Travers 2004)? The London Labour party, which included politicians who had been leading members of the GLC, campaigned vigorously for the re-establishment of a Londonwide authority to be included as a commitment in national Labour party manifestos, with the result that it was in the 1997 manifesto. As will be considered in Chapter 2, the Londonwide cross-party planning advisory body, LPAC, also advocated the re-establishment of an elected regional planning authority.

It is not unreasonable to comment that the re-establishment of a structure for London governance was not the highest priority for Tony Blair's New Labour government. It was the Conservative Major government which in 1994 had established a Government Office for London (GOL) to coordinate the work of national government departments in the capital. Labour ministers, like their predecessors, seemed reasonably comfortable with the direct relationship they and GOL had with the thirty-two boroughs and the City Corporation. The emphasis on public sector reform was based on direct relationships with the service providers such as hospitals and schools, and in fact over time the central government increasingly bypassed local authorities. Whereas the government acknowledged the need for a London advocate, it was not enthusiastic about creating a new regional agency with significant powers which would challenge central government, as the GLC had done, or annoy the boroughs, as the GLC had also done. The focus of the Greater London Authority Bill, piloted through parliament by the local government minister, Nick Raynsford, was in fact to constrain the powers of the Mayor. The creation of the London mayoralty was regarded as more of a symbolic act than a significant shift in the balance of power. The first Mayor was not to share this understanding.

Spatial planning in theory and in practice

Much of the extensive literature on the theory of planning and the role of theory in the revival of strategic spatial planning predates the introduction of the new framework for spatial planning in England in the 2004 Planning and Compulsory Purchase Act. Some more recent works do, however, reflect the introduction of new approaches in spatial planning within continental Europe, which both inspired and were promoted by the European Spatial Development Perspective published in 1999 (CEC 1999). Allmendinger (2002) sought to categorize approaches to planning theory into seven schools: systems theory, Marxist critical theory, new right theory, pragmatism, advocacy, postmodern and collaborative.

The application of *systems theory* to planning was expanded in Faludi's seminal work (1973). This promoted a systems approach derived from cybernetics and became a popular concept within the then emerging discipline of corporate management in the public and private sectors, as the only basis on which planners should proceed in their role as technocratic leaders. In retrospect this approach can be viewed as combining the belief in technocratic superiority of Sidney and Beatrice Webb with the futurology of H. G. Wells. This is perhaps unsurprising given the links between cybernetics and the US military and space programmes.

The most consistent advocate of the application of *critical theory* to planning and urban governance has been David Harvey. His approach to urban geography, set out in his initial classic work *Social Justice and the City* (Harvey 1973), has influenced a range of disciplines, including spatial planning and governance, as well as urban history, economics and international relations. Harvey's approach was followed by a number of academic planners in Britain including the team led by Patsy Healey who produced a set of conference papers as a critique of rationalist approaches (Healey *et al.* 1982). In this context, it is perhaps appropriate to recognize that a critique of the rationalist approach could be derived from active political engagement in the planning process as well as from a more purely academic theoretical approach. In the same period, another academic planner was seeking to apply critical theory of planning practice to a real life case study – the city of Oxford (Simmie 1981).

Allmendinger has studied both new right theory (Allmendinger and Thomas 1998) and then postmodern theory in some detail (Allmendinger 2001), a trajectory which itself demonstrates how industrious academics can be in generating new theories to seek to interpret or reflect new times.

New right theory is the term applied to the anti-planning approaches introduced by Margaret Thatcher and Michael Heseltine in the UK in the 1980s, which saw planning as a constraint on economic growth and a restriction on individual rights. It was a component of the neo-liberal approach to rolling back the power of the state and reducing state regulation of corporate and individual activity, and would be more appropriately called 'neo-liberal planning theory'. This led to the creation of simplified planning zones and new undemocratic planning agencies such as the London Docklands Development Corporation. The mid-2000s saw these theories returning as a central component of government ideology and practice under the government of Tony Blair, and they have had a direct impact on the practice of spatial planning in London, as will be demonstrated later in this book.

Postmodernist planning theory is more difficult to define. The term 'postmodern' is more an attempt to describe an epoch than a theory which can be applied to a discipline or practice. Allmendinger's book is after all called *Planning in Postmodern Times* rather than 'Postmodern Planning Theory'. A product of cultural and linguistic theory, the term 'postmodern' is most often used by Marxists disillusioned with Marxism to explain their own predicament and establish a new comfort zone. Postmodernism is in effect defined by what it is not: it is not positivist in that it rejects the concept that society is progressing in a positive direction. It argues that historical development can also be regressive and that society as a whole is fragmented and complex. Allmendinger is right to conclude that postmodernist theory cannot easily be incorporated into planning theory and consequently can have little impact on planning practice. It has been something of an unnecessary and unhelpful diversion.

Healey has set out the *collaborative* approach (Healey 1997), though this is later redefined as 'relational' planning, drawing on more recent European approaches and incorporating more 'institutionalist' approaches to the relationship between governance and spatial planning (Healey 2007).

Pragmatism in planning might not normally be considered as a separate theoretical approach. As defined by the American, John Dewey, pragmatism is 'the application of critical intelligence to concrete problems, rather than a priori theorising' (Festenstein 1997 p. 24 quoted by Allmendinger 2002 p. 116). Allmendinger considers pragmatism to be deeply theoretical, as the concept of a theoretically neutral decision-making process is itself predicated on a liberal democratic framework, in which planning and planners do not present any challenge to this framework. In contrast, *advocacy planning*, as promoted by Davidoff (1965), explicitly recognizes the power relations and conflicts between the state and citizens and between citizens with different interests. The role of the planner is to assist groups of citizens to play an active role in the democratic process, both by opposing the plans promoted by other parties and through promoting alternative plans. Originating in the United States in the turbulent 1960s, the advocacy approach was the basis for the establishment of the Planning Aid network in the UK.

Allmendinger's categorization of planning theories is largely historic, and is not applied specifically to the new concepts and frameworks for spatial planning. In contrast Salet and Faludi in their introduction to their pan-European study of *The Revival of Strategic Spatial Planning* (Salet and Faludi 2000) set out three different approaches to strategic planning. These are seen as 'streams' rather than narrowly defined categories. The first stream is the *institutionalist* approach. This seeks to relate planning theory to sociological theories of institutions in terms of economic, political and constitutional order, and incorporates Healey's concept of collaborative planning. Salet and Faludi distinguish between approaches which focus on *legitimization* and those which focus on *implementation*. Their second stream is termed the *communicative* or *discursive* turn in planning. This approach views planning as the 'symbolic encapsulation of social aspirations and the establishment of new referents for future action' (p. 8), based on the belief that the construction of a collective consciousness will generate new forms of social coordination. The third stream is termed the *interactive* approach to planning. This sees planning as dependent on the inter-relationship between different actors, recognizing the need for a balance between 'top down' and 'bottom up' planning and a more equal relationship between citizen and state.

This study of spatial planning in London was not preset within any one of these theoretical approaches, primarily because it is a case study of practice rather than an attempt to try to interpret practice through a predetermined theoretical conceptualization. Nevertheless, most of the theories summarized above can be seen as having some relationship to planning in practice, either as descriptors or as tools for analysis, and this will be considered in the concluding chapter.

It is interesting to note Davoudi's comment that recent years have seen an 'asymmetric' development in spatial planning – that, although postmodernist theorists, by way of the European Spatial Development Perspective and the 2004 Planning Act, introduced a new planning framework in England and Wales, based on the concept of 'spatial planning', most practising planners in the UK, whether at regional or district level, still operate on 'positivist' principles.

> The relational concept of spatiality, developed in other disciplines, has been rarely discussed in planning arenas and seldom influenced planning content. Hence, planners' conceptual interpretations of socio-spatial processes have remained surprisingly similar to the ones formed in the mid twentieth century by a positivist view of the world . . . nothing less than a paradigm shift is needed for translating the new relational, fluid and non-bounded understanding of space into the realm of planning practice.
>
> (Davoudi and Strange 2009 p. 243)

We will return in the final chapter to consider the extent to which Davoudi's conclusion applies to the recent trajectory of spatial planning practice in London, our capital and world city, which was to be the first UK city to which the new spatial planning concept was to be applied.

The literature on spatial planning in practice in London and other world cities

There is no comprehensive study of the history of regional planning in London. Michael Hebbert's *London: More by Fortune than Design* (Hebbert 1998) covers the period up to the mid-1990s and has the broader objective of being a history of the development of the city, rather than focusing on regional planning. There are a number of academic studies of specific periods in the London planning process, notably the two studies by Donald Foley (1963, 1972) and the study by Douglas Hart (1976) that cover specific periods or elements in some detail. Michael Collins's chapter in *Planning in London* (Collins 1994) gives the chronology but does not provide an assessment.

There are a number of comparative studies, which generally bring together essays in which each author covers a different world city, with editors attempting to find a common thread. Studies of this kind include *Metropolitan Governance and Spatial Planning* (Salet *et al.* 2003), with some twenty-seven contributors covering nineteen cities and regions, and *Making Strategic Spatial Plans: Innovation in Europe* (Healey *et al.* 1997), which has a total of fifteen different contributors covering some ten cities or regions. This format does not allow for an in-depth analysis within individual case studies. Moreover there is inevitably a focus on planning and governance structures and plan making, rather than on implementation and impact. Single or joint authored works such as Newman and

Thornley's *Planning World Cities* (2005) and Wannop's *The Regional Imperative* (1995), both valuable studies, can suffer from the same search for comparabilities, if to a less serious degree. Peter Hall's *The World Cities* (1966) remains perhaps the most useful as well as readable introductory study, despite being over forty years old.

Other comparative works have a more specialist focus: the numerous world cities studies following the approach of Saskia Sassen (2001) of ranking and categorization; studies which focus on the spatial consequences of economic change such as Andrusz, Harloe and Szelenyi's *Cities after Socialism* (Andrusz *et al.* 1996); or the more recent tradition of spatial analysis examining historical trajectories of urbanization, suburbanization, urban sprawl and re-urbanization in an attempt to project the future – a specialism which seems to be have been developed by academics in postsocialist cities such as Warsaw, Ljubljana and Liverpool. Another approach is to categorize forms of regional governance, contrasting centralized and decentralized regionalism, monocentricity and polycentricity as in Herrschel and Newman's work on the *Governance of Europe's City Regions* (Herrschel and Newman 2002).

There are also volumes of conference papers such as Hambleton and Gross's *Governing Cities in a Global Era* (2007), which seems to lack both theme and conclusion, other than that it comprises papers from academics across the world on contemporary city governance. A cynic could perhaps argue that the term 'globalism' serves primarily as a justification for international conferences. Other comparative studies select components of regional planning such as Peter Clark's edited urban historical comparative study of London and four other northern European cities, *The European City and Green Space* (Clark 2006), Martin Dijst's work on comparative city transport planning, *Governing Cities on the Move* (Dijst 2002), or William Neill's work on *Urban Planning and Cultural Identity* (Neill 2004), which seeks to compare the rather different types of cultural diversity and conflict in Berlin, Detroit and Belfast.

In terms of the academic literature published in English, it is perhaps Paris and New York which are best served, though it is significant that the most detailed studies are of a historical nature. The fullest study which analyses both plan making and impact in a single city is probably David Johnson's *Planning the Great Metropolis* (Johnson 1996), his study of the 1929 Regional Plan for New York, which follows the narrative and the assessment through to the 1960s. The study is supported by the numerous reports of the New York Regional Planning Association, including the Second and Third Regional Plans, as well as by studies of the work of the Regional Planning Association, such as that by Forbes Hays (1965).

Paris is fortunate to have five studies published in English, all of which are of a historical nature. Anthony Sutcliffe's classic study of Haussmann, *The Autumn of Central Paris: The Defeat of Town Planning 1850–1970* (Sutcliffe 1970), and David Pinkney's *Napoleon III and the Rebuilding of Paris* (Pinkney 1953) have now been followed by a fascinating study of an earlier period: Nicholas Papayanis's *Planning Paris before Haussmann* (Papayanis 2004*).* Nineteenth-century Paris is also the subject of the innovative spatial historical analysis of David Harvey in his *Paris: Capital of Modernity* (Harvey 2006), which combines historical, political, cultural and spatial analysis, a combination of which probably no other urban scholar is capable. Norma Evenson's *Paris: A Century of Change (*Evenson 1979) covers the period since Haussmann.

Of other detailed single-region studies, Gerald Burke's study of planning in the western Netherlands, *Greenheart Metropolis* (Burke 1966), remains useful, and for Moscow we have two studies originating in very different periods: E. D. Simon's study of *Moscow in the Making* (Simon 1937), written when the author was chair of Manchester's planning committee, and Timothy Colton's monumental study *Moscow: Governing the Socialist Metropolis* (Colton 1995). There are also useful studies of development of other major cities, including the case studies in the Bellhaven world cities series, regional studies such as the volume on Southern Europe edited by Wynn (1984), the volume on the Nordic countries edited by T. Hall (1991) and more recent studies such as Rowe and Sarkis's of Beirut (Rowe and Sarkis 1998), Broudeheux's of the development of Beijing (2008) and T. Hall's new volume on Stockholm (2008). A work which in my view best combines historical and geographical coverage is Robert Home's *Of Planting and Planning: The Making of British Colonial Cities* (Home 1997), which is masterful in both content and presentation, with British colonialism giving both historical continuity and almost global spatial comparisons. It has be stated that few of these works, with the notable exception of Harvey's work on nineteenth-century Paris, which adopts a critical Marxist perspective, and Mayerson and Banfield's work on Chicago, which adopts an explicit rationalist approach (Mayerson and Banfield 1955), seek to place their case studies within a theoretical framework. The study of planning theory and the study of planning practice have been, to a large extent, independent academic disciplines.

The most helpful previous study of the relationship between politics and planning in London in my view is Savitch's work *Post-Industrial Cities* (Savitch 1988*),* in which his study of London benefits from his comparative studies of Paris and New York. The volume was completed just as the GLC was being abolished, so can only speculate on the fragmentation of governance which followed. It nevertheless provides in its conclusion an analytical framework, to which I will return in the concluding chapter.

This book is neither primarily a historical study nor a comparative study. Although the next chapter does present a historical introduction, the focus of this work is on a single city, London, and on a limited time period: the eight-year term of Ken Livingstone as Mayor between 2000 and 2008. The new mayoral governance arrangements introduced for London in 2000 were based on a recognition that, without regional government, London as a world city was different from its peers. Although it took some elements from the American city mayor system, it should be recognized that the governance arrangements in London are different; even after the extension of powers introduced in 2008, the powers of the Mayor of London remain much more limited than those of the Mayor of New York, or for that matter, the Mayor of Paris. The UK remains a more centralized state than many other developed countries and, excepting devolution in Scotland, Wales and Northern Ireland, the principle of 'subsidiarity' has only limited application. The main purpose of some of the comparative studies referred to above is to contrast as well as compare; the transference of experience from one context to another may be limited. Whereas world cities may face similar challenges in terms of global economic changes and the increasing transience of the world's population in terms of residence and employment, the policy responses may be different in different contexts.

This book is therefore written primarily for those interested in London – academics and students, politicians, housing, planning and property professionals, as well as other London residents who are interested in what is happening in their city and want to get beyond the tabloid journalism they collect on their way to or from work every day. What is happening in London may nevertheless provide an interesting case study for those involved in or interested in the governance of other world cities in the developed world or even in the developing world – as a demonstration of the limitations of city government, but also of the need to focus on implementation and impacts as well as on advocacy and plan making. Few books on world city planning and governance try to do this. It is hoped that the combination of narrative, data presentation and analysis is of some value to academics and practitioners alike.

Chapter 2
Strategic planning in London before the Mayor

The first substantive plans for rebuilding London were drawn up by Christopher Wren, Robert Hooke and John Evelyn after the Great Fire of London in 1666 (Reddaway 1940, Whinney 1971, Baker 2000, Gilbert 2002, Cooper 2003, Jardine 2004). Other than more localized design and planning initiatives such as the work of John Nash in the area between Regents Park and Piccadilly Circus, there was a vacuum in London planning until the middle of the nineteenth century, with the interesting exception of John Claudius Loudon's pamphlet of 1829, *Breathing Places for the Metropolis*, which promoted a system of concentric green rings around London as part of a comprehensive plan for the metropolis, a plan which could also be applied in new colonial cities (Olsen 1964, Bell and Bell 1972, Summerson 1949, Loudon 1829).

In 1855, the Metropolitan Board of Works was established, with responsibilities relating to roadways, sewerage and water supplies across London. The MBW carried out an impressive programme of civil engineering works, supervised by its chief engineer, Sir Joseph Bazalgette (Halliday 1999). It did not however have an explicit town-planning function. More local projects were the responsibilities of local vestries (Owen 1982).

The London County Council, established in 1889, assumed the powers of the Metropolitan Board of Works, but also had housing powers. Its remit was limited to the County of London, comprising an area roughly equivalent to that now designated as Inner London. In this role, the LCC implemented a significant housing development programme, which complemented that undertaken by the boroughs (Collins 1994, Foley 1963). Planning was recognized as a distinct statutory function only with the 1909 Planning Act, which gave planning powers to the LCC and boroughs. These were extended in further legislation in 1919, which introduced a system of development control and gave the LCC and boroughs the power to prepare plans for undeveloped areas.

The first plan for London was drawn up by Raymond Unwin in 1929 (GLRPC 1929) for the Greater London Regional Planning Committee appointed by the Minister of Health, Neville Chamberlain. The committee comprised 45 members representing the LCC, the City Corporation, six county councils, the Standing

Joint Committee on the Metropolitan boroughs, the three non-London county boroughs of East Ham, West Ham and Croydon, and some 126 borough, urban and rural district councils (Cherry 1980). As well as making the radical proposal that planning should allocate land for development rather than focus on protecting open space, Unwin proposed the establishment of a Joint Regional Planning Authority with powers over major planning decisions. Neither recommendation was pursued. A second report in 1933 (GLRPC 1933) put forward a proposal for a green girdle around London, which was the basis of the Green Belt determined by the Green Belt (London and Home Counties) Act 1938 (Thomas 1970).

In 1943, the LCC published the *County of London Plan* (LCC 1943), for the area under its jurisdiction, prepared by the LCC architect J. H. Forshaw and Patrick Abercrombie, the Professor of Town Planning at University College, London. Drawing on the earlier approach of Patrick Geddes of survey-based planning and neighbourhood units, the plan produced a structure for a cellular organic metropolis. The plan was predicated on the decentralization of population from central London, the protection of open spaces, the systematization of the road network based on road classification and a new policy on residential densities. The Plan also put forward redevelopment proposals for those areas most affected by the blitz: Bermondsey and Stepney.

The City Corporation also took an early initiative to respond to the destruction caused by the blitz within the square mile. In 1944, it published a report of *Preliminary Draft Proposals for Post War Reconstruction in the City of London* (City of London Corporation 1944). This was later expanded by C. H. Horden and William Holford into a classic study which was both a historical analysis and a plan for the future: *City of London: A Record of Destruction and Survival*, which was published in 1947 (Horden and Holford 1947).

Given the geographical limit of the LCC's jurisdiction, a plan for the wider metropolitan areas was also required. Professor Abercrombie was this time commissioned by a Standing Conference on London Regional Planning established by the Minister of Works and Planning, Lord Reith. This *Greater London Plan* (Abercrombie 1944) extended the principles of the County of London Plan to the wider region, with four concentric rings – Inner London, Outer Suburban London, Green Belt and Outer Country, with decreasing density of population and employment – each defined by a ring road. The LCC planning committee, chaired by Lewis Silkin, who later became planning minister in the Attlee government, endorsed the design principles of the plan but not the specific targets for overspill and development density (Hebbert 1998, Young and Garside 1982, Saint 1989).

In the absence of a regional body for the whole of London, the responsibility for coordinating planning in the wider London and Home Counties region remained with the minister, who was none other than Lewis Silkin. Following the enactment of the 1947 Planning Act, the minister issued a Memorandum on London Regional Planning (Ministry of Housing and Local Government 1947), which required local planning authorities in the region to observe the policies in the 1944 Greater London Plan. This endorsed the policy on restraining London's growth, enforcing the Green Belt and implementing the policies of population dispersal and new road networks.

The LCC, using its powers under the new Act and in line with the memorandum, prepared a development plan for the County of London, which was submitted to the Minister for approval in December 1951 (LCC 1951) and, after a public inquiry, was approved in March 1955. The Plan assumed restraint in population growth. It set a framework of density zones of 70, 136 and 200 persons a hectare. It supported a slum clearance programme and comprehensive reconstruction of war-damaged areas. The Plan had a policy of zoning housing and employment sites, based on decentralization of employment as well as providing sites for schools and further education – education services were a LCC responsibility. In 1957, the LCC commenced a review of this plan, with proposals entitled *London Plan* published in 1960 (LCC 1960), and the revised plan was adopted in 1962 (LCC 1962). The main change was restrictions on office development and a reduction in the amount of land zoned for industrial use. There was a new focus on increasing residential development within the county boundary through increased densities, with the densities for some areas of central London being increased, though there were reductions in proposed densities in outer South East London. The plan promoted mixed use in central London and supported some decentralization of employment activity. The main population growth was in Outer London and so the development plans prepared for the nine boroughs with planning responsibilities in the Outer London area, all operating within the framework of the 1944 Greater London Plan, were also of significance.

Responsibility for wider regional planning remained with the central government, which in 1964 published the South East study (Ministry of Housing and Local Government 1964), in 1967 set up a South East Economic Planning Council as a new advisory body and then in 1970 published a Strategic Plan for the South East (Ministry of Housing and Local Government 1967). This plan, the successor to the Abercrombie plan of 1944, represented a policy reversal. Recognizing that the population of the region was in fact now growing, it proposed to meet this demand by planning five new growth areas, all based on strategic corridors: a south Essex growth corridor to Ipswich, a northeast Kent corridor including Ashford (both corridors in fact pre-empting the Thames Gateway and Ashford growth areas of the 2003 Sustainable Communities Plan), a south Hampshire growth area, an M4 growth area west to Reading and beyond (similar to the current Western Wedge), and a northwestern growth corridor to Milton Keynes and Northampton (similar to the M1 corridor proposed in the 2007 London Plan further alterations). A review of this plan in 1978 maintained the overall approach but scaled back the level of growth.

Meanwhile, following the 1960 report by the Herbert Commission, the government structure in London was reorganized in 1965, with the Greater London Council replacing the LCC with strategic planning responsibilities across the whole of Greater London, with local planning responsibilities transferred to thirty-two new London boroughs, which were amalgamations of pre-existing boroughs and districts, and the City of London Corporation. In a separate development, the 1968 Town and Country Planning Act introduced a new distinction between structure plans and local plans, so the new GLC became the structure plan authority, with the boroughs and the City Corporation being responsible for local plans.

Under its new powers, the GLC prepared a Greater London Development Plan (GLDP), as the first structure plan for Greater London (GLC 1969a, Foley 1972). The Plan statement was published in December 1969, supported by a report of studies. The report of studies was a substantial document including detailed studies of population and housing, employment, community services, recreation and open land and transport. The report assumed a continuing fall in population within the area, of between 650,000 and 850,000 people in the twenty-year period 1961 to 1981. The Plan's strategy for housing was therefore to deal with the obsolescence of the housing stock concentrated in Inner London, with the focus on rehabilitation rather than redevelopment, and to plan for the significant redistribution of population to Outer London. The trend of population movement from London to the wider southeast was welcomed as it was seen as 'easing the congestion from which London has suffered' (GLC 1969a para 2.12). The Plan did not propose targets for new housing at either regional or borough level, nor did it review the density policies of previous plans, though it did set out a categorization of areas in terms of the acceptability of high buildings. The Green Belt was to remain protected.

It was the transport proposals rather than any new policies on housing that were to cause controversy. The GLDP put forward proposals for a new primary road network, known as the 'motorway box'. With nearly 20,000 objectors to the plan, the public inquiry ran for a year (Eversley 1973). When the Plan was finally approved by the Secretary of State in July 1976 the motorway box had been abandoned, with the emphasis of the transport policy shifting to public transport. The government, while leaving housing targets as a matter for discussion between the GLC and individual boroughs, introduced into the Plan a new density policy. For family homes with gardens, the Plan proposed an upper limit of 85 habitable rooms an acre, whereas for mixed schemes the limit should be 100 habitable rooms a hectare. It was accepted that 'in central London, at strategic centres and at other locations with easy access to public transport, to open space, or other local facilities' higher densities may be suitable for non-family housing (GLC 1976 para 3.24). The Plan also commented that

> the expectation in regard to housing is that London will have a smaller population which will be better housed enjoying more space and better standards. The population will stop falling when the attractiveness of life in London including the availability of suitable employment, matches the attraction of life elsewhere. So long as London housing is inadequate in size, amenity and environment, and more costly, people will continue to leave in search of more acceptable standards. Thus the housebuilding effort is not only a matter of urgent social necessity but a basic factor in improving the living standards of Londoners.
>
> (GLC 1976 para 3.28)

In 1981, the GLC undertook an appraisal of the GLDP policies (GLC 1981). The main focus of the review was the need, in the light of the decline of London's manufacturing base, to produce plans for economic regeneration, including policies supportive of further office development in the central area. After extensive procedural wrangles with the central government, the GLC, now under an administration led by Ken Livingstone with George Nicholson as chair of the planning committee, published a draft revised plan in December 1983 (GLC 1983). This plan was focused not just on economic regeneration but on supporting those areas of Inner London where the population and employment had declined. The plan therefore designated a number of community areas, mainly on the fringes of the City and Westminster, where policies were aimed at protecting existing communities and stopping development, primarily central area office schemes, which were not regarded as of benefit to local residents (Nicholson 1990, 1992).

The proposals put forward a target of 203,000 homes over the ten-year period 1983 to 1992 (20,300 a year), and for the first time disaggregated the targets between new building and renovation at borough level. These targets were to be incorporated in borough Local Plans. Draft policy H04 also for the first time specified a tenure split: 'In Greater London as a whole the need is for 70% of provision to be for the public sector and 30% for the private sector'. Although the draft plan indicated targets for public sector renovation, it did not prescribe borough-level tenure split targets for the 20,300 new build target. Consultees were invited to propose appropriate figures (GLC 1983 policies H02–H04 and Appendix B footnote). Draft policy H08 in the Plan proposed 'normal maximum density' of 100 habitable rooms per acre (hra) for mixed housing and 85 hra for family housing. The norm minimum density was to be 70 hra. Local Plans were to identify zones in which the 85–100 range 'will be sympathetically considered' (ibid. draft policies H09, HO10). Draft policy H011 proposed that Londonwide 80 per cent of new developments should be houses with gardens, with Local Plans to set borough specific targets. Policy H012 stated that the GLC would set minimum standards for all housebuilding, covering layout, density, design, energy use, insulation and security. The plan also proposed a range of policies supporting renovation and discouraging clearance. A target of 4,500 wheelchair homes over ten years was proposed – equivalent to 2 per cent of proposed supply. Policies supported provision for a range of other housing needs groups and covered the needs of single-person households, the needs of women and the needs of ethnic minorities. A new London Area Mobility Scheme was also proposed. The draft Plan put forward a comprehensive set of planning and housing policies, many of which were to be replicated in the London Plan twenty years later. It could be argued that the continuity between the two documents reflected the role of Ken Livingstone in both administrations but also the continuity of planning advice from officers, notably from Drew Stevenson, who was chief strategic planner at the GLC and then planning advisor to the Mayor.

In September 1984, the GLC submitted a revised version of the new GLDP to the Secretary of State for approval (GLC 1984). The 203,000 target and the thirty-three borough targets were now disaggregated between homes to replace cleared housing (60,000 homes) and net additional dwellings (143,300) so the net target comparable with the later London Plan target was actually 14,300 a year. The 70 per cent public sector target, the density targets and the 80 per cent houses with gardens target were retained. The Plan did not prescribe tenure targets at borough level and this was left to individual boroughs with borough targets 'designed to relate to the need for a range of housing available on appropriate terms in each area' (ibid. para 3.39). As the Plan's preface recognized, the government had already announced its intention to abolish the GLC, and the Local Government (Interim Provisions) Act had already relieved the Secretary of State of his duty to consider proposals to amend the GLDP (ibid. preface). It is therefore not surprising that the Conservative Secretary of State decided not to consider the GLC's proposals and a plan that would have been the most comprehensive and progressive plan for London since 1944 was aborted.

With the abolition of the Greater London Council in April 1986, responsibilities for strategic planning in London returned to the central government (Pimlott and Rao 2002, Newman and Thornley 1997). A London Planning Advisory Committee was established on a statutory basis, comprising representatives of all thirty-three local planning authorities, to give advice to the Secretary of State on the carrying out of this function. Its tasks as laid down by parliament were:

i   To advise the London Boroughs on planning and development issues of common interest to them,

ii   To advise Government Departments on what the Boroughs think about planning and development issues; and

iii   To let local authorities around Greater London, and any bodies on which they and the London boroughs are represented, know what the London boroughs think about the issues.

(LPAC 1988a back cover)

LPAC was originally based in Romford in outer east London, but later moved to near Victoria Street in Westminster, very close to both Whitehall and the House of Commons. Its first chief planning officer was John Popper, who was later succeeded by Robin Clement and then by Martin Simmons. LPAC published a series of research studies and planning guidance, with a *Policy Issues and Choices* report in January 1988 (LPAC 1988a), which after a period of consultation led to *Strategic Planning Advice for London: Policies for the 1990's* being submitted in October 1988 to Nicholas Ridley, the Secretary of State for the Environment in the Thatcher government (LPAC 1988b, Graham and Hibbert 1999). The introduction to the document, signed by Sally Hamwee as chair of LPAC and her Labour and Conservative deputies, stated:

> Ours is a positive approach to London's future. We see the possibility of a city with a healthy economy which offers a high quality of life and opportunity to all its residents. We see some positive trends, achievements and assets. We also see some major problems. Many are to do with the physical environment and with the city's transportation system, but others reflect social and economic problems. We have identified four themes which we believe have made London what it has been at its best – London as a Civilised City, as a World City of Trade, as a City of Residential Neighbourhoods and Communities and as City offering Opportunities for All. We have also attempted to set forth the planning policies that would be necessary to ensure London's success into the next century, for all Londoners.

(LPAC 1988b p. i)

London boroughs were also represented on the South East Regional Planning Conference (SERPLAN), which was responsible for advising the Secretary of State on regional planning guidance for the wider South East region, guidance eventually published as Regional Planning Guidance (RPG9) (DETR 2001). SERPLAN was abolished in 2000 with the establishment of the mayoralty and the new regional assemblies for South East England and East of England, which took over the responsibility for advising the Secretary of State on strategic planning matters.

In 1989, the Secretary of State published the first version of *Strategic Guidance for London* (RPG3) (DoE 1989). The guidance, which was only thirteen pages long, focused on supporting London's economic growth and recognized the importance for the national economy of London's contribution to prosperity. It also gave high priority to the revitalization of older areas, maintaining the viability of town centres, sustaining and improving the amenity of residential districts and protection of the environment (Collins 1994 pp. 126–7, Simmons 2000).

LPAC produced annual reviews of trends and continued with its research programme. In 1991, LPAC published the results of a study by Coopers and Lybrand on the challenges facing London and the need for changes in governance arrangements: *London: World City* (Coopers and Lybrand 1994). By 1994, LPAC had developed a fourfold vision for London, which it set out in the 1994 LPAC Strategic Planning Advice (LPAC 1994a). The components were a strong economy, a good quality of life, a sustainable future and opportunities for all – themes which were to be taken up by the Mayor in his initial objectives for planning in London.

In 1994, as part of a process of regionalizing some central government functions, the Conservative government established the Government Office for London as one of nine government regional offices. A Minister for London was also appointed – John Gummer, who was succeeded by Nick Raynsford when Labour came to power in 1997. GOL acted as advisors to the Secretary of State on strategic planning matters in London, including consideration of borough Unitary Development Plans (UDPs) and call-in of individual planning applications. GOL also became responsible for preparing new regional planning guidance for London. In 2000, Nick Raynsford resigned in order to seek the Labour nomination for Mayor of London, in which he was unsuccessful. His successors, who served as ministers after the mayoral election, were Keith Hill, Jim Fitzpatrick, Tony McNulty and Tessa Jowell, none of whom seem to have had any significant influence on strategic planning in London.

The LPAC 1994 advice informed the revised *Strategic Guidance for London Planning Authorities* (RPG3), which was published by the Government Office for London in May 1996 (GOL 1996). As discussed in Chapter 3 below, whereas the guidance set out a framework for increasing housing supply in London, the only housing target in the guidance was a requirement for boroughs to provide 234,100 homes over the period 1992 to 2006, equivalent to 15,600 homes a year.

The government did not publish the final version of Strategic Planning Guidance for the South East until March 2001 (DETR 2001), a year after the Mayor of London came into office. As well as setting housing targets for the period 2001 to 2006 for each of the Home Counties, the document included within policy H1 that 'in London, provision should be made to accommodate on average an additional 23,000 households yearly'. This was based on the LPAC 1999 London housing capacity study, which was published by the Mayor (GLA 2000a).

The statutory responsibility and the initiative for plan making for London had passed to the Mayor. Together with the Mayor, the East of Regional England Assembly (EERA) and the South East of England Regional Assembly (SEERA) set up an Advisory Forum on regional planning for London, the South East of England and the East of England, known as the Inter-Regional Forum, to coordinate strategic planning across the three regions, but this committee had no statutory powers and was to prove largely ineffective.

Chapter 3
The new spatial planning framework for London

The Mayor and the Assembly

The Greater London Act 1999 created the office of Mayor and the London Assembly. The Mayor was to be directly elected and a new executive authority for the region, with a role that is similar to the directly elected mayors in American cities, though with more limited powers. The twenty-five Assembly members were also to be directly elected, with fourteen from constituencies and eleven from a regional list. The Assembly was not given any executive powers. Its role was to scrutinize the Mayor's activities. The Assembly's only effective power is the ability on a two-thirds majority to reject the Mayor's budget. The Assembly has a relatively small support office, which limits its ability to carry out investigations and reviews without external assistance. All other officers – initially some 500, but by 2008 over 700 staff – report through the chief executive to the Mayor.

The Mayor controls both the Greater London Authority and the other GLA group organizations: the London Development Agency (LDA), Transport for London (TfL), the Metropolitan Police Authority and the London Fire and Emergency Planning Authority. He is responsible for preparing strategies for London and must produce eight statutory strategies, covering spatial development, transport, economic development, air quality, noise, waste, biodiversity and culture. He has a general power to do anything to promote economic and social development and to improve the environment in London, within certain constraints. He has statutory obligations to promote health in London, sustainable development in the United Kingdom and equality of opportunity, when exercising his powers.

In 2007, a further Greater London Authority Act added to the Mayor's powers. This included expanding his strategic planning powers, taking over responsibility for the London Housing Strategy from the Government Office for London; added new duties in relation to reduction of health inequalities, climate change and energy; and established the London Waste and Recycling Board. Most of these new powers came into effect in spring 2008.

The first elected Mayor was Ken Livingstone, who had been leader of the Greater London Council before abolition in 1986, and then Labour MP for

Brent (D'Arcy and Maclean 2000, Hosken 2008). He was initially elected as an independent candidate, against opposition from Labour, Conservative, Liberal Democrat, Green and other independent candidates. In 2004, he was re-elected to a second term, this time as the official Labour candidate. In the May 2008 election, Livingstone was defeated by the Conservative candidate, Boris Johnson. The Mayor can appoint a Deputy Mayor. For most of the 2000–8 period, the Deputy Mayor was Nicky Gavron. The exception was 2004–5, when the Deputy Mayor was the Green Party Assembly member Jenny Jones.

No party has a majority on the Assembly. It comprises Labour, Conservative, Liberal Democrat and Green party members, together with members from the 'One London' party. In 2000, Labour and the Conservatives each had nine seats on the Assembly, with Liberal Democrats having four seats and the Greens having three; after 2004, the Conservatives became the largest party with nine seats, Labour falling to seven, Liberal Democrats with five, the Greens with two and One London, previously called the United Kingdom Independence Party, having two. Following the 2008 election, the Assembly comprised eleven Conservative members, eight Labour members, two Liberal Democrats, two Greens and one member of the British National Party (Table 3.1).

In 2000, the Assembly established a planning committee to scrutinize the Mayor's planning decisions. The committee, which has changed its name and remit several times, has also carried out a number of investigations on planning-related issues, some of which will be referred to below.

Under the 1999 Act as expanded by Government circular 1/2000 (GOL 2000), the Mayor became the strategic planning authority in London, a power previously reserved by the Secretary of State. The Mayor was given the responsibility for developing a Spatial Development Strategy (SDS) for London. This was the first of a new form of spatial plans, following the approach set out in the 1999 European Spatial Development Perspective (CEC 1999). The new approach was later extended to the other English regions, which under the 2004 Planning and Compulsory Purchase Act were required to develop Regional Spatial Strategies (RSSs).

Table 3.1 Party membership on London Assembly

	2000	2004	2008
Conservative	9	9	11
Labour	9	7	8
Liberal Democrat	4	5	3
Green	3	2	2
One London	0	2	0
British National Party	0	0	1

Box 3.1 gives the purposes of the SDS as set out in GOL circular 1/2000 (p. 4).

Box 3.1 Purposes of the Spatial Development Strategy

2.1   The Act provides that the Mayor shall prepare a Spatial Development Strategy and keep it under review. The SDS offers the opportunity for an integrated approach to shaping the future pattern and direction of development in London. It should provide a common spatial framework for all the Mayor's strategies and policies, as well as for the land use policies in Unitary Development Plans (UDPs).

2.2   The SDS must include the Mayor's general policies for the development and use of land in London, but it should also incorporate the spatial – that is, geographical and locational – elements of transport, economic development, environmental and other strategic policies for London, bringing them together in a single, comprehensive framework. It should adopt an integrated approach, embracing all aspects of physical planning, infrastructure development, and other policies affecting or affected by the distribution of activities. By doing so it should help to secure the effective co-ordination and targeting of activities and resources, and a consistent, holistic approach to the delivery of policy objectives. It should contribute to the achievement within London of sustainable development, a healthy economy, and a more inclusive society.

2.3   The SDS should provide guidance on the broad location of strategically important development. It may also contain policies and criteria for determining the acceptability of development proposals, where these raise issues of strategic importance. However, it should not incorporate detail more appropriate for borough development plans.

2.4   In order to provide a suitable framework for development plans and for investment decisions, a 15–20 year forward planning period should be assumed.

The SDS requirements are listed in Box 3.2 (GOL circular 1/2000 p. 9).

Box 3.2 Requirements of the Spatial Development Strategy

- set out a spatial strategy in the form of policies and proposals, supported by reasoned justification, distinguishing clearly between the two;
- identify clearly those policies and proposals relating to the development and use of land that are to be reflected in UDPs;

- illustrate the strategy, including relevant constraints, opportunities and proposals, in a key diagram (accompanied, where necessary, by additional inset diagrams), which may not be drawn on a map base;
- where appropriate, incorporate targets and milestones or performance indicators to measure the delivery of the strategy;
- be expressed in a form which facilitates monitoring and review (including partial review) of the strategy;
- include a statement of the regard that has been had to the matters covered in Section 2.(ii) above (these were stated as the general duties of the Mayor, the European context, the national context; and the regional context);
- be accompanied by a sustainability appraisal.

Under the 1999 Greater London Authority Act and circular 1/2000, local planning authorities in London (the boroughs and the City of London Corporation) were required to consult the Mayor on their Unitary Development Plans, with the Mayor able to object to Plans which were not in conformity with the approved Spatial Development Strategy. Under the 2004 Town Planning and Compulsory Purchase Act, the approved Spatial Development Strategy (which was to become known as the London Plan) was made a component of each London local planning authority's (LPA) development plan and consequently could be referred to in the determination of local (i.e. non-referable) planning applications as well as of strategic applications.

The 1999 Act also introduced a new concept of strategic development control – the ability of the Mayor to intervene in strategic development applications submitted to the thirty-three LPAs. The Act requires that planning applications in London be referable to the Mayor as being of strategic importance if they involve:

- the construction of 500 or more homes;
- major commercial development or infrastructure projects;
- development of over 30 metres (or 75 metres in the city, or 25 metres adjacent to River Thames);
- development on a protected wharf.

Under the 2007 Act, the referral threshold for residential development was reduced to 150 dwellings.

Local planning authorities were required to refer any such application to the Mayor as soon as it had been registered. The Mayor could then submit comments to the LPA. Where an LPA positively determined an application, the Mayor had power to veto such an approval where the application was not in conformity with the Spatial Development Strategy so long as this 'direction to refuse' was exercised within fourteen days of the LPA's decision.

The Greater London Authority compared with the Greater London Council

The Greater London Council in existence between 1964 and 1986 had been both a planning authority and a housing authority. The GLC was also a residential landlord, inheriting the stock built by the London County Council between 1889 and 1964, which was dispersed right across the Greater London area rather than located solely within the LCC boundary. The GLC had a housing investment programme and also continued to build housing in its own right. However in 1980, the GLC transferred its entire housing stock to the London boroughs, terminating its landlord function and limiting its role to being a strategic housing authority. The GLC nonetheless continued to undertake an investment programme. However, its strategies focusing on areas of deprivation and the need for renewal were dependent on borough support and cooperation for implementation.

With the abolition of the GLC, the strategic housing responsibilities were shared between individual boroughs and central government, acting through the Government Office for London. The GOL coordinated the development of a London Housing Strategy with the Housing Corporation, though initially this constituted only a brief annex to the national housing strategy guidance. Throughout the period, the London Research Centre (LRC), based on the former housing research, statistics and social surveys teams at the GLC, and supported by the thirty-two boroughs and the City Corporation, coordinated Londonwide housing research and information. Of particular significance for the development of housing and planning strategies in London was that the LRC conducted three major regional surveys in 1986, 1992 and 2002 providing analysis of housing costs, needs and affordability in London. With these evidence bases and analysis of other housing needs and market information, the LRC worked closely with LPAC, the individual boroughs, the Housing Corporation and the Association of London Government (ALG). The Association of London Government carried out a representative function for the boroughs, serviced meetings of the borough housing chairs and borough housing directors and published some Londonwide housing strategy material.

When the GLA was established in 2000, there was a decision by ministers that the GLA was to be limited to strategic functions and have no direct service delivery functions. Ministers, including the then Minister for Housing, Nick Raynsford, who doubled as Minister for London, decided not to give the Mayor any direct housing powers; the responsibility for the London Housing Strategy remained with the GOL and approval remained with the Secretary of State. The Secretary of State determined housing investment allocations to the thirty-three housing authorities, and the Housing Corporation managed the allocation of social housing grant made available by the central government for new housing association (HA) schemes. In fact, the 1999 GLA Act debarred the Mayor from any direct housing expenditure. It was only with the 2007 GLA Act that the Mayor was given responsibility for developing and publishing a housing strategy for London.

The Mayor's planning powers were much stronger than the planning powers operated by the Greater London Council. The GLC had been a plan-making body and was responsible for the Greater London Development Plan. As set out above, the Mayor had the responsibility for the new regional plan for London (the Spatial Development Strategy); under the 1999 GLA Act, borough plans had to be in general conformity with the plan. However, under the 2004 Planning and Compulsory Purchase Act, the Spatial Development Strategy was made part of the Local Development Plan framework for each borough and therefore could be used by a borough as a basis for determining local planning applications.

In having a power of veto in relation to strategic schemes, the Mayor's powers were significantly greater than those of the GLC, with the Mayor having decision-making powers over individual developments. Although the Secretary of State retained his call-in powers, the GLA Act transferred significant powers from boroughs to the new regional authority, for which there had been no precedent since 1889. It should also be recognized that these powers were significantly greater than those of the transitional regional planning body, the London Planning Advisory Committee, which existed between 1986 and 2000 and whose role was limited to providing advice to the Secretary of State on the government's regional planning guidance.

Housing in London in 2000

Tenure mix

The tenure mix of London's housing stock was significantly different from the rest of England, with a lower level of owner occupation and a higher level of local authority (LA) and housing association rented housing (Table 3.2; regional housing stock data for April 2000 is not available in a consistent format). London also had the highest proportion of privately rented housing.

Table 3.2 Dwellings by tenure at regional and national level

Region	Owner occupied	Shared ownership	Private rented sector	Social rented sector (LA)	Social rented sector (HA)	Total
London	56%	1%	17%	17%	9%	100%
South East	73%	1%	12%	7%	7%	100%
South West	72%	1%	13%	8%	6%	100%
East Midlands	72%	1%	10%	14%	4%	100%
Eastern	72%	1%	11%	12%	5%	100%
West Midlands	69%	1%	10%	14%	6%	100%
Yorkshire and Humberside	67%	0%	11%	17%	4%	100%
North East	63%	0%	9%	22%	5%	100%
North West	69%	1%	11%	14%	7%	100%
England (average)	68%	1%	12%	13%	6%	100%
England (thousands)	13,921	134	2,456	2,703	1,238	20,452

Source: 2001 census.

Housing needs and homelessness

When the Mayor was appointed, there was a serious shortage of housing in London, especially of affordable homes. There were nearly 200,000 households on council waiting lists – an increase of nearly 20,000 over the previous three years; the average house price was £190,000, having increased from £120,000 three years earlier – an inflation rate of 20 per cent a year; and the ratio between lower-quartile incomes and lower-quartile house prices had risen from 4:1 in 1997 to nearly 6:1 in 2000. Owner occupiers with a mortgage spent 24 per cent of their income on housing costs, council tenants 14 per cent, housing association tenants 15 per cent and privately rented tenants 23 per cent.

Homelessness acceptances were over 30,000 households a year, while there were over 50,000 households in temporary accommodation, of whom over 7,000 were in bed and breakfast. The backlog in unmet housing need was estimated at 110,000 households. Though not known at the time, the 2001 census was to show a significant increase in overcrowding over the previous ten years. There were 2.93 million households in London, with a growth rate of about 23,400 households a year. Completions were therefore running at about 5,000 homes a year short of what was needed to meet household growth, therefore increasing rather than reducing the backlog of unmet housing need.

The distribution of urban deprivation as measured in the official government index closely correlated with the areas of social rented housing. Projects in these areas were eligible for European Union cohesion policy structural funds under the Objective 2 category: designated areas facing structural difficulties.

Housing supply

Local authority housing stock had fallen from 618,000 homes in 1997 to 551,000 homes, a fall of 67,000 homes, not fully compensated for by the increase in housing association homes of 47,000 over the same period. Council house sales were still running at over 10,000 homes a year, whereas housing association new build rented completions were only 3,000 a year. Net total housing completions were static at about 19,000 homes a year between 1997 and 1999, with affordable completions of between 6,000 and 8,000 homes a year – averaging 38 per cent of the total.

Housing completions had fallen over the decade up to 2000, from a peak of 27,000 in 1988 to 17,000 in 1999.

House prices

As at April 2000, the average house price in London was £172,409. Prices varied significantly between boroughs (Table 3.3).

Table 3.3 Average house prices in London boroughs

Average house price	Boroughs
Under £100,000	Barking and Dagenham, Newham
£100,000–£149,999	Bexley, Croydon, Enfield, Greenwich, Havering, Hillingdon, Lewisham, Redbridge, Sutton
£150,000–£199,999	Brent, Bromley, Ealing, Hackney, Haringey, Harrow, Hounslow, Kingston, Lambeth, Merton, Southwark, Waltham Forest
£200,000–£249,999	Barnet, Islington, Tower Hamlets, Wandsworth
£250,000–£299,999	City of London, Hammersmith and Fulham, Richmond
Over £300,000	Westminster, Kensington and Chelsea

Source: HM Land Registry.

The Mayor's Housing Commission and the London Assembly housing report

Although the Mayor was not given housing powers, one of his first actions after his election was to establish a Housing Commission, under the chairmanship of Chris Holmes, the then director of the housing and homelessness campaign group, SHELTER. The purpose of the commission was:

> to inquire into London's needs for affordable homes, provide a firm foundation for the housing policies in the Spatial Development Strategy and set targets across London for all types of affordable housing.
>
> (GLA 2000a p. 3 para 1.1)

The commission comprised seventeen members from a range of public, private and voluntary sector organizations. It included the Mayor's housing advisor, Neale Coleman, Terrie Alafat, who was chair of the London borough housing directors' group, Karen Buck MP, the housing consultant Steve Hilditch, Charmaine Young from St George's developers, Mike Ward of the London Development Agency, Victor Adebowale from the homelessness charity Centrepoint, and Nigel Pallace, planning director from Hammersmith and Fulham. The group also included representatives from the Metropolitan Police, the National Health Service and academics. The Housing Corporation and Government Office for London had observer status. The commission was serviced by the Mayor's housing and homelessness team, which had been absorbed into the GLA from the London Research Centre. The commission did not include any members of the elected London Assembly.

It should be recognized that, even before the establishment of the Mayor's Housing Commission, there had been widespread joint working on development of a Londonwide housing strategy. Both the GOL and the Housing Corporation had involved a wide range of bodies, including the London Planning Advisory Committee and the London Research Centre, in drawing up successive London Housing Statements in 1999, 2000 and 2001, the forerunners of the Regional Housing Strategy. Officers of LPAC and the LRC also acted as advisors to the Association of London Government's member-level housing committee and housing directors' group, which generated a borough-led Housing Strategy for London, published in 2001 (ALG 2001a). This strategy was supplemented by a detailed Homelessness Strategy for London (ALG 2001b) and the London Housing Partnership initiative (ALG 1999), which brought together borough and Housing Corporation resources to fund an emergency programme of street property acquisition to meet the needs of homeless households. In addition the public/private sector London Pride Partnership had published a well-regarded review of priorities for strategic housing policy in London (London Pride Partnership 1998). The role of London Pride has been discussed by Newman (1995). LPAC, LRC and ALG officers took a leading role in writing the London Pride report.

The Mayor's Housing Commission completed a widespread consultation exercise, focusing on twelve key issues:

1. The need for affordable homes over the next 10 years including size, type and location of homes.
2. Definitions of affordability, including the potential role of privately rented housing.
3. The role of low cost home ownership and criteria for the Government's Starter Homes Initiative
4. The use of planning powers to secure affordable homes
5. The potential for the private rented sector to deliver good quality secure affordable homes
6. Providing affordable homes for the diverse needs of Londoners
7. Achieving socially mixed communities
8. How to regenerate estates without losing homes
9. Reducing the Right to Buy
10. Increasing choice and mobility
11. Tackling the dependence on using temporary accommodation for homeless families and single homeless people
12. Maximising the use of existing resources.

(GLA 206 pp. 107–9)

Making use of analysis of the London Household Survey 2000 to quantify housing need, a series of study visits during September and October 2000 and four working meetings, the Commission published the report *Homes for a World City*, in November 2000 – only eight months after the Mayor took office (GLA 2000b). As the Mayor had no housing powers, many of the recommendations focused on policies and targets for inclusion in the proposed Spatial Development Strategy (Box 3.3).

Box 3.3 Recommendations of Mayor's Housing Commission 2000

Half of new residential development to be affordable

The key recommendation was that the Mayor through the SDS should ensure that 'at least half' of new residential development should be affordable, with a provisional view that at least 35 per cent should be delivered as predominantly social rented housing targeted at meeting the needs of people on low incomes and that at least 15 per cent should be delivered as a mix of housing types targeted at meeting the needs of people on moderate incomes. The report also recommended, 'given the alarming gap between London's housing requirements and current levels of provision and estimated capacity, that the SDS include proposals for maximizing housing capacity in London, without jeopardising environmental sustainability, including the potential for increasing densities and for bringing more sites or non-residential buildings into use'.

Targets for affordable housing

The Commission proposed a target of 28,000 affordable homes a year, of which 20,500 homes should be social rent and 7,500 should be intermediate homes. This was based on seeking to meet the backlog of housing need and all newly arising need over a period.

Planning policies

The Commission also recommended a number of planning policies aimed at maximizing affordable housing output including:

- The requirement on a developer to provide affordable housing should be clearly stated in planning policy.
- The requirement should be applied to all sites capable of being developed as ten dwellings.
- Policy should achieve the maximum contribution from the private sector without jeopardizing the supply of land for housing.
- Affordable housing should normally be provided on site in any residential development. The acceptance of cash in lieu should be restricted to small sites and exceptional circumstances.
- The SDS should require affordable housing within all non-residential developments or a contribution to affordable housing off site.

- The SDS should set separate social rent and intermediate housing targets for each borough.
- The SDS should maintain high densities in central and Inner London and increase densities in Outer London, especially around transport routes, but without compromising sustainable residential quality principles.
- The SDS should contain a presumption against loss of affordable housing in regeneration schemes.

Strengthening government planning guidance

The Commission also recommended that the central government should strengthen its affordable housing guidance in PPG3 and circular 6/98 to provide more robust support to London and the boroughs in tackling housing needs.

Housing policies

The report also made a number of recommendation on other issues, such as use of publicly owned land, tax disincentives to property owners leaving properties empty, acquisition of private homes for affordable housing, reform of housing benefit and reference rents in the private rented sector, an inquiry on the modernization of the London private rented sector, new arrangements for housing mobility, improvements in housing advice services, and targets to phase out the use of bed and breakfast hotels as temporary accommodation.

New structures for developing and coordinating housing strategy

The Commission also recommended that the Mayor work with the Association of London Government representing the boroughs to agree a London Housing Strategy and establish a Regional Housing Forum, which would coordinate strategy across the public, private and voluntary sectors and identify priorities for action.

(GLA 2006 pp. vii–xvi)

In parallel with the work of the Mayor's Housing Commission, the London Assembly established an affordable housing scrutiny committee, to study the need for housing for key workers. This was under the chairmanship of Meg Hillier, the Labour Assembly member for Islington and Hackney, and later MP for Hackney. The committee, operating independently from the Mayor's office and the Mayor's housing and planning teams, employed Professors Christine Whitehead and Steve Wilcox as consultant advisors and held a number of investigative meetings with external witnesses from private and public sectors. The report *Key Issues for Key Workers* was published in February 2001 (London Assembly 2001), only three months after the Commission's report.

The report argued for the Housing Corporation to establish a Londonwide key worker housing scheme available to a wide range of key workers and for the development of more flexible shared ownership schemes, as well as changes in the London cost limits for the existing Starter Homes Initiative so that family homes could be included. The report's only recommendation on planning was that the deliverability of the 50 per cent affordable housing target should be tested. The Assembly report did not comment on whether the 15 per cent intermediate housing target was too low or too high. The report also recommended an upward review of the London weighting element within public sector salaries, to more fully compensate for the higher level of house prices in London.

The London Housing Forum and the London Housing Board

Following a recommendation from the Mayor's Housing Commission, the Greater London Authority and the Association of London Government established the London Housing Forum in 2001. This forum, chaired and serviced jointly by the two organizations, included representatives of a wide range of regional agencies. The Housing Corporation and GOL had observer status. Other public sector representatives included English Partnerships (EP), the LDA, and the London NHS. From the private sector, there was London First, the Home Builders Federation and the British Property Federation. From the 'voluntary' sector, there was the London Housing Federation representing housing associations and SHELTER, later joined by the London Tenants Federation, Homeless Link and the Federation of Black Housing Organisations. Membership was later extended to the Chartered Institute of Housing and representatives of the five sub-regional housing partnerships, with the group becoming some fifty members strong. The Forum set up four sub-groups: on homelessness, on housing supply, on regeneration and sustainable development and on the private rented sector. The groups had a significant role in contributing to the regional housing strategies and to Regional Housing Strategy conferences. However, with the establishment of the London Housing Board, the role of the Forum became more of a discussion group, with strategic direction on regional investment priorities increasingly determined by the Board, whose membership was intentionally limited to government agencies.

The London Housing Board was established by the government, through the GOL. This was part of a process of the government devolving functions to regions. Boards were established in all regions. The role of the Board was to supervise the development of regional strategies, a function which had previously been carried out, at least in theory, by the government regional offices, in partnership with the regional office of the Housing Corporation. In London, the Board, chaired by the Director of GOL, comprised representatives from the Housing Corporation, the ALG (renamed in 2006 as London Councils), the LDA and EP. As pointed out above, LPAC and LRC officers had contributed to previous London Housing Statements, and the GOL still largely relied on these officers, now working within the GLA, to assist with drafting the new strategies, though these new documents were more closely integrated with the government's new Sustainable Communities Plan. Before the transfer of strategy powers to the Mayor, three new strategies were published – *Delivering Solutions: London Housing Statement 2002, Homes and Communities in London 2003* and *Capital Homes London Housing Strategy 2005–2016* (GOL 2002, 2003a, 2005). The third of these documents sought to move beyond the normal one- or two-year timescale of earlier strategies and beyond the immediate housing investment funding bidding round.

Chapter 4
The development of the London Plan

The inheritance from the London Planning Advisory Committee

In parallel with the work of the Housing Commission, the Spatial Development Strategy team at the Greater London Authority, including staff transferred from the London Planning Advisory Committee led by Martin Simmons, initiated work on the Spatial Development Strategy. They had inherited a major programme of work from LPAC, which had been brought together prior to LPAC's abolition in a consolidated 'endowment' document (LPAC 2000a). The transition was assisted by the fact that the former LPAC chair, Councillor Nicky Gavron of Haringey, had, following her election to the London Assembly, been appointed as Deputy Mayor and Mayoral adviser on strategic planning. Another former LPAC chair, the Liberal Democrat Baroness Sally Hamwee, also became a member of the London Assembly, where she was to take a prominent role on planning issues. LPAC reports had been approved by a committee representing all thirty-three local planning authorities and represented a cross-party consensus, which meant that for a number of key policy areas, including planning for housing, the Mayor had a generally accepted starting point for his approach to the London Plan. Furthermore there was a legacy of key research and development studies, which would provide a substantial evidence base for the formulating of key planning recommendations relating to housing.

From a housing perspective, there were two main areas where LPAC had provided valuable guidance. First, LPAC had commissioned studies from Llewellyn-Davies on sustainable residential quality (SRQ). LPAC published in December 1997 *Sustainable Residential Quality: New Approaches to Urban Living* (LPAC 1997), and then in January 2000 *Sustainable Residential Quality: Exploring the Potential of Large Sites* (LPAC 2000b). The first study focused on small sites in and around town centres and showed how housing capacity could be increased by between 50 per cent and 100 per cent by relating location to relaxed car parking standards. The second study applied the design-led approach to large sites and produced a Location, Car Parking Density Matrix. The suggested density range varied from 150 habitable rooms per hectare (hrh) in remote suburban locations to 1,100 hrh in central locations well served by public transport. The design-led approach and SRQ design principles were recommended to boroughs in *Supplementary Advice on Sustainable Residential Quality on Small Sites* (LPAC circular 20/98) and

Supplementary Advice on Sustainable Residential Quality on Large Sites (LPAC circular 86/99).

LPAC had also commissioned a new Londonwide housing capacity study to reassess the residential development capacity within London. This study was undertaken jointly with all thirty-three local planning authorities and assessed components of potential capacity in each borough – large identified sites with capacity for ten or more homes, capacity from large windfall (unidentified) sites based on trend analysis, potential for residential provision from offices (both identified surplus offices and potential windfalls), small conversions, small sites and live work units. The study also considered the potential for non-self-contained provision in hostels and student accommodation and for vacant properties to be brought back into residential use. This study concluded there was a potential for 460,000 homes over a twenty-year period from all sources, or 23,000 homes a year. The report estimated potential by borough in five-year phases. This informed *Supplementary Advice on Housing Capacity* (LPAC circular 85/99). The full report was completed in March 2000 and published by the Mayor in September 2000 (GLA 200a).

LPAC had also published a number of other housing-related studies. These included a study of *One Person Households and London's Housing Requirements* by PS Martin Hamblin and the London Research Centre (LPAC 1998d); a report on *Offices to Other Uses* by London Property Research (LPAC 1996); a study of *Possible Future Sources of Large Housing Sites in London* by Halcrow Fox (LPAC 1998a); a study of *Dwellings over and in Shops* by the Civic Trust (LPAC 1998b); a joint report with the Association of London Government on *Affordable Housing, Regeneration and Sustainability in London* (LPAC and ALG 1997); and a report on *Cash in Lieu* payments for affordable housing under planning obligations (LPAC circular 76/97).

The role of LPAC was significant in setting the framework for the London Plan. The LPAC strategy advice represented a significant shift from the more protectionist policies of the GLDP amendments, in that it explicitly embraced economic growth based on the role of London as an international financial centre. It developed the principle of sustainable residential quality with its sophisticated approach to the question of residential density. Although focusing on the central area it also recognized the polycentricity of London centres and developed the notion of a town centre hierarchy. It also recognized the four growth corridors of Thames Gateway, Lee Valley, the western corridor and the Wandle valley, which were to be the basis of the London Plan key diagram. It was LPAC's work that enabled the Mayor to move to publishing a draft London Plan so quickly, and the Plan and the new approach to spatial planning it represented were to owe far more to the work of LPAC than to guidance from the central government, including the statutory Regional Planning Guidance.

The policy framework

The government's regional planning guidance for London and the southeast

Regional Planning Guidance 3: The Strategic Guidance for London Planning Authorities (GOL 1996) was published by the Government Office for London in May 1996. The document had a forward by John Gummer, the minister with special responsibility for London, who had been chair of the Joint London Advisory Panel, which had comprised public and private sector representatives.

RPG3 set borough targets for net additions to housing stock of 234,100 for the period 1992 to 2006, equivalent to 15,600 homes a year. These targets were derived from the LPAC 1994 housing capacity study and advice (LPAC 1994a,b). Boroughs were required to show how they proposed to exceed the minimum targets, including using vacant properties and sites and converting non-residential buildings to residential use. Boroughs were also required to assess housing needs, to identify locations suitable for affordable housing and to indicate the proportion of affordable housing to be sought on different sites. No Londonwide affordable housing target was set and boroughs were told to avoid setting a prescriptive target. Boroughs were also required to assess the need for special needs housing and set policies for meeting each need. Boroughs were required to assess the need for gypsy sites but told to avoid providing gypsy sites in the Green Belt or Metropolitan Open Land or on other areas of open space. The plan, unlike the 1944 Abercrombie plan, did not consider the issue of residential density.

As mentioned above, in March 2001 the government published *Regional Planning Guidance 9: Strategic Planning Guidance for the South East* (DETR 2001), which incorporated the 23,000 homes a year target derived from the 1999 London housing capacity study undertaken by LPAC and published by the Mayor. RPG9 did not, however, set targets at borough level; although the borough targets derived from the housing capacity study were included in LPAC guidance and used as a basis for monitoring by the Mayor and by other agencies, they did not have statutory effect until included in the published London Plan in February 2004.

The government's planning policy guidance on housing

Planning Policy Guidance on Housing (PPG3), published by the Department of the Environment, Transport and Regions in March 2000 (DETR 2000), applied to all regional and local planning authorities. Regional planning bodies, including the Mayor, were therefore required to ensure that policies proposed in regional policy guidance were in accordance with the new guidance. A special Annex A on London referred to the fact that the Mayor would be preparing a Spatial

Development Strategy and that the government would issue specific guidance for London in a separate circular.

Most of the guidance in PPG3 was aimed at local planning authorities. However, there were specific requirements of regional planning boards/regional planning guidance:

- Regional planning bodies should prepare regional planning guidance that 'aims to meet the likely housing requirements of their areas, based on a realistic and responsible approach to future housing provision, assessing both the need for housing and the capacity for the area to accommodate it' (para 4). However, by then referring to the separate arrangements for London set out in Annex A, there was an implication that this aim might not apply to London.
- Regional planning guidance should set out monitoring indicators, to be monitored through an annual report. Reviews should occur at least every five years or sooner. This requirement did not apply to London, as circular 1/2000 (GOL 2000), the separate arrangements for London, did not set any review timescale (para 8).
- Regional planning guidance may estimate the balance between market and affordable housing, 'but such estimates should be regarded as indicative only and should not be presented as targets or quotas for local planning authorities to achieve' (para 12).
- Each region should set out its own target for re-using previously developed land, consistent with the national target of 60 per cent. In this context it is significant that the London Plan was to include only a monitoring indicator and not a target (para 23).
- Regional planning guidance should identify major areas of growth (para 28).

PPG3 also gave guidance on the creation of mixed communities, delivering affordable housing, capacity assessment and site identification, land allocation and release, use of employment land, land assembly, mixed-use development, design, parking standards, rural housing and new settlements, though none of this guidance included explicit reference to a regional planning role.

Government Office for London circular 1/2000

GOL circular 1/2000 (GOL 2000) set out the requirements for the housing components of the SDS. This went well beyond the pre-existing RPG3.

The circular advised that the particular constraints on the supply of new land in London, the unique features of the London housing market and demographic trends should be taken into account in interpreting the national policy guidance set out in PPG3.

The circular referred to the *Draft Regional Planning Guidance for the South East* (RPG9: DETR 1999), which already included the London capacity figure of 23,000 a year assessed in the recent London housing capacity study. It stated that, 'unless there had been a significant change in circumstances, it should be unnecessary to reopen debate about the rate of housing provision in London' (GOL 2000 para 3.13).

The circular stated that any future review of the level of housing provision should have regard to housing need, the latest household projections, predicted levels of provision in areas adjoining London, and the social and economic needs of the capital (including the need for affordable housing). Attention was drawn to the need for the maximum use of previously developed land and the role of well-designed housing in improving the quality of urban life and promoting regeneration; the SDS should encourage more sustainable patterns of housing development linked to transport objectives. Any new target should be based on a further housing capacity study.

The circular stated that the SDS should set out a distribution of the overall rate of housing provision between boroughs as well as policies for achieving the rate and targets and indicators for monitoring. The circular also stated that the SDS should set out, 'where appropriate, policies and objectives for meeting particular types of housing provision need across the capital as a whole'. This wording was to prove significant. It was unclear what the phrase 'particular types of housing provision need' actually meant; whether this was type of housing in terms of built form or bedroom size or tenure and affordability or different types of housing need requirement. The circular was, however, clear that any guidance could be applied only Londonwide and not at local planning authority level.

Towards the London Plan

By the time of the publication of the Mayor's first strategic planning document – *Towards the London Plan* (GLA 2001a) – in May 2001, the parameters of the new strategic planning policies for housing were fairly well developed, as they could build on the work already undertaken by LPAC and for the Mayor's Housing Commission (Table 4.1).

The Mayor's statement was explicit about the fundamental strategic choice: he argued that the postwar policy of dispersing business and population from London was no longer valid, as the phenomenon of globalization had increasingly focused economic growth on capital cities as key gateways to national economies, and consequently for the previous fifteen years London had been growing both economically and in terms of population. The lack of strategic governance had weakened London's ability to plan to meet these challenges, with the consequence

Table 4.1 The chronology of the plan-making process

May 2000	Mayor and London Assembly take office
June 2000	GOL circular 1/2000
November 2000	Report of Mayor's Housing Commission published
May 2001	*Towards the London Plan* published
July 2002	*Draft London Plan* published
March–April 2003	Examination in Public (EiP)
July 2003	Report of EiP Panel published
February 2004	*London Plan* published

that New York, Paris and Berlin had improved their position as world cities relative to London. The option of attempting to rein back economic and population growth in London to reintroduce policies of dispersal was untenable and would compromise London's future development as well as damaging the UK's economy. The only realistic option was to accept the processes of economic growth, centralization and population increase and create adequate conditions for the city to achieve sustainable development. The Mayor believed that this growth would help pay for the many improvements in services and transport that London needed.

Given this context, and the overall objective of seeking to meet growth demands, *Towards the London Plan* used the 23,000 homes annual capacity from the capacity study and then took the 50 per cent affordable housing, 35 per cent social rent and 15 per cent intermediate targets from the Commission report. The statement also took the sustainable residential quality concept from the LPAC reports. It also recognized the need for supported housing, the need to improve existing housing stock and the need to 'protect and enhance those attractive features of residential areas which are valued by local communities – safety and security, privacy, amenity and open space'. It also stated that 'the application of new building technologies, including insulation, energy efficiency and air circulation, will promote health benefits and preserve natural resources'. It should be noted that, despite the publication of the Assembly's report on key worker housing, the Mayor's statement made no specific reference to the needs of key workers, the Mayor's view being that access to intermediate housing related to affordability of a range of household types and that specific groups of 'key workers' should not be given special priority.

The Mayor appointed two advisors to develop the draft London Plan. One was Robin Thompson, professor at the Bartlett School of Planning, University College London. He had been chief planner for Kent and Director of Development at Southwark as well as being a past president of the Royal Town Planning Institute. Drew Stevenson was the second adviser. He had been a professor at the University of East London as well as chief executive at Newham and chief strategic planner in the final years of the GLC with responsibility for the Greater London Development Plan. The Mayor also established an advisory group of external academics and professionals under the chairmanship of Sir Peter Hall, a professor at the Bartlett and leading advocate of city regional planning.

Professors Thompson and Stevenson were to work on a part-time basis in the Mayor's London Plan team not just through to the London Plan's adoption in 2004 but also through the early and further alterations examinations in Public in 2006 and 2007, leading for the Mayor in presenting his proposals through all three Examinations in Public. The role of Peter Hall's advisory group is more difficult to assess as it met privately and there is no public record of either its membership or its considerations, though it did include Martin Simmons, formerly LPAC chief planner, and Gideon Amos of the Town and Country Planning Association (TCPA). Sir Peter Hall gave evidence at the London Assembly Committee hearing on 17 July 2001 (London Assembly 2002a), to the effect that he did not consider that the London Plan dealt adequately with the relationship between London and the wider city region. In fact the advisory group was not allowed to see the draft London Plan before it was published and had no role in the finalization of the Plan, though Sir Peter did appear at the Examination in Public to represent the TCPA, of which he was president.

Demonstrating deliverability

In the eighteen-month period after the publication of the initial statement, the GLA published a series of technical reports to support the policy proposals. Three reports focused on the deliverability of the housing targets – both the overall target of 23,000 homes a year and the 50 per cent affordable housing target.

The Three Dragons report

The first issue was the most problematic one. As pointed out above, affordable housing output was running at between 7,000 and 9,000 new homes a year – 36–40 per cent of output – whereas applying the proposed 50 per cent target to the new housing capacity figure of 23,000 would require some 11,500 new affordable homes a year. There was considerable criticism from the development sector that the new target was not deliverable and would jeopardize the delivery by the market of an overall increase of affordable housing. The House Builders Federation (HBF), supported by the business-led group London First, argued that the new target would reduce rather than increase the affordable housing output; '50 per cent of nothing is nothing' became a common rallying cry.

The GLA commissioned the consultants Three Dragons (Lin Cousins and Kathleen Dunmore) and the Centre for Residential Development at Nottingham Trent University (Professor Michael Oxley and Dr Andrew Golland) to assess the deliverability of the proposed target. The consultants developed a model which assessed the relationship between cost and value of market-led developments, to test the ability to support affordable housing with or without subsidy through Housing Corporation grant. By using assumptions about land acquisition costs (£2m a hectare) and norm developer profit (15 per cent of sale value), the consultants ranked the thirty-three boroughs into those which could support the 50 per cent target without reliance on grant (the central London areas of the City, Westminster, Kensington and Chelsea, Camden, and Hammersmith and Fulham), boroughs which could deliver 50 per cent with the assistance of Housing Corporation grant at approximately the average grant per unit then available (most other Inner London boroughs, together with Ealing, Barnet, Merton, Kingston, Hounslow, Harrow and Bromley) and those where, even with grant, a 35 per cent target was the maximum deliverable (Lewisham, Greenwich, Newham and the remaining Outer London boroughs). The consultants concluded that, if 'surplus' profits from central London schemes could be used to support housing in lower value areas, then the proposed 50 per cent target would be deliverable across London as a whole. The report, *Affordable Housing in London*, published in July 2001, went on to suggest that boroughs be set either 35 per cent or 50 per cent affordable housing targets, depending on this categorization (GLA 2001b).

This report was useful to the Mayor in supporting his overall target. The model used by the consultants was criticized as being oversimplistic and for underestimating land acquisition costs. The GLA, in conjunction with the Government Office for London and in response to criticisms, commissioned an independent evaluation of the report and the model on which it was based from a separate set of consultants, Atis Real Wetherall. They concluded that, although the overall approach had validity, an average land price assumption of £3.7m a hectare, nearly double that assumed by Three Dragons, would be more appropriate. This therefore constrained the ability to deliver the 50 per cent target Londonwide unless more public subsidy were made available. This report was published in August 2002, with a response from Three Dragons and Nottingham Trent University being published the following month (GLA 2002a,b).

Speeding up delivery

The second piece of research related to the question of how to raise housing output to the proposed capacity-based target of 23,000 homes a year. The GLA collaborated with the House Builders Federation to commission a consultancy team led by the University of Westminster and London Residential Research. The team, comprising Chris Marsh, Geoff Marsh, Kelvin McDonald and Fiona Sadek, was asked to consider the development constraints on residential development. The study examined the operation of the house-building industry in London, examined the extent to which allocated housing sites were or were not developed, and undertook case studies in six boroughs, interviewing both planning officers and property professionals. In their report, *Future Housing Provision: Speeding Up Delivery*, published by the GLA in February 2002, the consultants identified a range of constraints: physical difficulties on site, high infrastructure costs and site assembly problems. Most developers recognized the need to provide an element of affordable housing. The recommendations focused not on policy changes but on improving inter-agency working and planning practice. The report argued that the Spatial Development Strategy needed to set clear and unequivocal standards on density and parking and affordable housing and also set a clear policy framework for planning obligations (GLA 2002c).

Planning obligations

The need for a clear policy framework for planning obligations, often known as section 106 agreements after the relevant clause of the 1990 Planning Act, led to the GLA commissioning a third study. Professor Rob Lane, also of the University of Westminster, reviewed the operation of planning obligations in London. This study reviewed policy and practice on planning obligations nationally and in London, building on the analysis published in Chris Marsh and Geoff Marsh's study of *Planning Gain 2001* (Marsh and Marsh 2001), but also conducted a new questionnaire-based survey of London boroughs' policy and practice. Rob Lane's report (GLA 2002d)concluded that, although planning agreements had been used for over thirty years as a means of securing acceptable development and use had increased considerably in London over recent years, government guidance was overrestrictive relative to the legislation; this caused uncertainty for all parties.

Lane noted inconsistencies in borough practice and inadequate staffing in most boroughs leading to a failure to take full benefit of the opportunities available. He considered that pooling arrangements could be used more widely and suggested it would be essential that the Mayor's Spatial Development Strategy set a framework for planning obligations Londonwide. He did not consider that there was a need for new primary legislation but argued that government guidance needed to be updated. He noted that only 14 per cent of dwellings in residential developments of ten or more homes could be considered to be affordable and was disappointed at the limited provision in mixed-use schemes which included a commercial element.

Lane argued that the revision to existing government guidance as set out in circular 1/97 on planning obligations and circular 6/98 on affordable housing should encourage pooling arrangements based on an assessment of needs related to a group of developments in an area. The costs of meeting those needs over an appropriate timescale and planning obligations for affordable housing should apply to all residential development (rather than just schemes of fifteen or more units in Inner London and schemes of twenty-five homes or more in Outer London as specified in circular 6/98) and to appropriate commercial developments. Lane made a number of other recommendations for changes in government guidance:

a   to make it clear that when a facility needs to be off site it can be provided in another borough if this is demonstrated to be an acceptable means of meeting the needs of the development;
b   to provide clearer advice on appropriate policies, which may be included in development plans;
c   to provide a more specific requirement of financial openness to ensure that there cannot be an accusation of 'deals behind closed doors';
d   to require developers to submit financial appraisals for schemes in which planning obligations are proposed to demonstrate the viability of development and the possible need to access other sources of funding; and
e   to make available model agreements to provide consistency between authorities.

Lane also argued that the Mayor should be entitled to be a party to section 106 agreements and that this change could be made through secondary legislation.

Lane drafted a policy for incorporation in the SDS as a strategic framework for planning obligations in London, and outlined the content of a best practice guide for London.

Lane proposed a general planning obligation policy for the SDS, which he contended was consistent with pre-existing government guidance. This would require boroughs to state in their Unitary Development Plans that:

a   development would not be permitted unless it made appropriate provision or contribution towards requirements which are made necessary by, and are related to, the proposed development;
b   development proposals which have an impact beyond the application site must be accompanied by an impact assessment and show how any measures required to mitigate these impacts are to be met;
c   that applicants be required to finance the full cost (capital and revenue costs), or if appropriate a contribution towards the full cost, of all such provision which is fairly and reasonably related in scale and kind to the proposed development and its impact on the wider area; and

d   the obligations must specify the nature and timing of all provision, both on and off development site, made necessary by or contributing to the success of development.

Lane also proposed a policy requirement in the SDS that boroughs should decide on priorities for planning obligations, in which it would not be viable for all to be met, but that 'the provision of affordable housing should generally be treated as the highest priority' (GLA 2002d p. 88).

As will be seen later, the policy included in the draft SDS was to be simplified from that proposed by Professor Lane, with public transport given equal priority to affordable housing, whereas the proposed best practice guide was never published.

The *Draft London Plan*

The housing policies proposed in the *Draft London Plan* published in July 2002 (GLA 2002e) were not significantly different from the proposals set out in *Towards the London Plan* and the series of research reports published subsequently. Some studies of the early period of the development of the London Plan (Thornley *et al.* 2002, West *et al.* 2002, Rydin *et al.* 2004) have pointed to a conflict between political and professional advisers to the Mayor and debates over whether an economic growth- and transport-led agenda or an environmental sustainability approach should be the overarching paradigm for the Plan. There is no evidence that either of these issues had any significant impact on the development of the key housing-related policies. Both the overall housing target and the approach to affordable housing were consensus based and in practice taken as a given. The overall objective of responding to the demands of economic and population growth as set out in *Towards the London Plan* remained, though the draft Plan had an increased emphasis on achieving growth in the most environmentally sustainable manner. The Mayor in his Introduction to the new document set out his vision as:

> to develop London as an exemplary, sustainable world city, based on three interwoven themes:
>
> * strong, diverse long term economic growth
> * social inclusivity to give all Londoners the opportunity to share in London's future success
> * fundamental improvements in London's environment and use of resources
>
> (GLA 2002c p. xii)

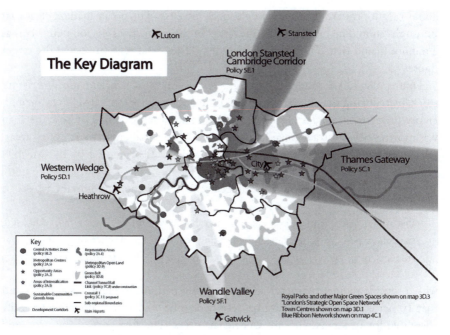

Map 4.1 London key diagram. Source: GLA (2004a).

The main policy content of the draft Plan was grouped into six themes:

- making the most sustainable and efficient use of space in London;
- making London a better city for people to live in;
- making London a more prosperous city with strong and diverse economic growth;
- promoting social inclusion and tackling deprivation and discrimination;
- improving London's transport; and
- making London a more attractive, well-designed and green city.

The core housing policies on housing supply and affordable housing fell within the second theme.

Housing supply

The first two draft policies (3A.1 and 3A.2) related to the new housing provision target of 23,000 and set out the new borough targets derived from the 1999 housing capacity study, including (in contrast with housing targets in other regions) provision of bedspaces in non-self-contained accommodation and assumptions about vacant properties being brought back into use. The policy made it clear that boroughs should include the relevant target in their Unitary Development Plans as a minimum and that UDPs should include policies 'that seek to exceed the target figures'.

Draft policy 3A.3 required boroughs to promote the efficient use of existing stock, by reducing the number of vacant, unfit and unsatisfactory dwellings through empty property strategies. This proposed policy was an example of how the Plan was moving beyond traditional land use issues into broader strategic policy areas, taking on board some of the non-land use objectives promoted by the Mayor's Housing Commission.

Draft policy 3A.4 on Housing Choice combined a general requirement

> that new developments offer a range of housing choice in terms of the mix of housing sizes and types, taking account of the housing requirements of different groups, such as students, older people, families with children and people willing to share accommodation

with a specific requirement that all new housing be built to lifetime standards and that 10 per cent of new housing be designed to be wheelchair accessible or easily adaptable for residents who are wheelchair users. The first part of the proposed policy was uncontentious, whereas the latter part was contentious as it was seen as introducing a specific standard, which would normally be a matter for building regulations, into a statutory planning document.

Draft policy 3A.5 on Large Residential Developments required boroughs to prepare, in consultation with local communities and other stakeholders, area development frameworks for all large residential sites of 10 hectares or more, or that could accommodate more than 500 dwellings. These plans were to include the provision of suitable non-residential uses, such as offices, workspaces, restaurants, leisure facilities, and local shops and services. Boroughs were encouraged to assess the need for community and ancillary services such as local health facilities, schools and public open space.

Affordable housing

The next section of the draft Plan set out policies for affordable housing. Draft policy 3A.6 set out a definition of affordable housing. This was more specific than the guidance in PPG3 required, as it separately categorized social housing (defined as housing usually provided by a Registered Social Landlord or housing authority, using public subsidy, at levels no higher than Housing Corporation target rents) and intermediate housing (defined as sub-market housing substantially above Housing Corporation target rents, but substantially below market rents). The definition of intermediate housing was to be based on affordability – targeted at households on moderate incomes (roughly between £15,000 and £35,000 a year), who were unable to access the housing market. The draft policy also stated, somewhat contentiously, that, 'in some cases, low cost market housing' would also be considered as affordable. The supporting text explained that this would be 'where its price is close to other forms of intermediate housing'.

After replicating the assessment of housing need included in the report of the Mayor's Housing Commission, and referring back to the Three Dragons/Nottingham Trent University report on affordable housing in London, the draft Plan stated that the Mayor had adopted a target that 50 per cent of all dwellings should be affordable and that, within the overall target, he sought to achieve 35 per cent social rented housing and 15 per cent intermediate housing. The draft Plan did not include the 50 per cent Londonwide target explicitly in the proposed plan policies.

Draft policy 3A.7 set out the basis for boroughs to set affordable housing targets. Without any reference to the Londonwide targets, the policy required boroughs to 'set an overall target for the highest reasonable number of affordable homes to be provided taking account of regional and local assessments of need, the promotion of mixed and balanced communities and potential sources of supply'. These sources were then listed as local authority developments, including estate renewals; Registered Social Landlord developments; low-cost market housing, where it can be shown to be affordable; private residential development negotiations secured through planning agreements or conditions; vacant properties brought back into use; and provision from non-self-contained accommodation. Draft policy 3A.8 then set out targets by borough for the negotiation of affordable housing in individual schemes. These targets, based on the Three Dragons/Nottingham Trent University report, were 50 per cent for central London and other higher-value boroughs, and 35 per cent for the remaining boroughs. The draft policy stated that:

> Boroughs should apply these targets sensitively when negotiating with developers for affordable housing in residential or mixed use schemes that include housing, taking account of individual site costs, economic viability, including the availability of public subsidy and other planning objectives.

The proposed policy also stated that 'Boroughs should seek to achieve a range of affordable housing following the guide 70:30 for social rented to intermediate housing'. The wording and intention of these two policies was to generate considerable debate in the Examination in Public.

The draft Plan also assumed that affordable housing requirements should apply to all sites, including sites with a capacity of a single dwelling. It was argued that, given the shortage of housing in London, there was a case for amending the existing guidance on the unit thresholds at which the planning policy requirement for a proportion of affordable homes applies as set out in the government's circular 6/98, which set a threshold of twenty-five for Outer London and fifteen for Inner London. Although the GLA thought it had government support for this revision, at the Examination in Public it was to be discovered that this was not in fact the case.

Draft policies 3A.9 and 3A.10 set out a framework for the use of planning obligations to provide affordable housing. Priority was to be given to on-site provision, with boroughs required to state in their UDPs the exceptional cases in which payment in lieu of on-site provision might be acceptable. Boroughs were advised to set out in Supplementary Planning Guidance (SPG) the basis on which such payments would be calculated, based on the principle that the developer should not benefit from an obligation being transferred from on-site to off-site provision.

Draft policies 3A.11–3A.15 covered secondary matters which were not primarily land use issues: the promotion of sub-regional approaches to the provision of affordable housing, the provision of special needs housing, the needs of travellers and gypsies and the avoidance of loss of housing and affordable housing through estate regeneration and the avoidance of loss of hostels and shared accommodation.

Density

The proposed residential density policy was set out in the design chapter of the Plan as draft policy 4.3. Under the heading 'Maximising the potential of sites' the proposed policy stated that 'The Mayor will and boroughs should ensure development proposals achieve the highest possible intensity of use compatible with local context, design principles and with public transport capacity'. The draft policy stated that 'Boroughs should develop residential and commercial density policies in their UDPs in line with this policy. Residential development should conform to the density ranges set out in Table 4B.1'. (This table was the density, location and parking matrix taken from the Llewellyn-Davies 1997 and 2000 reports for LPAC – Table 4.2 – and set the ranges from 30–50 units per hectare (150–230 hrh) in suburban sites with poor public transport access to 240–435 units per hectare (650–1100 hrh) for flatted development with limited car parking provision in central locations with very good public transport access.) The draft policy then stated that 'The Mayor will refuse permission for strategic referrals that under-use the potential of the site'. For commercial developments, plot ratios should be at least 3:1 and 5:1 for sites with good public transport access and located in central London and some opportunity areas.

Table 4.2 London Plan density matrix: density location and parking matrix (habitable rooms and units per hectare)

			Car parking provision	High 2–1.5 spaces per unit	Moderate 1.5–1 space per unit	Low < 1 space per unit
		Predominant housing type		Detached and linked houses	Terraced houses and flats	Mostly flats
Location	Accessibility index	Setting				
Sites within 10 mins walking distance of a town centre	6–4	Central				650–1100 hr/ha 240–435 u/ha Ave. 2.7 hr/u
		Urban			200–450 hr/ha 55–175 u/ha Ave. 3.1 hr/u	450–700 hr/h 165–275 u/ha Ave. 3.0 hr/u
		Suburban			200–300 hr/ha 50–110 u/ha Ave. 3.7 u/ha	250–350 hr/ha 80–120 u/ha Ave. 3.0 hr/u
Sites along transport corridors and sites close to a town centre	3–2	Urban			200–300 hr/ha 50–110 u/ha Ave. 3.7 u/ha	300–450 hr/ha 100–150 u/ha Ave. 3.0 hr/u
		Suburban		150–200 hr/ha 30–65 u/ha Ave. 4.4 hr/u	200–250 hr/ha 50–80 u/ha Ave. 3.8 u/ha	
Currently remote sites	2–1	Suburban		150–200 hr/ha 30–50 u/ha Ave. 4.6 hr/u		

Source: GLA (2004a).

Planning obligations

Proposed policies on planning obligations were included in Chapter 5 'Delivering the Vision' of the draft London Plan in the section on mechanisms for implementation. Under draft policy 5.3, borough policies were required to reflect strategic as well as local needs; affordable housing together with public transport improvements should be given the highest importance with priority also given to learning, skills and health facilities and services. Draft policy 5.4 was a simplified version of the criteria proposed in Professor Lane's research report. The proposed policies also included the Mayor's wish to establish pooling arrangements and to be party to appropriate section 106 agreements. The policies also referred to the Mayor's wish to see legislation changed to explicitly extend requirements to impacts beyond the development site. The draft Plan also included a reference to the Mayor's concern that large increases in land values, much of which are attributable to the planning system or to public investment, should be recouped to reinvest in the public interest – a significant point given the government was beginning to consider the reform of the planning obligation regime.

Public consultation

The draft Plan was subject to a public consultation exercise. The GLA arranged an extensive programme of consultation meetings, with an additional consultation structure for voluntary sector organizations. Organizations and individuals had three months in which to make written responses. Over 650 responses were received, comprising over 12,000 specific comments. All responses were categorized as Support, Objection or Comment. It should be noted that a respondent who was in general support of a policy but sought a minor amendment could be categorized as an objector.

Responses to housing policies were categorized as shown in Table 4.3.

Opposition was greatest to the Mayor's proposal that he should have a strategic role in planning obligations and the proposed density policies. There was also a wide range of objections to borough housing targets, despite these being derived from the thirty-three boroughs through the housing capacity study undertaken by LPAC. The policies on affordable housing including on- and off-site provision and payment in lieu were also contentious. Even the proposals for partnerships and sub-regional coordination met with considerable opposition. The policies with greatest support were those on effective use of stock, including vacant dwellings, and on special needs housing and provision for gypsies and travellers – policies which were advocating borough action rather than being seen as prescriptive and interventionist.

Table 4.3 Consultation responses on the *Draft London Plan*

Policy no.	Policy heading	Support	Object	Other comments	Total responses	Support as % of total
3A.1	Increasing London's supply of housing	37	51	20	108	34
3A.2	Borough housing targets	24	52	17	93	26
3A.3	Efficient use of stock	31	12	6	49	63
3A.4	Housing choice	45	41	18	104	43
3A.5	Large residential developments	24	17	9	50	48
3A.6	Definition of affordable housing	23	46	23	92	25
3A.7	Negotiating affordable housing in individual schemes	41	88	36	165	25
3A.8	Affordable housing targets	32	91	24	147	22
3A.9	On- and off-site contributions	29	30	3	62	47
3A.10	Payments in lieu	27	34	9	70	39
3A.11	Partnership approach and sub-regional frameworks	15	14	2	31	48
3A.12	Special needs housing	16	5	2	23	70
3A.13	London's travellers and gypsies	11	1	3	15	73
3A.14	Loss of housing and affordable housing	22	10	7	39	56
3A.15	Loss of hostels, staff accommodation and shared accommodation	17	12	5	34	50
4B.3	Maximising the potential of sites	43	94	20	157	29
5.3	Priorities in planning obligations	21	109	18	148	14
5.4	Planning obligations	13	67	8	88	15

Source: Analysis of responses to consultation as published by GLA at http://www.london.gov.uk/mayor/strategies/sds/responses/policy.jsp.

Strengthening the evidence base

The GLA team needed to strengthen their evidence base for the forthcoming Examination in Public. The GLA therefore continued to publish research reports to support its policy proposals. Reports which impacted on the housing proposals included *City of Villages: Promoting a Sustainable Future for London's Suburbs* by the consultants URBED in August 2002 (GLA 2002f), a report on *Investigating the Potential of Large Mixed Use Housing Developments* in August 2002 (GLA 2002g) and revised *GLA Population and Household Forecasts*, based on the 2001 census, published in January 2003 (GLA 2003a). The GLA also published a report on affordable housing thresholds by Three Dragons, Nottingham Trent University and Roger Tym in March 2003 (GLA 2003b). This was jointly commissioned with GOL and the Department of Communities and Local Government (DCLG) and examined the case for a reduction in the threshold at which an affordable housing requirement applied. Despite providing evidence for a lower threshold in London than the current circular 6/78 guidance, it did not endorse the draft London Plan assumption of a zero threshold; it considered five units to be the lowest practical threshold.

The Examination in Public

The Examination in Public, chaired by Alan Richardson, ran for six weeks in March and April 2003. In preparation for the EiP, the Panel invited submissions in response to a number of questions:

- How realistic are the draft Plan's population and household growth assumptions in the light of the emerging post 2001 Census projections?
- How realistic are the housing provision figures for the subregions, London boroughs and Corporation of London in the light of the latest housing capacity assessments carried out by those authorities?
- Are the draft Plan's policies for achieving additional housing provision, including proposals for higher densities, realistic and sustainable? Are these policies compatible with the needs of local communities and with the aim of creating a higher quality environment?
- Do the policies in the draft Plan adequately address the housing needs of all sections of the community in terms of the type of accommodation and the supply of affordable housing? Is the assessment of London's overall housing need realistic?
- Should the Plan contain overall and borough targets for affordable housing provision and are the proposed 50% and 35% figures appropriate? Does the Three Dragons and Nottingham Trent methodology provide an adequate foundation for the approach in the Plan?

• How are the proposed Borough targets for affordable housing to be applied and what are the mechanisms available for delivery? Are the proposed policies for requiring affordable housing in all development regardless of size and in mixed use developments workable and justified?

(GLA 2003h pp. 12–13)

The first major discussion in the housing sessions of the Examination in Public was on the relationship between the housing target and the identified housing need, as the capacity-based target of 23,000 was clearly below the identified need of 31,900 homes a year. By the date of the EiP revised household projections had in fact increased this latter figure to 33,600 homes. The house builders argued that the target should be higher. GLA officers responded that the target had to be capacity based, and that until a new capacity study had been undertaken it was not known whether a higher target was deliverable, and there could be no sound basis for distributing any higher target between boroughs. The Panel's conclusion was that the Plan should include an aspirational target and that a new target following a new capacity study be added to the London Plan by 2006. Policy 3A.1 in the final Plan published in February 2004 (GLA 2004a) included the new statement that 'The Mayor will seek the maximum provision of additional housing in London towards achieving an output of 30,000 homes per year from all sources'. The borough targets as published in the draft Plan were adopted as the basis for monitoring up to 2006. The Panel also strengthened the policy on the role of empty homes in increasing effective supply and required boroughs to have comprehensive strategies and monitoring.

The second major debate was over the 50 per cent affordable housing target. The house builders first wanted the affordable housing target fixed as a unit target at 10,000 rather than as a proportion, and then argued that the 50 per cent target should be made conditional on the 30,000 being agreed. The Panel agreed with GLA officers that the Londonwide 50 per cent target should remain as drafted rather than be made dependent on an increase in overall output.

There was then a debate over the density policies in the Plan. A number of boroughs argued that density policy was a matter for borough determination. The Panel endorsed the GLA view that, to ensure effective use of capacity across London, there needed to be a consistent policy and that the framework set out in the London Plan was an appropriate one. Consequently the matrix as set out in the draft Plan was adopted without amendment. Despite opposition from the Forum of Amenity Societies, the objective of maximizing capacity was left unchanged. Although the Panel recommended more flexibility for boroughs, the final wording of the adopted plan was 'Boroughs should adopt the residential density ranges set out in Table 4.B1' which was in effect no weaker than the sentence 'residential development should conform to the density ranges set out in Table 4B.1', to which the Panel had objected. Once the Plan was adopted the Mayor objected to any borough UDP that neither adopted the matrix nor included a borough matrix consistent with the London Plan matrix.

The basis for setting borough targets for affordable housing was a source of considerable confusion both in terms of the questions asked by the Panel and in terms of the discussion. A number of parties at the EiP interpreted the targets proposed for the negotiation of affordable housing in individual major developer-led schemes (which varied between boroughs, with some at 35 per cent and some at 50 per cent) as if they were boroughwide targets applying to supply from all sources. The London Plan's definition of 'all sources' included supply from small sites, including affordable housing only schemes, hostels and shared housing, and long-term vacant units returning to permanent use.

PPG3 and other government guidance actually precluded the setting of boroughwide affordable housing targets by the regional planning authority. The GLA was also concerned that the impression had been given that lower affordable housing targets, for example a 35 per cent target, would be acceptable as a boroughwide average in those boroughs where values were relatively low. The GLA therefore accepted the Panel's view that the contentious borough table be deleted and that boroughs be given flexibility to negotiate affordable housing outputs in individual private residential and mixed-use schemes. This would be based on seeking 'the maximum reasonable amount of affordable housing', recognizing that targets should be applied flexibly, taking account of individual site costs, the availability of public subsidy and other scheme requirements.

The policy on setting boroughwide targets was strengthened; whereas the draft policy 3A.7 made no reference to the Londonwide targets, the policy adopted in the final Plan was explicit that 'boroughs should take into account . . . The Mayor's strategic target for affordable housing provision that 50% of provision should be affordable and, within that, the London-wide objective of 70% social housing and 30% intermediate provision.' This critical change, although not prescribing borough targets, which would have been in breach of PPG3, put the onus on a borough proposing a lower target to demonstrate that they had had regard to the Mayor's Londonwide target, and justified a mayoral objection where this could not be demonstrated.

There were four other contentious issues. The draft Plan had assumed that an affordable housing requirement would apply to all sites, irrespective of size. The Government Office for London, on behalf of CLG, had objected to this as being inconsistent with circular 6/98. The GLA would have accepted a norm threshold of ten. The Panel therefore required the text to be amended to state that boroughs should not normally set a threshold over fifteen and they were encouraged to set a lower threshold through the UDP where this was justified and consistent with government guidance. As will be demonstrated below, this failed to ensure consistency of approach across London and the threshold issue was to remain contentious and become a matter for review in the further alterations in 2007.

The second issue was the proposed policies (3A.9 and 3A.10) on on-site and off-site contributions and 'payments in lieu' of on-site provision of affordable housing. The Panel was persuaded by GOL and the boroughs that this was not a strategic matter and that there was no need for Londonwide consistency. This conclusion was to prove ironic when PPS3 (Policy Planning Statement) later gave national guidance on the issue and ODPM/CLG and the Treasury were to commission a series of reports examining why practice was inconsistent and opportunities for effective planning obligations not utilized. The GLA retained the wording of its proposed policy guidance as text in the final Plan, and the issue of payments in lieu was later picked up in the *Housing Supplementary Planning Guidance* (GLA 2005a). The Panel also made two significant changes to the two draft policies on planning obligations. The statement in Policy 5.3 that 'The Mayor will seek secondary legislation to enable him to be a party to appropriate s106 agreements' was deleted following unanimous objection from boroughs, while the requirement that all borough UDPs include policies which reflected the Mayor's priorities of affordable housing and public transport was also deleted. It is significant that the adopted Plan included strategic priorities for planning obligations and a reference to pooling – policies going beyond existing national government guidance.

There was a strong lobby at the EiP from developers building student housing and from agents acting on behalf of universities, who wanted all housing for students defined as affordable and therefore contributing to the 50 per cent target. The GLA, supported by some boroughs, objected to this on the basis that student housing was not available to other households in housing need, that student requirements had not been included in the estimates of the need for social rented and intermediate housing which had informed the proposed 35 per cent and 15 per cent targets and that, if student housing were treated as affordable, its provision would be at the expense of provision for households in greater priority need – households in need of self-contained permanent housing – rather than short-term provision in cluster flats or hostels for students. The Panel supported the student housing lobby, although there did not appear to be any basis for this in government guidance. The Mayor decided not to accept the Panel recommendation on this issue on the basis that applications for student housing should be considered on their merits as a specific form of housing provision. The Mayor agreed that, where a higher education institution was providing a student development within a campus site or on a site not suitable for family housing, so long as no open market housing was being provided, the requirement for social rent and intermediate provision would not be pursued.

The final and in many ways most contentious issue was the proposal in Policy 3A.4 that all new development be built to lifetime homes standards and that 10 per cent of new development be built or easily adaptable to the full wheelchair standard. The house builders objected strongly to these proposals, whereas GOL argued that the matters were for national building regulations rather than for a statutory regional plan. The GLA responded that there were critical issues of undersupply and disadvantage to vulnerable client groups, and that, given the space requirements and cost implications of providing to meet such needs, the issue had to be dealt with at the planning stage; the building regulation stage was too late in the process. The Panel supported the GLA position. GOL continued pursuing its objection and only reluctantly conceded that this difference of view was insufficient grounds for direction of non-adoption of the Plan by the Secretary of State.

The adopted London Plan and housing

The housing policies in the adopted London Plan were consistent with the original policy intentions set out in both *Towards the London Plan* and the *Draft Plan*. The key policies on housing targets and affordable housing were actually strengthened relative to earlier drafts and the unintentional implication that some boroughs could deliver only 35 per cent of housing as affordable removed. On the two controversial issues of lifetime homes and student housing, the Mayor sustained his original position against objections from central government and the Panel respectively. The main substance of the strategic policies on density and planning obligations was retained, with clarifications on implementation left to Supplementary Planning Guidance. The need to increase housing capacity beyond 23,000 was recognized. The Mayor's approach was to take revised targets through an early alteration to the London Plan after a new housing capacity study was endorsed. The regional 50 per cent target, far higher than in any other approved regional plan, was endorsed as was the new principle for separate targets for social rent and intermediate housing. Moreover the Plan set out a clear relationship between the regional target, borough targets and application of targets to individual sites with a new focus on development viability central to the planning approval and planning obligation negotiation process.

The Plan was the first Regional Spatial Development Strategy and therefore included policies that were not solely land use based and which relied on other powers, agencies, strategies and funding for their implementation. The Plan also set a number of targets which could be monitored and used as a basis not only for checking the general conformity of borough plans but also as a basis for mayoral intervention. This included veto of strategic development schemes referable by local planning authorities. The 2004 Planning and Compulsory Purchase Act was an unexpected bonus in that it made the London Plan a component of each borough's Local Development Plan Documentation and consequently a basis for local planning decisions. The housing policies in the Plan were also to serve as the basis for the Mayor's draft housing strategy published in 2007 and in fact it could be argued that the later strategy added little to the Plan policies as adopted.

It is also significant that the Plan was adopted before the end of the mayoral first term. The whole Plan process took less than four years and was achieved with a quite surprising degree of consensus – both factors due substantially to the preparatory work of LPAC. It should be remembered that neither the 1929 Unwin nor the 1944 Abercrombie plan was statutory – their status was advisory, although the 1944 plan was later endorsed by ministers. After a long gestation period from the original 1969 statement, the first Greater London Development Plan was only adopted in 1976, with the motorway box proposals excluded, whereas the 1984 proposals fell as the GLC was abolished. Discounting RPG3 (London) published in 1996 and RPG9 (Greater South East) published in 2001, both by the central government, the London Plan is only the second statutory plan for London proposed and published by a democratically elected regional authority. Furthermore, it was adopted within four years of the powers being obtained. It is, therefore, not an inconsiderable achievement by the Mayor and his planning team. The Mayor had achieved his objective of getting his Plan adopted before the end of his first term. In June 2004, Ken Livingstone was re-elected for a second four-year term, this time as the official Labour candidate, back in favour with the Labour government, though no less 'his own man'.

Key issues in the plan-making process

Political direction and the compact city agenda

The fact that the Mayor had his own vision of London's future, and was as an individual the strategic planning authority for the city, gave a clear political direction to the London Plan. Nicky Gavron as Deputy Mayor for most of the plan preparation period was advisor to the Mayor on strategic planning matters and chaired the Spatial Development Strategy steering group, but the role of Richard Rogers as the Mayor's advisor on architecture and urbanism was also significant. The foreword to the draft London Plan was signed by both Gavron and Rogers, and Rogers's support for high-rise development and views on design were to have more influence over the Mayor than Gavron's more environmentalist perspective. Rogers had previously set out his vision in the book *A New London*, many of these arguments also being set out in the report of the Urban Task Force which he chaired for the Deputy Prime Minister, John Prescott, in 1999. He was to publish in November 2005 his own independent review of progress against the original recommendations, an initiative which was to annoy Prescott (Rogers and Fisher 1992, Rogers 1999, Rogers 2005). Rogers also published two popular books advocating the compact city approach, the first of which was based on his Reith lectures, and the Mayor's urbanism unit under his direction was to publish its own guide to how higher densities could be achieved (Rogers 1997, Rogers and Power 2000, GLA 2003c).We will return to this issue in a later chapter.

The objectives of the SDS, derived from the European Spatial Development Perspective's threefold vision of economic growth, social inclusivity and improvements to the environment, was a statement of Livingstone's personal position. Rydin *et al.* (2004) consider that there was a tension between economic growth and environmental objectives. Livingstone asserted that there was not a conflict between these two objectives and the Plan as a whole does not acknowledge any such conflict.

The structure of the GLA, with the Mayor having executive authority, and the Assembly's role limited to scrutiny, meant that there was no need for collective political responsibility or agreement on the process of developing the Plan.

The business sector and the pursuit of growth

Livingstone's commitment to the economic growth of London was based on a close alliance with the representative bodies of London's private sector, with London First in the leading role but also involving the Confederation of British Industry (the CBI), the London Chamber of Commerce and Industry (LCCI) and the House Builders Federation. Thornley *et al.* (2002) focused on the close working relationships between the Mayor and these private sector bodies, and the key role of Livingstone's economic advisor, John Ross, in supporting market-led employment growth, besides the fact that the leader of the City Corporation, Dame Judith Mayhew, also sat on the Mayor's cabinet of advisors as city and business advisor. In a separate article, Thornley (1999) examined the lobbying by London First and the work of London Pride in promoting policies which supported economic growth; a later article argued that the Mayor gave the business sector a privileged role within his policy development framework (Thornley *et al.* 2002).

This campaign proved successful in convincing the Mayor and his advisors, an outcome perhaps surprising given the left-wing anti-capitalist stance previously taken by Livingstone and Ross. Ian Gordon, in a study of the 'global city rhetoric' in the London Plan, refers to the global city focus of the plan as a 'trump card' used by the Mayor 'in order to establish legitimate claims to resources controlled by central government' and that this claim was bolstered 'through a credible pattern of interaction with the relevant business interests' (Gordon 2003). The evidence from the plan-making process, including the Examination in Public, was that the private sector was an integral component of the pro-growth consensus, which had developed in the pre-mayoral and early mayoral period. This helped to ensure that the growth-based plan was endorsed, and that they were prepared, if reluctantly, to live with some of the mayoral policies which were less in their favour, such as the affordable housing requirement. In this sense, the Mayor won over the private sector into accepting components of his broader social justice agenda as much as the private sector had won over the Mayor to a market-led plan.

The London Plan as the first Regional Spatial Strategy in England

The London Plan was the first Regional Spatial Strategy adopted by a regional planning authority under the new regional governance arrangements. Although the London Plan was technically the Spatial Development Strategy published under the powers granted to the Mayor by the GLA Act 1999, it was recognized as the first of the new type of regional plan and a precedent for the Regional Spatial Strategies to be developed by the eight regional assemblies for non-London regions under the 2004 Planning and Compulsory Purchase Act. The government guidance on plan content as set out in the GLA Act and GOL circular 1/2000 was very broad. Not only was Planning Policy Statement 11 on Regional Spatial Strategies published only in July 2004, after the publication of the London Plan, but also it does not apply to London. Given that the London Plan goes far beyond traditional land use issues, it is surprising that there were so few challenges from either objectors or the Panel to the Plan content.

As far as housing policies were concerned, the Panel's conclusions were rather curious – for example the proposed policy on off-site contributions to affordable housing planning obligations was removed. It was not considered to be a strategic matter, though the wording of the policy survived as supporting text. The Panel supported the strengthening of the policy to require boroughs to develop empty property strategies and monitor their effectiveness – a policy that would traditionally be seen as an element of housing strategy rather than planning strategy. It was also unexpected that the 2004 Planning and Compulsory Purchase Act retrospectively gave development plan status to the published Plan – in that it allowed boroughs to use the Plan policies and for other parties to make reference to them, in the determination of planning decisions by the borough as a local planning authority. This status was different from the traditional role of a strategic plan, or for that matter county structure plan, in setting a framework for local borough/district plans rather than as a basis for determination of individual planning applications.

Nevertheless, given its nature as a strategic plan rather than a land use allocation document, a number of relatively minor changes were required to the draft Plan to ensure that no sites were red-lined and any designation of areas, such as the Central Activities Zone or an Area of Opportunity or Strategic Employment Location, was indicative only. The specific boundaries were to be determined by the borough plan, though there was to be a delay before boroughs could adopt new core strategies or site allocation development documents under the new 2004 Act framework. One rather curious anomaly was that, when the Secretary of State directed the City of Westminster to adopt different affordable housing targets for sites within the CAZ and for sites outside the CAZ, the direction largely depended on the indicative CAZ boundary identified in the London Plan, and a specific CAZ boundary then had to be included in Westminster's document. A boundary that could not be fixed by the regional body, as it was not a strategic matter, was in effect determined by the Secretary of State.

Regionalization: government, the Mayor and the boroughs

It should be noted that in London the power to publish and adopt the strategic plan was with the Mayor rather than the Secretary of State. This is in contrast with the new powers granted to regional assemblies outside London by the 2004 Act, whereby the regional assembly recommended the RSS to the Secretary of State and the Secretary of State could direct amendments. The Examination in Public Panel reported to the Mayor, whereas outside London the Panel reported to the Secretary of State. Curiously, this is a distinction which was not initially acknowledged by the Panel appointed in 2006 to consider the early alterations to the London Plan. However, given that the Secretary of State reserved the power to direct the Mayor not to publish the Plan, and consequently suggested amendments that would ensure he would not use this power, the distinction is mainly technical. Nevertheless it allowed the Mayor to refer to the SDS as the 'Mayor's Plan', in a manner that would not apply in the other regions, where, given the history of RSSs to date, the extent of amendments made to regional assembly draft RSSs by the Secretary of State has made it clear that these plans are being imposed by the central government on unwilling assemblies.

Despite the transfer of strategic planning powers to the Mayor, the Government Office for London retained some planning functions on behalf of the central government. GOL was responsible for advising the Secretary of State whether the draft London Plan conformed with national planning policy. GOL also continued to advise the Secretary of State on calling in individual planning applications – a power which had not been transferred to the Mayor. In practice, the planning team at GOL continued to operate as a parallel strategic planning authority. GOL planners appeared to check every sentence of the draft London Plan against every national planning policy document and formally object to every statement that was not fully consistent. In addition they continued policing the borough Unitary Development Plan system still operating under the pre-2004 legislation.

This process was further complicated by the fact that the central government was consulting on a range of changes to policy guidance. The Secretary of State had issued a series of proposals on changes to Planning Policy Guidance 3. Some proposed amendments had been brought into effect; others had not. The government had also consulted on a range of options for changing the planning obligations regime and in the 2004 Act was to enact legislation for a new optional planning charge scheme. This was then abandoned in favour of Planning Gain Supplement (PGS). Two years later they were to drop this in favour of a proposal for a Community Infrastructure Levy (CIL). The GLA, having sought to draw up planning policy in line with government proposals, then found the policies objected to by GOL on behalf of the central government on the grounds that the government had not yet formally issued revised guidance based on their proposals and consequently could not support any policies in the plan which were not in accordance with the pre-existing PPG3. Boroughs were caught in a similar trap: if they tried to follow the London Plan policy or the Mayor's interpretation of national policy, their policies could be objected to by GOL. If they did not follow London Plan policy they could be objected to by the Mayor.

It was difficult for the Association of London Government to mount a coordinated opposition to plan policies. Individual boroughs had objections to individual London Plan policies, as each borough had its own interests, and political control of boroughs varied. Few boroughs, for example, objected to the housing targets, which had been derived from a study in which they had been fully engaged. Most boroughs supported a Londonwide 50 per cent affordable housing target, and the plan was not prescriptive as to targets for individual boroughs, especially with the removal of the borough site target table which had categorized boroughs. The boroughs argued for more flexibility on the division between social rent and intermediate housing and the Mayor conceded minor wording changes but maintained his Londonwide target for a 70:30 ratio between social rent and intermediate housing. Boroughs generally supported the proposal for tighter definitions of affordable housing than were included in PPG3.

So, whereas boroughs had a concern that the Mayor would intervene more in matters they saw as primarily their responsibility, the policies were based substantially on LPAC guidance to which they had been party. Objecting boroughs were isolated and as a result unable to sustain objections. Given that the London Plan was far more comprehensive than RPG3 had been, boroughs were more constrained by London Plan policies than they had been by previous regional guidance, so there was in fact a shift of power from both the central government and the boroughs to the Mayor; but this shift, at least at the time of Plan adoption in 2004, was generally accepted. As far as the London Plan was considered, the Mayor was seen as both adopting justifiable policies and operating in a reasonable and non-adversarial manner. From the strategic planning perspective, at least in terms of the making of the London Plan, the new experiment in regional government was seen as successful.

Community engagement

Engaging the community in a strategic plan for a region of 7.5 million people is not an easy process. As a regional plan sets general directions but not site-specific land use allocations, it is difficult for an individual to assess specific impacts on one's own interests. Nevertheless in a city such as London there are extensive networks of lobbying groups and individuals, some with a national perspective but London based, some with a regional focus, some borough based, some much more localized. Developers with specific proposals are also interested in how new strategic policies will impact on their schemes and their profitability. In the stage between *Towards the London Plan* and the draft Plan, and between the draft Plan and the Examination in Public, the GLA held hundreds of presentation and consultation meetings – some at regional level with specific interest groups, others at sub-regional level. There was a concentrated effort to engage voluntary sector bodies.

At the formal pre-EiP submission stage, 650 organizations submitted 12,000 specific comments. The Examination in Public was dominated by the regional bodies: the Government Office for London, the Association of London Government, London First and the House Builders Federation. Of the voluntary sector bodies, the London Forum of Civic and Amenity Societies was probably the most effective. In terms of the housing sessions of the EiP, Chris Holmes as former chair of the Mayor's Housing Commission played a significant role. Few of the local groups were selected by the Panel to participate in the EiP. Many of their concerns were not considered to be of a strategic nature and they were left to pursue their points through other policy consultation processes, including those on the Sub-regional Development Frameworks (SRDFs) discussed below.

It is difficult to identify elements of the plan which changed as a result of the extensive community engagement process. The groups most dominant in the formal strategic plan-making process were those professional regional representative bodies who had been engaged in the earlier processes undertaken in the pre-mayoral period by LPAC and through organizations such as London Pride. They were generally seeking fairly minor changes to a generally agreed consensus to which they were party, rather than arguing for an alternative position. The exception was some elements of the environmental lobby who argued for a no growth option, but these interests were marginalized by the alliance between the Mayor and the business lobby and did not impact significantly on the debates on the housing policies in the plan.

The missing inter-regional dimension

Representatives of the East of England (EERA) and South East of England (SEERA) Regional Assemblies made submissions and participated in the EiP. Sir Peter Hall had expressed the view that the Plan did not adequately consider the relationship of London to the wider metropolitan region. There was, however, no substantive challenge to the Plan's explicit assumption that London would meet its needs within the London boundary – the whole basis of the 'compact city' plan for more intensive development. This was to a large extent because it was in the interest of the two neighbouring regions that London adopted the self-containment principle, however unrealistic that might be, as it allowed them to develop their own Regional Spatial Strategies on the basis of no net out-migration from London. This also allowed them to propose lower housing targets than would have otherwise been necessary, which was politically convenient given the hostility within both regions to higher levels of housing development. SEERA and EERA were later to welcome the Mayor's increased housing target, as this allowed them to propose relatively low levels of housing growth. This strategy was to unravel as the government published higher household population growth projections while the South East and East of England Plans were in the consultation and Examination in Public stages. These developments were also to impact on the EiP into the London Plan early alterations in 2006. It is not insignificant that the 2003 EiP recognized the deficiencies in the Mayor's consideration of inter-regional issues and recommended that further policies be developed (GLA 2003d).

Professionals, political advisers and consultants

It has already been noted that the London Plan vision, especially the 'world city' and 'compact city' components, was largely politically driven by Ken Livingstone. Although the Mayor appointed Professors Stevenson and Thompson to advise on the Plan and to give the Plan some status in the planning profession, external consultants were used to provide support for preset plan policies, rather than to examine alternative scenarios or challenge preset assumptions. The series of technical reports written by consultants for the GLA were clearly 'technical' reports, with the GLA ensuring these did not raise awkward issues. To take one example:

SDS technical report 1 on *Affordable Housing in London* (GLA 2001b)was used to support the Mayor's argument that a 50 per cent affordable housing target was deliverable. When a separate report was published by Atis Real Wetherall, which challenged this assumption (GLA 2002a), the GLA published a further technical report by Three Dragons as a riposte (GLA 2002b).

Another example was the report on affordable housing thresholds, also by Three Dragons (GLA 2003b). The purpose of this report had been to support the Mayor's proposition that affordable housing thresholds should be set at zero. The central government through GOL and ODPM was also a party to this report. Although the consultants supported lowering of the threshold from the norm of fifteen in Inner London and twenty-five in Outer London, ODPM was not convinced of the case for setting a new norm threshold at zero, ten or fifteen. The report's conclusions remained ambivalent, though they were later used by the central government to support lowering of thresholds to ten in specific boroughs.

The Panel's report led to a number of minor changes to the Plan, but there were nevertheless a number of cases, for example policy on student housing, in which the Mayor and his advisors discounted Panel recommendations. The Mayor was required to publish reasons for his decisions. However, the London Plan team and the consultant professors were only one element of the mayoral decision-making process, together with the Mayor's political advisers, notably Neale Coleman, Eleanor Young and John Ross. They had a significant input into both the draft Plan and the final Plan. Collectively, they operated a power of veto on behalf of the Mayor, a process in which both the Deputy Mayor and the Mayor's professional advisers were sidelined. In this context, external consultants had minimal impact on the Plan's policies; they were generally pleased to be associated with the Plan and were wary of making any specific criticism of the detailed Plan content.

Conflict and consensus

Planning is normally regarded as adversarial: a plan-making body proposes a plan and a range of agencies and individuals then oppose it. Certainly the Examinations in Public into the South East and East of England plans were adversarial. Those regional assemblies had to defend their plan proposals from agencies who were opposed to development, including county councils, most district councils and the organized environmental lobby, and also against the central government, which demanded higher levels of development. Despite the range of submissions to and participants in the London EiP, the London Plan examination was far more consensual. This partly reflected the wide consultation on the Plan's preparation but also reflected the consensual approach developed by LPAC. It also reflected a rather unusual set of circumstances: support for the growth strategy from both the central government and the business sector; support from the environmental lobby with the the Campaign for the Protection of Rural England (CPRE) endorsing increased housing growth in London and densification to protect the Green Belt both within and outside London; support from EERA and SEERA for the compact city assumption. Potential opponents of the Plan were divided. The London Assembly had no majority party and the Association of London Government, representing the boroughs, did not have a very coherent position, which left individual borough objectors isolated.

Neither the Panel nor the government had grounds for requiring significant changes to the Plan. The Mayor and his advisers, keen to get the Plan published before the 2004 elections, were generally happy to accept minor changes of wording and give commitments to an early review of the Plan to consider outstanding issues such as housing capacity and waste policy. Given the difficulty faced by other regions in getting RSSs adopted under the new planning regime, and the similar problems in local planning authorities getting core strategy local planning documents approved, though imperfect, the London Plan can be presented as a successful example of consensus planning at a strategic level.

Government and governance

In establishing the mayoralty in 2000, the government was responding to a demand from the business lobby, supported by the findings of a number of academic studies, notably those emanating from the Greater London Group at the LSE, that London needed more coordinated government and its own public voice. However, the government also took the view that it wanted a small strategic regional body rather than a body which was responsible for service delivery. The GLA was not to be another Greater London Council. It was therefore more than a little ironic that the elected Mayor was none other than the last leader of the GLC, Ken Livingstone, whose ambitions for the mayoral role and powers went far beyond the government's. New Labour, in following the American model for a city mayor, had not thought through the consequences of the powers being taken by someone they did not favour. Moreover the powers of the Assembly were so limited as not to allow for any effective constraints to be put on the Mayor, especially as no political party had a majority. The mayoral elections introduced a concept of celebrity politics from America, with New Labour slow to realize that none of their possible candidates – Frank Dobson, Nick Raynsford, Nicky Gavron or Trevor Phillips – could compete with Ken Livingstone in the celebrity stakes. The Conservatives and Liberal Democrats also found themselves unable to compete on these terms.

Livingstone both before and after election used his independent status to adopt what is generally called a 'big tent' approach to his role. Recognizing his powers were limited, he was quick to make alliances, by appointing Assembly members to key paid positions at the Metropolitan Police Authority, the London Development Agency, Transport for London and the London Fire and Emergency Planning Authority. That key Assembly members were put on the mayoral payroll clearly weakened the Assembly. Coopting key external figures such as Judith Mayhew, leader of the City Corporation, Glenda Jackson MP, Diane Abbott MP and George Barlow of the Peabody Trust onto his advisory cabinet was also an important step. In practice this was symbolic, as the advisory cabinet soon stopped functioning, with the role replaced by the Mayor's own personally appointed advisers, soon given the status of 'directors'. This allowed them to overrule the Mayor's professional staff. Nevertheless the image of the 'big tent' was maintained, primarily because of the Mayor's continued working relationship with the business sector.

As the spokesman for London, and a figure seen as representing London and more effective than the succession of Ministers for London, Ken Livingstone soon discovered that his influence was far greater than his powers. A quick scrutiny of press articles and questions at the Assembly's question time with the Mayor demonstrates the extent to which the Mayor was asked for a view, and freely gave it on matters far beyond his remit. The Mayor could publish a strategy on matters ranging from noise pollution to higher education, which had authority even though he had no powers on either issue. What the government had not predicted was the demand for the Mayor to have greater powers, demands which were widely supported by the private sector.

This reflected the Mayor's two key successes – the introduction of congestion charging and the winning of the 2012 Olympic Games. Ken Livingstone's rejoining the Labour party was also significant, though it could be argued that this was of more benefit to the Labour party than it was to Ken Livingstone. Nevertheless, the Mayor, through his control of Transport for London and despite his opposition to the government's private/public partnership funding regime, was given control of London Underground, and then given some influence over commuter rail franchises. The government's willingness to increase his planning powers and give him some strategic housing powers, which are discussed below, reflects government recognition of the Mayor's achievements. These achievements were not primarily in the areas of planning and housing. The view that the experiment of the mayoralty as a structure of government has been successful is quite widely held both within and outside central government. It is however important to recognize, and the continuing role of the Government Office for London demonstrates this, that this perspective represented more frustration with the boroughs than a belief in decentralization of powers from central government. Thornley, in the London chapter in *Metropolitan Governance and Spatial Planning* (Thornley 2003), concluded that, while the central government had retained control over London government through regulation and funding, the Mayor's use of political and symbolic power was likely to raise new conflicts with the central government.

The Mayor and his advisers were very successful in persuading the government that the Mayor was able to deliver policies while local boroughs could not. The fact that the Mayor delivered very little directly, whereas boroughs with constrained resources and powers generally had continued to deliver services, was something that the central government and others continued to ignore. Ken Livingstone was an extremely successful propagandist. He demonstrated that his strategies were positive and progressive, without having responsibility for their delivery. It can be concluded that, as the Mayor's key strategy, the London Plan was a great success, and demonstrated an exemplary achievement both as process and as plan. The remaining chapters of this study will now focus on implementation of the Plan, a matter not as yet considered by other studies.

Chapter 5
From policy to implementation

The challenges of implementation

A plan without a mechanism for implementation is no more than a plan. The implementation of the London Plan depended on borough plans, Unitary Development Plans under the pre-existing statutory framework, incorporating the policies in the London Plan, and on both strategic planning applications referable to the Mayor and locally determined applications being determined in line with the policies set out in the Plan. There was no precedent either for ensuring that local plans were in conformity with a regional plan; nor was there any precedent for a regional planning body operating development control functions in relation to specific planning applications. The adoption of the Plan represented a fundamental change in the strategic planning framework for London. It represented a shift in the balance of power between the Mayor, the boroughs and the central government with GOL as its agent.

There was also a new political dimension. In 2000, the Mayor had been elected as an independent candidate. By February 2004 he had been adopted as the Labour party candidate and in May 2004 he was elected for a second four-year term, this time as a Labour Mayor. The Mayor's relationship with the central government had improved. With the success of the congestion charge policy, Labour ministers now saw Livingstone as an asset rather than as a liability. The government, as represented by GOL, had been generally supportive of the Mayor's position on planning at the Examination in Public, though raising minor issues of wording not being fully consistent with national guidance. The relationships with boroughs also had an increasingly political aspect. Although the Mayor was far from being a Labour party loyalist, it was queried whether he would treat boroughs with different party political control in a consistent manner. There was also the question of the role of the London Assembly. The Mayor had paid little regard to the Assembly's representations at the various stages of the London Plan consultation. He had resented the attempts of the Assembly to intervene in his consideration of both borough plans and individual strategic cases and had been annoyed when the Assembly published a report *Behind Closed Doors* scrutinizing his planning decisions (London Assembly 2002b). Whereas the Assembly committee had had no role in relation to individual planning applications, the Mayor changed the role of the Assembly planning committee in the process of considering borough planning documents from one of predecision consultation to an arrangement for postdecision notification.

The Sub-regional Development Frameworks and the Supplementary Planning Guidance

Unlike other Regional Spatial Strategies, the London Plan is not required to have an Implementation Plan. Although it includes a set of indicators for monitoring and reporting in the statutory annual monitoring report, there is no implementation programme with timescales. Instead the Mayor decided to publish a set of sub-regional planning documents, which would not set new policy but would give further guidance on planning at sub-regional level. Guidance on implementation of plan policies would be given in a series of Supplementary Planning Guidance documents. Although the sub-regional approach was consistent with the sub-regional approach in the 2004 Planning and Compulsory Purchase Act, there is no statutory basis for either sub-regional frameworks or regional supplementary planning documents. It is worth noting that the sub-regional planning provisions within the 2004 Act were a gesture to the county councils who were seeking a continued planning role following the abolition of county structure plans.

In the absence of any statutory requirement for or guidance on sub-regional planning within London, there was considerable uncertainty as to what the purpose of the Sub-regional Development Frameworks was. The London Plan asserted that 'the SRDFs will have a major role in helping to implement this plan by supplementing policy and aiding delivery between the strategic and local dimension'. London Plan policy 5A stated that the SRDFs

> will build upon existing partnership arrangements operating within the sub-regions, and will include arrangements for involving boroughs, including those in neighbouring sub-regions and authorities in adjoining regions, statutory agencies including the NHS and Environment Agency, infrastructure providers, and representatives from the private sector, voluntary sector and community groups.
>
> (GLA 2004a p. 222)

As the SRDFs were not able to put forward new policies, the documents were primarily descriptive. With sub-regions comprising between four (the North sub-region) and twelve boroughs (the East sub-region), boroughs within groupings shared little common identity (Map 5.1). The East sub-region sought to reflect the new Thames Gateway definition by including boroughs north and south of the river, which had previously had limited geographical or political connection, but

Map 5.1 The 2004 London Plan sub-regions. Source: GLA (2004a). Used with permission.

included the City Corporation, because of its new relationship with Canary Wharf in Tower Hamlets. This left a hole in the Central sub-region, which effectively became West End dominated with Westminster and Kensington and Chelsea being the leading boroughs in the process. The logic of splitting the Central Activities Zone between two sub-regions was questionable. The sub-regions generally did not replicate existing inter-borough arrangements – for example the South London Partnership included Wandsworth, which was in the Central sub-region, and the North London Alliance went wider than the four sub-regional boroughs. The closest correlation was in West London, where the borough-led West London Alliance had already developed close cross-borough cooperation at member and officer level. From a housing perspective, the sub-regions made little sense, as, except for East London, there was a separation between Outer London (generally areas of lower housing stress but with significant potential new housing supply) and Inner London (generally areas of higher stress but with more limited supply potential). The sub-regions therefore contrasted with the more sectoral arrangements established by the Housing Corporation and the ALG, with each area including a mix of inner and outer boroughs. These different five sub-regions already had sub-regional partnerships operating, and in some cases had developed sub-regional housing strategies. The GLA was therefore obliged to publish analysis of housing need and capacity in two sub-regional formats: one for the SRDFs and a separate one for the pre-existing sub-regional groupings.

There were some limited attempts within the SRDFs to identify common issues within a sub-region, given the supply/need mismatch between sub-regions. With surplus capacity in East London and deficits in other sub-regions, especially the Central and West sub-regions, the critical issue was the relationship of a borough's need and supply context to that of the region as a whole, rather than to its immediate neighbours, some of which would be in another sub-region anyway, depending on which grouping was used. The SRDFs were therefore of limited use, other than in aggregating data and describing, in very general terms, the challenges facing an area. They neither provided adequate planning information on Opportunity Areas and Areas for Intensification identified in the London Plan, as had been intended, nor had detailed and costed projections of infrastructure requirements as had been considered – primarily because it was not possible to agree estimates with other statutory bodies such as the Department for Education and Science and the five Regional Health Authorities, soon to be re-organized into a single London Health Authority, but with strategic planning responsibilities transferred to thirty-two primary care trusts. The SRDF process, though staff intensive and involving considerable external consultation, was unproductive for GLA staff as for external consultees, given the lack of clarity as to purpose of the SRDFs. The process, however, initiated a dialogue between GLA planning staff and a wide range of statutory and non-statutory external bodies, with some significant progress being made in terms of exchange of information, if not quite coordinated joint planning and investment, with the utility providers: gas, electricity and water supply.

In the published London Plan, the intention to publish a number of Supplementary Planning Guidance documents was stated. The London Plan listed eleven SPGs, some of which had been published in draft prior to the publication of the London Plan in February 2004 (GLA 2004a). The full list was:

- Accessible London;
- Industrial Capacity;
- Housing Provision;
- Affordable Housing;
- Urban Design Principles;
- Sustainable Construction and Design;
- View Framework Management;
- Land for Transport;
- Renewable Energy;
- Meeting the Spatial Needs of Diverse Communities;
- Retail Needs Assessments.

The two draft Housing SPGs were published separately for consultation, but were published as a single combined SPG in November 2005 (GLA 2005a). Both SPGs were based on a significant research basis, so it is necessary to first consider the research process and outputs. The content and consultation on the Housing SPG is considered later in this chapter.

The 2004 housing requirements study

The housing requirements assumptions in the London Plan had been based on work undertaken in 2000 for the Housing Commission report. Although a summary of the assessment had been included in both the Commission report and the draft London Plan, by the time of London Plan adoption it was recognized that the assessment was both out of date and not sufficiently detailed to support the required guidance on the implementation of the London Plan housing policy on housing choice. The GLA therefore commissioned external consultants, Opinion Research Services (ORS), to make an assessment of the need and demand for housing in all sectors – market, social rented and intermediate – for the full plan period to 2026. Rather than the traditional approach of assessing backlog of housing need and then adding on forecast household population growth, the study was based on a stock flows analysis, which projected forward the interaction of supply and demand over the twenty-year period, assessing the extent to which demand could be met by households moving between dwellings. The analysis was therefore based on assumptions about more effective use of both the existing stock and future supply in terms of occupation levels – predicating a reduction of overcrowding and a reduction in, though not the complete abolition of, underoccupation (GLA 2004b).

The study produced an overall housing requirement of 35,400 new homes a year, compared with the London Plan estimate of 33,600 and the then housing capacity-based target of 23,000 homes a year. The most significant conclusion of the study was, however, not this overall increase in the requirement, but its distribution in terms of affordability/tenure category and bedroom size mix. It was assessed that some 59 per cent (20,800) of the annual requirement was for social rented housing, 7 per cent (2,500) for intermediate housing, and 34 per cent (12,100) for market housing. This contrasted with London Plan targets of 35 per cent, 15 per cent and 50 per cent respectively. The study also concluded that, within the social rented sector, there was a significant need for larger family homes; 41 per cent (8,600) of the 20,800 need was for homes with four or more bedrooms. This contrasted with the demand for market homes, which was predominantly for smaller homes. The main intermediate demand was for one-bedroom homes, but also for four-bedroom homes. The study therefore raised the issues of whether the London Plan target for social rented housing was high enough and whether planning policy should or could seek to increase the proportion of larger homes, especially in the social rented sector.

The development appraisal toolkit

The Mayor's team had recognized that development viability was critical to the achievement of the London Plan's 50 per cent affordable target. The assumptions in the original Three Dragons report had generated significant debate and, as discussed above, the London Plan was amended to shift the focus from borough-level targets to the assessment of individual schemes to demonstrate that the maximum reasonable amount of affordable housing had been achieved. The GLA, initially with some financial support from the Housing Corporation, commissioned Three Dragons and Nottingham Trent University to develop a scheme-specific version of the original residual value model. The purpose of the model was to allow the GLA, local planning authorities and the Housing Corporation to assess whether individual development proposals could deliver 50 per cent affordable housing and still be profitable for the developer. From the GLA's perspective, the model would assist the Mayor's use of his strategic planning powers to decide whether or not to allow schemes which did not meet his full policy objectives, on the basis that the appraisal demonstrated that they were achieving the maximum affordable housing deliverable in the specific circumstances. From the Housing Corporation's perspective, the assessment would determine whether or not the provision of social housing grant would deliver affordable housing which would be additional to that which could be supported by the development value of the private development.

The consultants devised a financial model, which could operate either on preset default data on costs and values, set at borough level, or on the basis of scheme-specific data provided by the development. Scheme-specific data could be compared with borough-level defaults, which would be updated on an annual basis. The toolkit model also made assumptions about developer profit, financing costs and the overheads of the developer, the building contractor and the provider and manager of the affordable housing provider, which was normally, though not always, a housing association. The initial assumption of developer profit on market housing was 15 per cent of value, with an assumption that the builder of the affordable housing would make a 10 per cent return on cost. The model allowed for different mixes of market housing, intermediate housing including shared ownership and sub-market rented provision, and social rented housing to be modelled, together with different mixes of units in terms of built form, density, internal space standards and bedroom size mix, and different levels of grant to be assessed. The model also allowed for the consideration of different levels of contributions to the costs on non-residential development or services through planning obligations.

GLA practice was that, where a residential planning application referred to the Mayor under his strategic planning powers (i.e. schemes with 500 or more homes) did not meet the 50 per cent affordable housing target or the 35 per cent social rent benchmark, or did not provide an appropriate bedroom size mix, a toolkit appraisal was required to justify the underperformance of the proposal. Appraisals should also be submitted to the local planning authority. The GLA and the local planning authority would also use this information to discuss with the Housing Corporation appraisal assumptions on the availability of social housing grant for a scheme, but also whether an additional grant could be made available to support an increase in the amount or type of affordable housing proposed. The boroughs as local planning authorities were also encouraged to ask applicants to submit appraisals for schemes below the 500 threshold where the planning application would be determined locally. The GLA and the Housing Corporation London region published a joint statement advising that appraisals would be used to inform both the planning decision process and the Housing Corporation's investment process. This was important as at a national level the Housing Corporation's investment policy statement made it clear that the Housing Corporation would only provide grant for private-led 's106 schemes' where grant was used to provide additional affordable housing. This approach was often referred to as the 'open book' approach, though this term was misleading because the appraisals, which contained commercially sensitive data, were generally kept confidential between developers and planning authorities.

Private developers were initially reluctant to provide appraisals to the GLA and boroughs and the approach was opposed by the developers' representative body, the House Builders Federation. However, as developers realized that commercial confidentiality was not breached, and that both the Mayor and some boroughs would not support an application unless an appraisal was submitted, over time all major developers in London cooperated with the appraisal approach. Developers' consultants became skilled in using the toolkit, with some local authority planning teams struggling to master the process. Toolkit appraisals were to become a central feature of the London residential development process and a feature of a number of planning inquiries.

The GLA issued an updated version of the toolkit each year, based on reassessment of benchmark costs and values. The 2007/8 version of the model included additional features: a check on whether social rented housing and intermediate housing was affordable in terms of the London Plan definitions, a feature sought by the boroughs, and an ability to model development cash flows over a full scheme development period, which for larger schemes could be up to twenty years, a feature sought by developers. This allowed for the modelling of different timing of costs and receipts, for example the payment of s106 contributions or the sale of completed homes. Since the publication of the toolkit by the GLA, a number of versions of the model have been produced for use in other parts of the United Kingdom, for example Cornwall, the Home Counties around London, Cambridgeshire and Wales, each with its own set of area-specific cost and value benchmarks. There has also been some interest in developing the financial appraisal approach to planning decisions in other countries.

The mixed-use study, the Central Activities Zone and the city fringe

One of the issues central to the viability of a site for housing development is the relative value of the existing use of the site or a potential alternative use. Many of London's development sites did not have a specific land use zoning within a borough's Unitary Development Plan or the Local Development Document equivalent prepared under the new local planning framework introduced by the 2004 Planning and Compulsory Purchase Act. Many sites were zoned for 'mixed use development', which could envisage a combination of different land uses including residential, industrial, commercial, retail, hotels or leisure. The GLA therefore commissioned a study from consultants, London Residential Research and CBRE, to examine the relationship between different use values in different locations. The study was published in March 2004 as the *Mixed Use Development and Affordable Housing Study* (GLA 2004c). This study examined the relationship between housing and commercial development within the Central Activities Zone, the commercial centre of London and other town centres, and proposed mechanisms for appropriate development of city fringe sites, including consideration of 'in lieu' contributions from commercial developments to support the development of affordable housing on other sites. The study also provided use value information which could be used as part of the development appraisal system to ensure that affordable housing requirements imposed on residential schemes did not reduce development returns below returns achievable through other permitted uses. This would in effect push a developer away from pursuing a residential development, but could also assist consideration of the mix of uses on a specific site which would best support affordable housing This was in a context where it was generally not possible legally to impose an affordable housing requirement on a non-residential development.

Where a borough's definition of a mixed-use site specified that 50 per cent of the site should be developed as housing, such as in the central London boroughs of Westminster and Camden, an affordable housing policy requirement could be applied to that residential proportion. In boroughs where policy and zoning was less specific, it became difficult to obtain a contribution to affordable housing, other than through seeking to demonstrate that a non-residential development, such as an office or shop, itself generated a need for affordable housing and therefore justified a planning obligation for this purpose. The report was also used to support draft guidance on application of mixed-use policies in different locations, which was included in the draft *Supplementary Guidance on Housing Provision* published by the Mayor in December 2004.

The Supplementary Planning Guidance on Housing

Although the London Plan was itself a substantive document, the Mayor decided to publish a series of Supplementary Planning Guidance documents to give guidance on implementation of Plan policies. Whereas there were legal provisions for local planning authorities to issue Supplementary Planning Guidance to support implementation of approved Unitary Development Plans, there were no provisions in the 1999 Greater London Authority Act or in circular 1/2000 on this issue. The 2004 Planning and Compulsory Purchase Act also did not include any provisions for SPGs for Regional Spatial Strategies. However, there was little challenge to the mayoral decision to issue SPGs. The government had two main concerns: that the SPGs did not create new policies, as this was a matter for the London Plan itself, and that any guidance given did not conflict with national planning guidance. It was this second factor that was to generate difficulties with the production of the Housing SPG, as government guidance was itself in a fluid state. Under the provisions of the 2004 Act, the government was committed to a programme of producing Planning Policy Statements (PPSs) to replace the pre-existing Planning Policy Guidance (PPGs). Although a number of proposed changes to the pre-existing PPG3 on housing had been floated, no revised PPG3 had been issued, and work on PPS3 was at an early stage at the time GLA officers were drafting and consulting on their own proposed planning guidance for housing. PPS3 was not in fact published until November 2006.

The draft Affordable Housing SPG was published first in July 2004. Much of the content derived from the housing requirements study's analysis of housing need, demand and affordability. The London Plan had been innovative in disaggregating the government's PPG3 definition of affordable housing into two sub-categories: social housing and intermediate housing. It is important to note that these definitions were not tenure specific, but related to household income levels. Although council and housing association rents were subject to the rent target system introduced by the central government in 2002, the GLA was also concerned that service charges, which were not subject to government or Housing Corporation regulation, could make rented housing unaffordable for lower-income groups. Consequently the GLA introduced into its social rent definition the criterion that housing costs for social housing, comprising rent and service charges, should not exceed 30 per cent of net household income. This was later to become a sensitive issue. Since the target rent system introduced by the government included a 25 per cent value-driven component, target rents climbed in line with property value increases; with the increased focus on flatted mixed-tenure development, service charges also increased. The housing costs to the occupant of many new rented housing association schemes, including Housing Corporation-funded schemes, therefore breached the 30 per cent net income guidance. This was especially the case for larger homes in higher-value locations. The draft SPG also made it clear that housing let on the basis of short-term tenancies was not counted as social housing. However, it was also proposed that private rented housing which met affordability criteria, was accessed on the basis of housing need and was let on a tenancy of five years or more could be treated as meeting a planning policy target for social rent. This was intentional and was an attempt to attract private investment in affordable, good-quality secure and regulated or licensed rented housing to supplement the traditional council and housing association provision.

The London Plan definition of intermediate housing was also clarified in the SPG. The London Plan had set the target income range at between £15,000 and £40,000 a year. Based on a 3.5 mortgage–income multiplier, the top of the range would allow for the purchase in the lowest quartile of the market on an unsubsidised basis of a property with a value of £140,000. A household on an income below £40,000 would either need financial support to buy into the open market, or be able only to part-buy a home – for example through shared ownership. Owing to increases in house prices, by the time the final SPG was published in November 2005, the income threshold for market access had climbed to £49,000. By February 2008, this market access threshold was to climb to £58,600. The GLA was concerned that, in order to meet the London Plan definition, developers were focusing on providing smaller shared ownership or discounted market units just below the threshold. The SPG therefore made it clear that a range of sizes should be provided and that provision should be across the income range, with average intermediate housing costs being affordable by households in the middle of the range – on incomes of £27,500 a year in 2004 – a monitoring target that increased to £38,000 by February 2008.

The draft SPG also sought to deal with the complex issues of how boroughs set affordable housing targets and how targets were to be applied to specific schemes. In Chapter 3, reference was made to the published London Plan introducing an explicit link between the regional target, borough targets and the application of targets to individual schemes. The government's PPG3 and related guidance had made it explicit that affordable housing targets were a matter for determination by the boroughs as local planning authority. However, if boroughs were free to set targets below 50 per cent, the London Plan 50 per cent target was at risk. The SPG sought to make it explicit that boroughs in setting their own local target had to take into account regional needs as assessed in the London housing requirements study, and could not just rely on a local assessment. The Guidance also made it clear that boroughs with surplus development capacity should make a contribution to Londonwide needs. Locally based targets would justify low affordable housing targets in the more prosperous Outer London boroughs, while not helping to relieve the pressures in Inner London boroughs, generally with limited development capacity. It was also made clear that 50 per cent should not be seen as an upper limit. In order to reduce social polarization across London as a whole, where existing proportions of social housing were below the then 26 per cent average, higher proportions of affordable housing could be justified. This was introduced partly to support Hammersmith and Fulham, which had adopted a monitoring target of 65 per cent – the only borough whose target was higher than the Mayor's 50 per cent. This guidance was to prove important in supporting the borough's objections to boroughs such as Westminster, Bexley or Bromley, which were proposing borough targets below 50 per cent.

The draft SPG gave further guidance on the balance between social rented and intermediate housing. The 70:30 social rent–intermediate ratio in the plan was a Londonwide objective and never intended to be prescriptive at borough or scheme level. The SPG argued that a local target split should nonetheless reflect broader mixed and balanced communities objectives; a borough with high proportions of social rent could shift the balance more to intermediate provision, whereas a borough with less social rent or where shared ownership was not viable for most middle-income households, as was the case in some suburban boroughs, could shift the balance towards rented housing. Some boroughs adopted ratios of 80:20 or 90:10, with the Mayor's support, while other boroughs with high existing social rented stock and little intermediate housing proposed 60:40 or even 50:50. The Mayor accepted a 50:50 split as acceptable in the most disadvantaged areas; he did not support a borough-level intermediate target above 40 per cent.

The draft Guidance also dealt with the mechanisms for determining 'the maximum reasonable amount of affordable housing' required by the London Plan which would be considered as deliverable in an individual scheme. The Guidance stated that individual schemes should be subject to a development appraisal, which would assess the maximum affordable housing output in relation to the strategic targets that 50 per cent should be affordable, of which 70 per cent should be social housing. Although the Guidance did not prescribe a methodology for this assessment, it explicitly recommended the use of the Three Dragons model, discussed above, with this recommendation supported by a joint statement with the Housing Corporation. This approach was justified by reference to paragraph 17 of government circular 6/98, which required a planning authority to ensure that a planning obligation did not make a development unviable. The GLA contended that this requirement could be tested only through a financial appraisal and that only through a financial appraisal could an applicant challenge the policy requirement of the planning authority. PPG3 and subsequently PPS3 failed to clarify this point despite representations from the Mayor and despite a series of research reports, some of which were funded by the government, which recommended financial appraisal as the best mechanism for informing s106 agreements. It is significant that, despite the ambiguity in government guidance, the GLA's interpretation, and requirement for financial appraisal, was never subject to legal challenge. The outcome of the financial appraisal practice will be considered in the next chapter.

The draft Affordable Housing SPG was followed in December 2004 by a draft SPG on Housing Provision. The main purpose of this document was to assist local planning authorities in implementing the housing supply targets in the London Plan. Most of the guidance was uncontentious, giving advice on efficient use of stock, empty property strategies, the identification of large and small sites and the potential for mixed-use development including new homes on underutilized employment sites. The draft guidance, however, dealt with two more contentious issues: the appropriate density of development for a specific site, and the appropriate mix of dwellings in terms of bedroom size mix, for any specific site.

On the issue of density, the London Plan had included a density matrix which included the categorization of three types of neighbourhoods: central, urban and suburban, with each type generating different density ranges for developments. Each range was then varied according to the Public Transport Access Level (PTAL) with different ranges given for different forms of development: flatted/mix of flats and terraced houses and detached and semi-detached houses. Although the GLA and Transport for London published a Londonwide PTAL map (Map 5.2), which gave advice to boroughs and developers on the PTAL assessment for a specific site, the Mayor had not previously mapped London according to the three neighbourhood categories. This made it difficult for both the developer and the borough as local planning authority to assess the appropriate density for a specific site: the density consistent with the principles of sustainable residential quality set out in the London Plan.

The GLA decided to publish a neighbourhood character map (Map 5.3). This was based on 2001 census data on the built form of existing residential development, but also reflected the relationship of a site to a town centre – with neighbourhoods near a metropolitan town centre treated as of a central character.

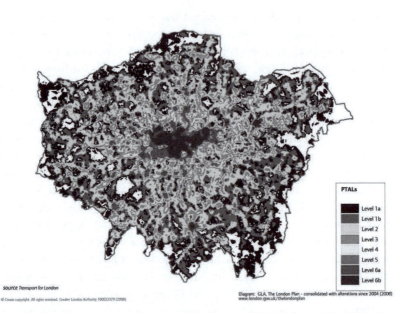

Map 5.2 Public Transport Access Level. Source: GLA (2004a). Copyright ONS. Licence number: 10004924. Property of Transport for London, permission obtained from TfL.

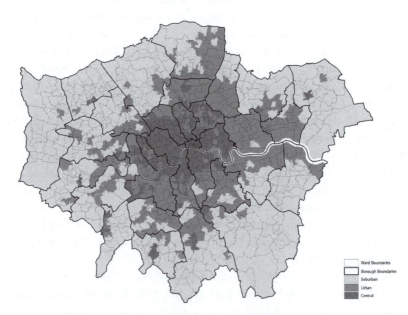

Map 5.3 Neighbourhood character map. Source: GLA (2005a).

This was consistent with the density matrix in the London Plan. The map was criticized from two directions. Some boroughs and community groups wanted areas characterized as central to be treated as urban and areas categorized as urban to be treated as suburban, to reduce the likelihood of what they considered to be overdevelopment. Inevitably, there was a contrary argument from developers that the categorization limited their ability to develop higher-density schemes, which would normally be more profitable. There was also a view that, even as indicative guidance, the map would be interpreted as prescriptive to individual sites, that that was beyond the strategic remit of the Mayor and that site density was a matter for individual local planning authorities to determine.

There was a parallel debate on the guidance on housing mix. The draft Affordable Housing SPG included bedroom size mix targets for each affordability category (market, intermediate and social rent) derived from the 2004 housing requirements study summarized in the previous section. The London Plan policy on housing mix only provided general guidance that new developments should offer a range of housing choices in terms of the mix of housing sizes and types. For this to be achieved, the GLA considered it necessary that guidance was given on what mix was necessary to achieve this objective. Although the proportionate requirement for larger social rented homes, at 41 per cent four bedrooms or more, was much higher than current outturn, or mix guidance in individual borough planning documents, the argument was widely accepted as the case was evidenced not just by the requirements study but also by waiting times for larger properties on borough waiting lists, and the evidence of increased overcrowding. The guidance on market units was contentious. The requirements study had concluded that two thirds of new development in the market sector should be for family-sized homes, at a time when market output was dominated by smaller units. Developers objected to both the figures on the basis that market demand for smaller units remained high and that demographic projections showed a continuing increase in the number of single people. Their main objection was one of principle: that it was not for planning authorities to tell developers what to build. They would build only what was most profitable for them – they objected to what they considered to be 'the nationalisation of the private property market' (House Builders Federation 2005).

Following extensive consultation, in November 2005 the two draft documents were combined as the *Housing Supplementary Planning Guidance* (GLA 2005b). Part of the delay had been waiting for the government to publish substantive revisions to PPG3 or to publish a Housing PPS. Despite the government publishing a draft PPG3 revision, the final document did not appear and the Mayor decided he could not wait any longer. Interestingly, the main reason for the delay over the finalization of government guidance was also a hostile response from the house builders to suggestions that planning authorities should give guidance on the mix of market sector homes. When the final SPG was published, there was only one substantive change. The neighbourhood character map was dropped, which left boroughs to draw up their own density guidance maps, though these still had to be consistent with the density matrix and neighbourhood character definitions in the London Plan. The guidance on housing mix for all sectors was left substantially as drafted. The annex to the draft Housing SPG on applying mixed-use policies in different locations was also dropped, as this was considered inappropriate to guidance and best dealt with through the Sub-regional Development Frameworks. Once published, the Guidance established a detailed framework for the implementation of planning policy for housing across London. It gave more detailed and relevant, as well as up-to-date, guidance than the out-of-date national PPG3, and was widely used by boroughs in drafting their own planning guidance on housing. Boroughs and developers were generally appreciative of the framework it set, which encouraged greater commonality of policy and greater consistency in the determination of planning applications across London.

General conformity and the transitional Unitary Development Plans

Under the provisions of the 1999 GLA Act and GOL circular 1/2000, London borough plans – Unitary Development Plans under the pre-2004 planning framework and Local Development Documents under the 2004 Act framework – had to be in 'general conformity' with the London Plan. There was no legal definition of 'general conformity'. The London Plan included over 150 policies. The Mayor was of the view that every policy in the Plan was strategic, so that all boroughs should comply with each policy in the Plan. It should be noted that many of these policies were not in themselves prescriptive. The Mayor had a case, as some policies in the draft Plan had been deleted following government representations or recommendations from the Examination in Public Panel as not strategic. Consequently he argued that any policies remaining in the published Plan must be, by definition, of a Londonwide strategic nature. The Government Office for London however took a different view, considering that general conformity required conformity only where lack of conformity would lead to material damage to the integrity of the strategic plan as a whole. Although draft proposals were circulated by the Mayor in March 2004, it was not until July 2006 that the Mayor was able to issue his formal guidance note *General Conformity with the London Plan* – over two years after the Plan had actually come into effect (GLA 2006a). The Mayor's argument that the delay was partly due to confusion in central government guidance was overstated, as ministers had included guidance on the concept of 'general conformity' in Planning Policy Guidance 12 issued in September 2004.

There was a difficulty in that neither the 1999 GLA Act nor the 2004 Planning Act gave the Mayor the power to amend Local Development Documents which were not in 'general conformity' with the London Plan. The Mayor could only state his objections, which would then be considered by the Examination in Public into the Local Development Document, which might or might not be taken into account by the minister in approving such a Document. Planning officers at GOL who advised the minister were to be selective as to which policies they considered to be matters of general conformity. As far as housing policies were concerned, GOL supported the Mayor on overall housing targets but was not consistent in supporting the Mayor on affordable housing targets or density policy.

An additional factor weakening the Mayor's ability to bring his adopted Plan into effect quickly was that nearly half the boroughs were still in the process of drafting, consulting or finalizing their pre-2004 Act Unitary Development Plans. For some boroughs, this process had been under way for five or more years. In these cases initial drafts predated the Mayor's coming into office in May 2000, irrespective of the draft London Plan in 2002 and the Plan's publication in 2004. Boroughs argued that it was too late in the process to have regard to newly emerging strategic policies, especially if their plan had already been subject to public inquiry and inspector's report and/or representations from the central government. Government Office for London planners, keen to get the UDPs approved before the July 2007 deadline, were reluctant to support the Mayor on objections, especially where any amendments would require the borough to open up a new round of consultation. This reluctance, however, still did not stop GOL intervening to request boroughs to amend and reconsult on changes ministers sought. That the 2004 Act made planning inspectors' recommendations binding on local planning authorities, though oddly not binding on the Mayor in relation to the London Plan, introduced a further complication, as boroughs often found themselves caught between conflicting guidance from three sources: the inspector, the Mayor and GOL acting on behalf of ministers.

This confusion led to a number of inconsistent outcomes in this transitional period. First, the Mayor was relatively relaxed about UDPs at a postenquiry stage which did not include a 50 per cent affordable target. Greenwich and Lewisham, UDPs reaching the final stage just after February 2004, were allowed to proceed on the basis of 35 per cent targets, on the basis of rather loose commitments to bring forward reviews of these policies. In the case of Harrow, the borough agreed to raise its boroughwide target to 50 per cent while leaving a lower site-specific target. This was achievable without a further round of consultation, which led to the plan being adopted just before Labour lost control of Harrow to the

Conservative party. The case of Westminster was to prove the most contentious. There had been a long history of antagonism between Ken Livingstone and the Conservative-controlled Westminster City Council, partly attributable to the fact that his housing adviser, Neale Coleman, had been a leading Labour councillor in the authority. Westminster had long advocated a 30 per cent housing target. However the Mayor's strenuous representations direct to ministers, bypassing the ambivalent planning officers at GOL, pressurized the minister into requiring Westminster to adopt the 50 per cent affordable target on a boroughwide basis. However, as part of a compromise, Westminster were allowed to keep the 30 per cent target for sites within the Central Activities Zone, which comprised about 80 per cent of the borough area, with the 50 per cent target applying only to the largest sites outside the zone. The minister also required Westminster to adopt a threshold of 10 units for sites to which the requirement applied, but Westminster managed to get approval for a complicated staircasing arrangement by which sites of between ten and eighty homes required only a lower proportion of affordable housing. This dispute delayed the adoption of the Westminster plan by nearly two years.

Following the Westminster case, ministers and GOL planners became more supportive of the Mayor's position. This was notably the case in relation to the first two borough core strategies drawn up under the 2004 Act arrangements. Both Redbridge and Havering, boroughs in outer East London which were Conservative controlled, proposed affordable housing targets of only 35 per cent. The Mayor strenuously objected to these targets on the basis that neither borough had provided evidence for a target lower than the 50 per cent target in terms of the criteria set out in the Housing SPG. In both cases, the Mayor was supported by the independent planning inspector and, with the support of ministers, both boroughs amended their plans to include the 50 per cent. The plans were adopted in May 2008 and July 2008 respectively.

The 2004 Act included the provision that, where a planning document under the pre-2004 Act system had not been replaced by a new plan prepared under the new legislation by July 2007, the borough had to get agreement from ministers that the old policy could be saved. The Mayor was consulted on this process and, not surprisingly, objected to saving any borough policies which were not considered to be consistent with the London Plan. This in fact meant that the Mayor objected to the saving of any borough affordable housing target below 50 per cent.

Development control interventions and appraisals: achieving consensus on the GLA's approach

The Mayor's main planning power related to his ability to intervene in strategic planning cases. Some 200–250 developments were referred to him each year. About 80 per cent of these projects included a residential component. The referral process was in two stages: the Mayor was consulted by the local planning authority when a strategic application was submitted and then, once the LPA was seeking to determine the application, the Mayor had a ten-day period to decide whether or not to direct the LPA to refuse the application. The Mayor had to base his representations and use of direction on his published policies.

In the majority of cases, the Mayor would allow the LPA to proceed with determining the application. However, about 20 per cent of cases came back to the Mayor for a second-stage decision. He used his veto power selectively – generally in fewer than ten cases a year, and in most of these the direction to refuse was withdrawn after changes were made to the proposal. The financial appraisal process became key to the consideration of housing schemes, as it was applied to any scheme referred to the Mayor which did not meet his policies. Despite initial hostility from house builders, once the GLA officers had demonstrated that they would respect the commercial confidentiality of scheme financial data, most developers and their consultants collaborated in the appraisal process. In fact private consultants soon became very adept at using the appraisal process to justify their projects. Although the GLA trained up over 100 borough planning staff, as well as Housing Corporation London regional staff, limited staff resources and officer turnover often meant that boroughs and the Housing Corporation relied on the GLA's appraisals.

Nevertheless the appraisal system was helpful in setting a consistent approach to scheme appraisal across London – at least for strategic schemes. Moreover it enabled the Mayor's officers to negotiate improvements to schemes in terms of compliance with mayoral policies. GLA officers, sometimes working jointly with borough planning officers, were able to increase numbers of affordable housing units within schemes, but also to change the composition of the affordable housing element – generally through increasing the proportion of social rented housing relative to intermediate provision, or through increasing the number of larger homes. The Mayor's success was limited and a fuller analysis of the outputs from schemes considered by the Mayor is given in Chapter 6. It is important to note that the planning decisions were taken personally by the Mayor at fortnightly meetings, on the advice of his planning decisions unit. The meetings were also attended by the Deputy Mayor, Nicky Gavron for most of the period, and by officers from the London Plan team, the London Development Agency and Transport for London.

Neither the applicant nor the borough concerned was represented. The meetings were held in private and therefore not open to scrutiny, a matter which was of concern to the London Assembly's planning committee, who published a critical report on the matter. Once a decision was made, the decision letter and the officers' report to the Mayor on which it was based were published on the Mayor's website.

The Mayor also received pre-application presentations from developers on major schemes. These tended to be held at a relatively early scheme design stage, and were an opportunity for 'iconic' architects to impress the Mayor. These were closed meetings, though on occasions officers from the relevant local planning authority were invited. The presentations often happened without the Mayor being fully prebriefed by his planning officers. The discussions therefore tended to focus on aspects of the model or graphic presentation given by the architects rather than on scheme content or policy compliance. The Mayor was not backward in expressing a personal opinion on the design of a scheme – a risky strategy for an architect whose project might not impress, but also potentially problematic for officers who had to advise on policy compliance issues at a later stage.

The Mayor's conflicting priorities

The London Plan implementation process was slower than had been expected. The implementation of housing policies still contrasts well with progress in some other policy areas. The housing policies were fairly explicit with specific targets, and both borough plans and individual development proposals could be tested for policy compliance. It is not insignificant that most of the controversies over borough plans focused on housing issues – notably the Mayor's representations in the case of the Westminster, Havering and Redbridge plans. The policies in the plan and the comprehensive planning advice were based on sound evidence and were difficult for individual applicants to dispute. As has been shown above, support from the government was more ambivalent, with GOL planners supportive in mayoral disputes with boroughs over total housing provision targets, but more ambivalent when it came to affordable housing issues. The Mayor was not helped with the inconsistencies and prevarication within the central government policy process, especially the delays over finalizing PPS3, the mixed messages over whether planning policy could seek to steer the mix and type of market housing, and also the continuing confusion over the affordable housing threshold issue.

One disappointment was the failure to make much progress in coordinating the planning decision process with the Housing Corporation investment decision processes. Despite the joint statement between the GLA and the Housing Corporation, many of the schemes which were the subject of a planning application had not been submitted to the Housing Corporation for funding. In the absence of clarity over funding, it was difficult to ensure that a planning decision could actually be implemented. This issue will be considered further in a later chapter. Similarly, the lack of certainty over the funding and phasing of social infrastructure could act as a constraint on residential development. The Sub-regional Development Frameworks were therefore much weaker documents than the infrastructure plan which had been intended.

There were also policy conflicts within the London Plan and within the Mayor's office. Housing policy objectives were not the only mayoral priority. Whereas affordable housing targets were a key focus of the Mayor's first term in office, from 2004 onwards much of his attention focused on energy renewables and broader climate change-related policies, including increasing attention being given to carbon emission reduction targets. Under the influence of Richard Rogers, his advisor on architecture and urbanism, he focused increasingly on design issues, including the impact of the London skyline, centring on his increasing enthusiasm for high-rise developments. Where individual schemes were concerned, the Mayor was often enthusiastic about promoting non-residential elements, whose lack of profitability would impact on the housing output, employment schemes in unattractive areas often promoted by the LDA, or high-profile leisure or tourism provision, often part of a strategy for regenerating unpopular areas. Examples of loss of affordable housing potential to other policy objectives include the inclusion of an aquarium in the scheme at Silvertown Quays in Newham, the inclusion of exhibition space in the Potters Field development next to City Hall and the proposal for a swimming pool in the Coin St Community Builders tower at Doon Street in Lambeth. Other schemes, such as Convoys Wharf in Lewisham or Wandsworth Riverside, involved cross-subsidy to employment uses. In other cases such as the Dalston junction scheme or the proposed scheme at Bromley South station, residential development value was to be used to support transport improvements rather than affordable housing. Some of these issues will be considered further in later chapters. The next chapter will first present a detailed analysis of housing outputs in London in the period of Ken Livingstone's mayoralty.

Chapter 6

The impact of spatial planning on housing outputs

London housing outputs

Overall housing completions

Housing output in London increased significantly between 2000 and 2008. Housing completion monitoring in London is net of homes lost through demolition but does include new hostel bedspaces and long-term vacant properties returning to use. These two categories are combined as other supply in Table 6.1.

By 2006/7 total output had risen to 31,430 – 8,430 homes above the 23,000 target – but it fell back to 28,199 in 2007/8, below the new housing output target of 30,500. This was primarily because there was an increase in long-term private sector vacant property, which is treated as a net loss in supply. Net additions from new build and conversions showed a small increase.

Table 6.1 Housing completions

	Net additions from new build and conversions	Other supply	Net total completions	Target applying	Net completions as % of target
2001	18,156	5,895	24,051	23,000	105
2002	17,056	4,475	21,531	23,000	94
2003/4	21,045	4,861	25,906	23,000	113
2004/5	22,885	4,479	27,364	23,000	119
2005/6	24,009	4,300	28,309	23,000	123
2006/7	27,290	4,142	31,432	23,000	137
2007/8	27,569	630	28,199	30,500	92

Source: GLA London Plan Annual Monitoring Reports 1–5.

Notes
Other supply comprises net additional hostel bedspaces and long-term vacant properties returning to use.
GLA monitoring changed from calendar years to financial years in 2003/4.

Table 6.2 Regional housing completions

Region	2000/1	2001/2	2002/3	2003/4	2004/5	2005/6	2006/7	2007/8	% increase
London	14,492	13,927	15,670	19,394	24,063	18,809	21,846	20,750	43
South East	21,839	21,815	22,745	24,280	25,692	28,209	27,698	30,170	38
East	16,026	15,616	17,844	18,395	19,885	20,251	22,616	22,230	39
South West	14,972	15,598	15,729	15,984	17,411	18,761	19,499	18,990	27
West Midlands	14,094	13,373	13,872	13,843	14,153	16,191	15,097	12,550	−11
East Midlands	13,675	14,102	14,875	14,375	15,465	16,886	18,171	17,390	27
North East	6,641	6,429	5,607	5,939	7,132	7,637	8,193	8,180	23
North West	18,172	15,835	18,197	17,752	14,905	20,619	18,110	20,310	12
Yorkshire and Humberside	13,344	13,171	13,200	13,996	14,187	16,035	16,461	15,680	18
England	133,255	129,866	137,739	143,958	155,893	163,398	167,691	166,250	25

Source: DCLG Housing Statistics.

This increase can be compared with changes in housing completions in other regions over the same period (Table 6.2). Unfortunately, the regional completions data published by the central government have not in the past netted out demolitions and include only conventional supply – they exclude new hostel bedspaces and vacant properties returning to use.

These government figures, despite undercounting London's output, nevertheless show London as having the largest increase in housing output over this period: 51 per cent compared with a national average of 26 per cent. The total England figure for 2007/8 of 166,250 is to be compared with the government's completion target of 240,000 – completions were only 69 per cent of target.

Affordable housing completions

The GLA's dataset shows an increase in affordable housing output in London over this period from 7,728 homes to 10,394 homes (Table 6.3). However, as a proportion of total net housing output, affordable housing output has been lower since the London Plan was adopted than in the period before the Mayor took office. Average affordable outturn had been 38 per cent in 1997–99, and remained at an average of 38 per cent in the first four years of the mayoralty. However, the proportion fell to an average of 34 per cent for the four years after the London Plan was adopted. Whereas overall conventional housing output increased by 45 per cent between 2000 and 2007/8, market output increased by 51 per cent, while affordable output increased by only 34 per cent.

Table 6.3 Market and affordable completions in London

	Net new affordable homes	Net new market homes	Net conventional completions	Affordable as % of total completions
2000	7,728	11,770	19,498	39.6
2001	7,502	10,005	17,507	42.8
2002	6,021	11,035	17,056	35.3
2003/4	7,173	13,872	21,045	34.1
2004/5	7,515	15,370	22,885	32.8
2005/6	7,696	17,117	24,813	31.0
2006/7	9,435	18,081	27,516	34.3
2007/8	10,394	17,805	28,199	36.9

Source: GLA London Plan Annual Monitoring Reports. Data from GLA London Development Database. Figures related to conventional supply only.

Table 6.4 Social rent and intermediate completions

Year	Social rent units	Intermediate units	Social rent as % of affordable	Intermediate as % of affordable
2004/5	4,612	3,112	59	41
2005/6	5,664	2,977	65	35
2006/7	5,982	4,712	56	44
2007/8	5,313	5,081	51	49
Total	21,571	15,822	58	42

Source: London Plan Annual Monitoring Reports.

Table 6.5 Planning approvals by sub-region

	North	North East	South East	South West	West	London
2000/1	7,591	6,128	5,960	6,561	6,317	33,365
2001/2	6,336	5,418	5,616	7,530	6,124	31,024
2002/3	11,020	10,113	9,066	8,038	7,304	45,541
2003/4	8,368	9,138	16,053	7,733	5,011	46,303
2004/5	12,605	15,724	9,234	8,533	14,549	60,645
2005/6	16,330	15,006	5,844	8,878	9,499	55,557
2006/7	15,882	9,575	13,352	12,665	9,016	60,490
2007/8	12,712	36,001	12,617	10,203	8,909	80,442
Total	90,844	107,103	77,742	70,141	66,729	412,559
% of total	22	26	19	17	16	100
% increase	67	487	112	56	41	141

Source: This table is taken from GLA London Plan *Annual Monitoring Report* 5 (February 2008) and uses the new sub-regional groupings introduced by the 2008 alteration to the London Plan.

The balance between social rent and intermediate housing output

Performance in relation to the Mayor's 70:30 social rent–intermediate target has been poor. Output figures were not monitored in the early years of the mayoralty, and are still not a key output indicator monitored in the Mayor's London Plan *Annual Monitoring Report*, despite having been a key mayoral policy objective. However figures for 2004/5 to 2007/8, the period since the London Plan was adopted, are in Table 6.4.

Planning approvals

There was a fairly steady increase in homes receiving planning consent between 2000 and 2006/7, with a doubling of consents over the seven-year period.

Table 6.5 gives total consents each year by sub-region and for London as a whole. The monitoring system changed from calendar year to financial year from 2003/4.

This shows an increase in development activity in terms of planning consents in all sub-regions, with the greatest proportionate increase in activity in North East London. At the end of March 2008, there were 61,156 dwellings under construction and 111,485 consented units for which construction had not started.

Bedroom size mix

In relation to the bedroom size mix, output has been disappointing. Table 6.6 gives requirements as assessed in the 2004 housing requirements study.

Housing completions in 2007/8 were actually distributed as shown in Table 6.7. Output in all sectors was predominantly one-bedroom (including studio) and two-bedroom units. Output of three-bedroom and larger units was actually higher in the market sector than in the social housing sector, where it was most needed. Only 201 four-bedroom or larger social rented homes were completed – only 2 per cent of the annual estimated requirement of 8,200 homes.

It should be noted that the Mayor has no mechanism for monitoring compliance with the policies on 100 per cent lifetime homes and 10 per cent wheelchair homes. The GLA was to publish a consultant's report in August 2008 on the monitoring of lifetimes home outputs (GLA 2008b).

Table 6.6 2004 net annual shortage or surplus: bedroom size and tenure

	1 bed	2 bed	3 bed	4 bed +	Total
Social	4,000	11,200	(3,200)	8,600	20,800
Intermediate	4,400	200	(4,300)	1,900	2,500
Market	3,000	5,100	4,200	(100)	12,100
Total	11,400	16,500	(3,200)	10,600	35,400

Source: GLA 2004 housing requirements study (GLA 2004b).

Figures in brackets are surpluses.

Table 6.7 2007/8 completions: bedroom size and tenure

	1 bed	2 bed	3 bed	4 bed +	Total
Social	1,787 (29%)	2,657 (43%)	1,232 (20%)	588 (9%)	6,242
Intermediate	2,297 (45%)	2,591 (51%)	164 (3%)	37 (1%)	5,089
Market	7,984 (39%)	9,590 (47%)	1,934 (9%)	1,010 (5%)	20,518
Total	12,068 (38%)	14,838 (47%)	3.330 (10%)	1,613 (5%)	31,849

Source. London Plan *Annual Monitoring Report* 5. Data from GLA London Development Database.

Housing density

It is in relation to density policy that there has been the most radical shift in output. As described above, the density policy matrix set ranges for development density that relate to SRQ principles, incorporating public transport access and neighbourhood character including town centre location. Borough plans were also required to adopt not just the principles of the density policy but the density matrix and apply it to individual locally determined schemes.

As discussed above, Transport for London has mapped public transport access and the GLA published a map of neighbourhood character in the draft Housing Provision Supplementary Planning Guidance. It was recognized that, following the application of these principles, there was a capacity for higher development densities in some central locations, and also for increased densities in more suburban locations with good public transport access that were near district centres. The London Plan set a performance indicator that 95 per cent of developments should be consented at densities within the appropriate range.

In Chapter 5, reference was made to the Public Transport Access Level map and the neighbourhood character map. It is possible to combine these maps, the two key components of the London Plan density policy, to produce an indicative density policy map (Map 6.1). This then allows an analysis of whether individual developments are consistent with the London Plan guidance.

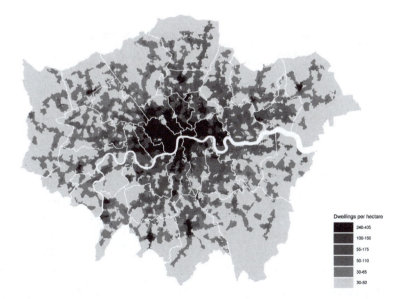

Dwellings per hectare

■	240-435
■	100-150
■	55-175
■	50-110
■	30-65
■	30-50

Map 6.1 Density guidance map. Source: GLA (GLA seminar presentations, 2006). Permission obtained.

The GLA operates the London Development Database, which records all planning consents. It has therefore been possible to monitor the density of all consented schemes relative to the appropriate density range as set out in the London Plan. The performance indicator stated in the 2004 London Plan was that 95 per cent of all consents should be within the appropriate density range. For the four years since the adoption of the London Plan, the results are in Table 6.8. This demonstrates that, for the first two years, some two thirds of schemes were approved at densities above the appropriate range, with the proportion falling to a third in 2006/7, but increasing again in 2007/8.

There has been a clear correlation between the density at which a scheme has been approved and the bedroom size mix of a scheme. The higher density the scheme, the lower the proportion of family-sized homes (Table 6.9).

Mayoral policy included an explicit intention to increase overall densities. Table 6.10 shows that development densities have doubled over the last few years. Government data gives densities on completion. However, the Mayor's London Development Database monitors densities at planning consent. As the table demonstrates, average Londonwide development densities have increased from 59 dwellings per hectare (dph) for 1999–2002 completions to 137 dwellings per hectare for 2006/7 permissions.

These figures of course disguise variations between boroughs. As shown in Table 6.11, borough-level densities vary between densities of 50 dph in suburban

Table 6.8 Planning consents: compliance with London Plan density policy (%)

	2004/5	*2005/6*	*2006/7*	*2007/8*
Above range	62	65	32	55
Within range	31	28	50	40
Below range	8	7	18	5

Table 6.9 Density and bedroom size mix (%)

Density	*1 bed*	*2 bed*	*3 bed*	*4 bed*	*5 bed*	*6 bed +*	*Total*	*3 bed +*
Under 30 dph	8	14	25	26	18	9	100	78
30–64 dph	11	49	25	12	2	1	100	40
65–149 dph	31	56	10	2	<1	<1	100	13
150–239 dph	29	41	21	8	<1	<1	100	30
240–434 dph	40	46	11	2	<1	<1	100	14
435 dph +	47	45	7	<1	<1	<1	100	8

Source: London Housing Federation and London Councils (2006) sourced from GLA analysis of 2005/6 planning consents in London Development Database.

dph: dwellings per hectare.

Table 6.10 London development densities 1999–2008

	1999–2002 completions	2001–4 completions	2004/5 permissions	2005/6 permissions	2006/7 permissions	2007/8 permissions
Average density in dph	59	64	125	131	137	145

Sources: Completions: CLG land use change reports; Permissions: London Plan Annual Monitoring reports.

Table 6.11 Borough development density: planning consents 2007/8

Density	Boroughs
Under 50 dph	Bromley, Havering
50–99 dph	Barnet, Bexley, Enfield, Harrow, Hillingdon, Hounslow, Kingston, Merton, Richmond
100–149 dph	Barking and Dagenham, Camden, Croydon, Ealing, Haringey, Redbridge, Sutton, Waltham Forest
150–199 dph	Brent, Kensington and Chelsea, Lewisham, Wandsworth
200–299 dph	Greenwich, Hackney, Hammersmith and Fulham, Islington, Lambeth, Southwark, Westminster
300–399 dph	Newham
400 dph +	City, Tower Hamlets

Source: London Plan *Annual Monitoring Report* 4 (Mayor of London February 2008).

boroughs such as Bromley and Havering, and average development densities over 300 dph in docklands boroughs such as Newham and Tower Hamlets.

These borough average figures themselves disguise individual hyperdense schemes. In the eighteen-month period April 2006 to September 2007, there were in fact 513 schemes at densities over 435 dph (the top of the highest range in the London Plan). The highest-density scheme recorded was Woburn Place, Camden, at 2,462 dph.

The built form of new development

There has also been a significant change in the built form of development. The proportion of homes built as houses as opposed to flats has fallen. However the most radical shift has been a return to developing high-rise residential units, as shown in the number of schemes referred to the Mayor of over ten floors (Table 6.12; the mayoral referral threshold is 30 metres, so schemes of ten floors will normally be referred to the Mayor.) Even more significant is the fact that in only one of these schemes (a scheme in Stratford High Street in Newham) did the

Table 6.12 Development proposals over ten storeys high

	Schemes	Units
2003/4	1	45
2004/5	7	833
2005/6	23	6,122
2006/7	14	3,725
2007/8	39	13,331

Table 6.13 High-rise schemes by borough

Borough	Number of towers	Highest tower (floors)	Average height (floors)
Tower Hamlets	31	48	22
Southwark	12	51	26
Newham	10	45	23
Croydon	7	44	25
Hackney	5	50	26
Lambeth	5	43	23
Westminster	4	43	34
Islington	3	39	28
Sutton	3	20	15
Barking and Dagenham	2	23	18
Brent	2	23	21.5
Ealing	2	12	11.5
Lewisham	2	15	12.5
Redbridge	2	24	19.5
Wandsworth	2	28	21
Bexley	1	17	
City of London	1	35	
Greenwich	1	22	
Havering	1	14	
Hounslow	1	25	
Kensington	1	27	

Mayor consider that the project might constitute overdevelopment. The issue of mayoral planning interventions will be considered further below.

The distribution of blocks in these schemes between boroughs is shown below, noting that some schemes involved more than one tower. Table 6.13 gives information on the highest block in each borough and the average height of towers in the borough. The following boroughs had no proposals for schemes over 10 floors high (source: analysis of mayoral referrals 2003–8):

- Inner London: Camden, Hammersmith and Fulham;
- Outer London: Barnet, Bromley, Haringey, Harrow, Hillingdon, Kingston, Merton, Richmond, Waltham Forest.

Space standards

An analysis was undertaken of space standards in a sample of some thirty-five major developments which were subject to development appraisals between July 2006 and July 2007. This information is not generally available in a useable form from planning applications. The data represented information provided by the developer at the time of the application and does not necessarily reflect the space standards of homes when completed. The analysis, which provides average space standards by tenure and bedroom size, provides clear differentiation between market, social rent and intermediate housing (Table 6.14).

In the private sector, there are studio flats averaging 33 sq m. It should be noted that the Housing Corporation did not fund studio flats either as social rented or as intermediate provision. For one-bedroom homes, the average space provided is just over 50 sq m for both social rented and intermediate housing, with the market sector figure being only slightly higher. For two-bedroom, three-bedroom and four-bedroom homes, the space in private sector homes is much larger than for social rent, the differentiation increasing from 20 sq m to 140 sq m. Interestingly, space standards are lower for intermediate housing than for social rent for most unit sizes, demonstrating that in practice the Housing Corporation applies its Housing Quality Index (HQI) standard only to social rented housing. The sample of schemes included private sector penthouse flats with an average size of 442 sq m – nearly three times the size of an average three-bedroom social rented home.

This concern led to the Mayor commissioning a review of space standards. This review and its conclusions are considered in Chapter 7.

Table 6.14 Space standards (square metres)

	Social rent	Intermediate	Market
Studio			33
1 bedroom	54	52	76
2 bedroom	109	104	125
3 bedroom	123	117	193
4 bedroom	146	152	288
Penthouse			442

Source: GLA data on scheme appraisals 2006/7.

The Mayor's intervention in borough housing targets

The above analysis relates to all development in London, irrespective of whether the schemes were locally determined, referred to the Mayor, subject to appeal or called in for decision by the central government. As stated above, the Mayor as the strategic regional planning authority has two powers of intervention: he can object to a local plan which is not in 'general conformity' with the London Plan, and he can direct a local planning authority to refuse a strategic planning application which is not in accordance with London Plan policies.

The London Plan sets housing output targets for each borough. Generally borough plans adopted the targets in the 2004 London Plan; if they did not, the London Plan targets took precedence. Only two boroughs – Islington and Redbridge – sought to ignore the new, generally higher, targets derived from the 2004 housing capacity study, and were compelled by the central government, which supported the Mayor's objections, to adopt the Mayor's new targets. In Islington's case, the planning inspector instructed Islington to withdraw the non-compliant plan. In Redbridge's case, the plan was amended.

Although the London Plan could not prescribe borough affordable housing targets, after the adoption of the London Plan in February 2004 the Mayor objected to any borough proposal to set a target lower than 50 per cent. In 2002, only five boroughs operated 50 per cent targets, including Hammersmith and Fulham with a monitoring target of 65 per cent. By February 2008, sixteen of the thirty-three London boroughs had adopted the 50 per cent target, while several others were consulting on adopting the 50 per cent target. There was a lengthy test case in Westminster, which had proposed a 30 per cent target; after strenuous representations by the Mayor the council was eventually directed by the central government to adopt a boroughwide 50 per cent target, although it was allowed to apply a 30 per cent target to sites within the Central Activities Zone. However as will be discussed below, the adoption of a new policy target did not in itself increase the output of affordable housing. Some boroughs with low affordable housing targets, such as Barking and Dagenham and Enfield, had high affordable housing output proportions, whereas others with high targets, for example Hillingdon, Barnet and Harrow, had relatively low affordable housing outputs. Despite the Mayor's assertions to the contrary, there was also little correlation with the party political control of the borough.

A number of boroughs failed to save their old Unitary Development Plan affordable housing targets by the July 2007 deadline; the targets lapsed with the coming into effect of the 2004 Planning and Compulsory Act provisions for new plans, the Local Development Document regime. By 2008 a further ten boroughs were in effect operating the London Plan target by default, bringing the total number to twenty-six, including Redbridge and Havering, which amended their Local Development Document target to 50 per cent, leaving only six with targets below 50 per cent: Bromley on 25 per cent, Bexley, Greenwich and Lewisham on 35 per cent, and Lambeth and Richmond on 40 per cent. Significantly, three of these boroughs were under Labour party control with three under Conservative control.

A schedule of borough policies in 2002 and 2007 is given in Table A.1 in the Appendix.

Actual performance in delivering affordable housing between 2003/4 and 2007/8 is shown in Table 6.15, presented by London Plan sub-region. A schedule of performance by borough is given in Table A.2 in the Appendix. Over the five-year period, 22 per cent of housing output was social rent, with 13 per cent as intermediate housing, giving a total of 35 per cent affordable as compared with the 50 per cent target. Social rent output was proportionately highest in the West and North sub-regions, with intermediate housing proportionately highest in the West. Overall, affordable housing output as a proportion of total output was lowest in the Central and South sub-regions.

There was limited correlation between borough policy and borough output as shown in Table 6.16. Boroughs with affordable housing targets of 50 per cent did not necessarily consistently achieve higher affordable housing output than boroughs with targets of 25 per cent, 30 per cent or 35 per cent. However, boroughs with 50 per cent targets had a median output of 40 per cent affordable housing – 10 per cent below the London Plan target – while boroughs with lower targets had a median output of only 30 per cent – 10 per cent lower still. Hammersmith and Fulham had both the highest target and the highest proportionate affordable housing output.

It is also interesting to analyse policy and output by the political control of the borough. Table 6.17 demonstrates that, on aggregate, Labour-controlled boroughs had higher affordable housing policy targets and output, followed by Liberal Democrat boroughs and then by Conservative boroughs. A number of boroughs changed political control in 2006, but this would have had little impact on housing completions until after 2007/8.

Labour boroughs also had on average higher proportions of social rent completions, with an average of 25 per cent of output, with Liberal Democrat boroughs averaging 21 per cent and Conservative boroughs 18 per cent. It is interesting that Labour boroughs also had the highest proportion of intermediate housing output at 15 per cent, followed by Liberal Democrat boroughs at 14 per cent, with Conservative boroughs achieving only 8 per cent.

Table 6.15 Affordable housing performance by sub-region, 2003/4 to 2007/8

Sub-region	Social rent	Intermediate	Affordable	Total	Social rent (%)	Intermediate (%)	Affordable (%)
Central	6,055	4,515	10,570	34,392	18	13	31
East	9,124	5,456	14,580	41,775	22	13	35
West	4,884	3,701	8,585	19,815	25	19	43
North	3,259	1,463	4,722	13,116	25	11	36
South	4,019	1,633	5,652	17,384	23	9	32
London	27,341	16,768	44,109	126,482	22	13	35

Source: London Plan Annual Monitoring Reports 1–5. Conventional completions.

Note: this table is on the basis of the original 2004 London Plan sub-regions. 2003/4 taking as starting point for analysis 50 per cent affordable housing target initially published in draft London Plan in June 2002.

Table 6.16 Affordable housing output relative to borough policy

Borough policy target as at 2004 (%)	Number of boroughs	Borough	Affordable output 2003/4 to 2007/8 (%)	Median (%)
20	1	Bromley	26	26
25	5	Barking and Dagenham	43	32
		Enfield	40	
		Hillingdon	33	
		Redbridge	28	
		Wandsworth	16	
30	3	Bromley	26	31
		Sutton	44	
		Westminster	23	
33	2	City of London	19	22
		Kensington and Chelsea	25	
35	6	Bexley	25	30
		Greenwich	22	
		Havering	22	
		Lewisham	37	
		Newham	42	
		Tower Hamlets	32	
40	4	Islington	43	31
		Lambeth	26	
		Merton	28	
		Richmond	25	
50	11	Barnet	20	40
		Brent	45	
		Camden	34	
		Croydon	44	
		Ealing	42	
		Hackney	47	
		Haringey	48	
		Harrow	28	
		Hounslow	43	
		Southwark	43	
		Waltham Forest	42	
65	1	Hammersmith and Fulham	69	69

Source: GLA London Plan Annual Monitoring Reports. See also Tables A.1 and A.2 in Appendix.

Table 6.17 Borough affordable housing targets and output by party political control

Borough political control 2002–2006	Number of boroughs	Average policy target at 2004 (%)	Average output 2003/4 to 2007/8 (%)
Labour	17	36	40
Liberal Democrat	5	32	35
Conservative	10	23	26

Note: table excludes City Corporation, whose members were all Independents.

Mayoral intervention in strategic development applications

The Mayor's intervention in strategic planning cases also produced mixed results. Strategic cases were generally housing schemes of 500 or more homes, but also included smaller high-rise schemes and mixed-use schemes that involved a smaller number of homes but departures from local plan land use allocations. Nearly 800 schemes were considered by the Mayor between July 2003, when the GLA monitoring system was established, and April 2008. These comprised some 157,065 homes, equivalent to six years of the total London development completions. Of these schemes considered by the Mayor at the initial consultation stage prior to the local planning authority's determination, some 56,343 homes were recorded as affordable – 36 per cent of the total. In addition the schemes involved provision of a further 710 affordable homes off site: on sites outside the specific planning application. This 36 per cent figure is only slightly above the 34 per cent proportion of all approvals, including approvals locally determined without reference to the Mayor.

Although in a few cases the Mayor's intervention would lead to an increase in affordable housing units, this rarely added more than a few affordable units in the few schemes where scheme revisions were made. In practice, the Mayor's intervention appears to have had little impact on the overall affordable housing outturn. In fact there is evidence that the schemes considered by Ken Livingstone in his last couple of years as Mayor have involved lower proportions of affordable units than schemes locally determined. For example, the affordable housing proportion within mayoral referrals fell from 40 per cent in 2003/4 and 2004/5 (above the London norm) to 34 per cent in 2005/6 and 2006/7 and then to 30 per cent in 2007/8 – below the London norm of 34 per cent. The reasons for this reduced affordable housing output from major schemes will be considered further below, but included increasing difficulties with financial viability of schemes and increased focus by the Mayor on planning policy outputs other than affordable housing.

The Mayor had also stated that affordable housing output should be split 70:30 between social housing and intermediate housing. It has already been mentioned that, over the three-year period 2004/5 to 2006/7, affordable housing output across London was roughly 60 per cent social housing and 40 per cent intermediate housing. For the schemes considered by the Mayor, over the five-year period 2003/4 to 2007/8, the proportionate split was actually 53 per cent social housing to 47 per cent intermediate, with the social rent proportion of 63 per cent in 2003/4 falling to between 48 per cent and 51 per cent in the subsequent years – the average in the three years consistent with the Londonwide dataset being 49 per cent. So the larger schemes considered by the Mayor generally had a significantly lower proportion of social housing and a higher level of intermediate housing than schemes which were locally determined. This reflected a combination of viability issues and the built form of the developments – many of the major schemes considered by the Mayor being high-rise schemes and/or hyperdense schemes in which provision of significant numbers of family social rented homes was not appropriate. Although in a few cases the Mayor's intervention led to an increase in such homes, the impact of these interventions was marginal. With the mayoral support for high densities and high rise, it was inevitable that the provision of family-sized social rented units was squeezed.

The characteristics of development schemes

An analysis of the characteristics of a sample of London development schemes has been published separately (Bowie 2008a). This analysis showed that, although there were some schemes which countered the general pattern, the higher the development, the lower the proportion of affordable housing and the lower the proportion of family-sized homes, defined as three bedrooms or larger, and the higher the proportion of small homes, defined as studios and one-bedroom flats. There was also some correlation with density, the clearest link being the higher the building, the higher the proportion of small homes. There was also some evidence that the higher the density, the smaller the internal space standards within a home, both for studios and for one-bedroom flats, and for three-bedroom homes where they were provided. There was less of a correlation with floor height, though space standards were generally highest for low-rise development.

Conclusion

It is difficult to assess the impact of the Mayor's planning policies as distinct from the impact of external factors such as market demand and the availability of central government funding. It should be noted that central government planning policies changed during the period, especially with the introduction of Planning Policy Guidance 3 on housing in 2006 (DCLG 2006a). The analysis presented in this chapter, however, has demonstrated that, while there was an increase in overall housing output in London between 2000 and 2008, the increase in affordable housing output was lower, so affordable housing as a proportion of overall output actually fell. There was an increase in the proportion of affordable housing which was intermediate provision, and a fall in the proportion which was social rented. Output of social rented housing was well below the targets set by the Mayor, both in proportionate terms and in terms of homes completed.

Homes built were generally one- and two-bedroom homes, whereas the main requirement for social rented homes was in fact larger family-sized homes. Development densities doubled and there was an increase in the proportion of development proposals coming forward as high-rise developments. There was little evidence that the adoption of the Mayor's 50 per cent affordable target by boroughs had increased affordable housing output, as there was little correlation between targets and output at borough level. Moreover the Mayor's intervention in strategic planning applications did not appear to have any significant impact on affordable housing outturn, and the affordable housing proportion in schemes considered by the Mayor actually fell in the last few years of his mayoralty. We will return in later chapters to consider the reasons for this disappointing outcome.

Chapter 7
Revising the spatial plan

The 2004 housing capacity study and the new housing target

The approved London Plan had set out the objective of reviewing London's housing capacity to seek to increase the target from 23,000 homes a year to 30,000 homes a year. As stated above in Chapter 4, the Mayor and his advisors had resisted pressure from both the central government and the Home Builders Federation to adopt the higher figure in advance of a new study. The GLA, however, moved quickly to undertake a new assessment, recognizing that the 1999-based study was out of date. The GLA commissioned the consultants ERM to undertake an assessment of methodologies which could be used for a new study (GLA 2003e).

One of the problems with the earlier study was that it had been partly dependent on estimating windfalls – the potential housing output from sites which had not been identified. This assessment had been to a large extent trend based, and led to some boroughs, notably Lambeth and Haringey, being set higher targets than were deliverable. This was partly attributable to the fact that, with the published report listing specific sites assessed, sites which boroughs were reluctant to declare as suitable for housing and likely to be available were not included in the site-specific assessment. Supported by the ERM study, the GLA decided that, rather than limiting detailed site assessments to sites already allocated for housing, the new study should instead assess all potential housing sites, including sites in other uses and/or not allocated for housing in Unitary Development Plans, but that site details would not be published.

The ERM study developed a methodology for appraising the factors which would determine whether a site or part of a site could be appropriate for housing, before assessing the likelihood of the site being developed in one of four phases. The intention was to develop new borough targets which would be effective from 2007/8 to 2016/17 as well as give an indication of potential longer-term capacity.

The phases were therefore set as:

- Phase 1: 2004/5 to 2006/7 (three years);
- Phase 2: 2007/8 to 2011/12 (five years);
- Phase 3: 2012/13 to 2016/17 (five years);
- Phase 4: 2017/18 to 2026/7 (ten years).

Phase 1 was to cover capacity expected to be realized between the April 2004 site assessment date and the new target coming into effect in 2007/8.

What was perhaps most innovative about the new approach was its use of intranet and geographic information system (GIS) facilities. The GLA bought a number of land use datasets, including a dataset of all sites allocated for housing in UDPs, and these were mapped onto a GIS system. The data and maps were then available on an intranet system for boroughs to amend or exclude. The GLA set the site assessment threshold at 0.5 ha. Sites in protected Green Belt and Metropolitan Open Land were excluded from the original assessment, together with sites which were Strategic Employment Locations. There was then a set of criteria for excluding other sites, such as sites with a strategic operational use, sites which had been recently developed and sites with no prospect of being brought forward for development in the twenty-three year study period. The first stage of the site search identified some 4,500 sites above the threshold. Once the initial exclusion assessment had been completed, there were some 1,500 sites assessed as having some housing potential. Importantly, this included sites in industrial or commercial use, which were considered as having housing potential, either because the sites were considered surplus to employment requirements or, more commonly, because the site was considered to be underutilized and therefore more intensified use could protect or even increase employment generation and enable some housing development. With over 95 per cent of development in London being on previously developed land, the effective use of developed and previously developed land was essential.

Where sites had consents or published planning briefs, the consent or brief set the capacity assumption. For other sites, the density policy and ranges set out in the London Plan were applied to individual sites. Sites were plotted on the density map given in Chapter 6 (Map 6.1), which as described above was derived from the PTAL and neighbourhood character maps given in Chapter 5 (Maps 5.1 and 5.2) which had been published in the draft Housing Provision SPG. In each case density was assessed at the midpoint of the appropriate range.

For each large site, an assessment of capacity was undertaken, having regard to constraints.

Constraints were categorized as follows:

- strategic constraints:
  - air pollution;
  - flood risk;
  - noise pollution from aircraft;
  - pylons across site;

- local constraints:
  - ownership;
  - poor local social infrastructure;
  - environmental setting;
  - site contamination;

- planning policy:
  - Designated Employment Site in borough UDP;
  - other employment site which borough wished to retain.

Each factor, which could be assessed as low, medium or high constraint, had an impact on the proportionate probability of the site being developed.

Map 7.1 gives the distribution of the large sites identified as having housing capacity. It does not, however, include the 20 per cent of sites assessed which had not been publicly identified. Boroughs had insisted this information be kept confidential, as identification of the potential for housing on a site in other use was likely to fuel speculative land purchases as well as potentially prejudicing consideration of individual development proposals through the planning process. The map nevertheless shows that, although there is a concentration of sites in Inner East London, there were sites in every borough.

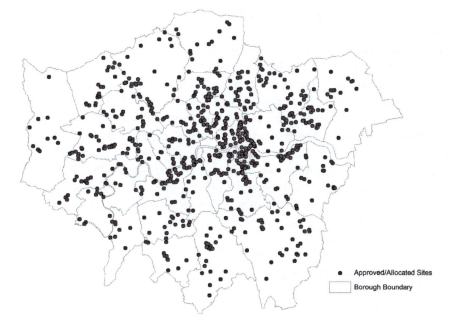

Map 7.1 Large sites. Source: GLA (2005a).

As well as assessing the capacity of large sites, the study also assessed the capacity for development of sites below the 0.5-ha threshold. This was assessed through a combination of assessing the historic trend of consents and completions in each borough from the GLA's London Development Database and an assessment of borough policy on small site development. This was to be a contentious process as the GLA assessed the capacity of individual boroughs to increase small site output through higher densities on appropriate sites – so a borough with very low density of development on small sites, such as Bromley and Bexley in South East London, was assumed to be able to deliver an increase of 50 per cent through small-scale intensification, whereas central London boroughs such as the City, Westminster and Camden with existing high development densities were assumed to have reached a limit of potential intensification. Coinciding with the public debate over the character maps in the draft Housing Provision SPG referred to in Chapter 5, these small site capacity uplift targets reinforced the view in some suburban neighbourhoods, sometimes supported by local councillors, that the Mayor wanted to build on their back gardens. For example, in Southwark, councillors and the local paper, the *Southwark News*, ran a 'Save our Villages' campaign. The issue was to dominate the public inquiry into Southwark's own Unitary Development Plan.

The capacity study also assessed the potential capacity from the other two supply components within the adopted London Plan target: supply from the provision of new hostels – mainly student housing promoted by specific universities – and supply from the bringing back into permanent use of long-term vacant properties. The first assessment was undertaken from considering historic trends and the limited information available on plans for university expansion and new student housing development. The second assessment was undertaken by analysing data on long-term private sector vacancies in each borough and setting a target that in each borough this could be reduced to 1 per cent of total private sector stock within 10 years – a target that had already been achieved by a third of boroughs.

Before finalizing the housing capacity estimates, the GLA needed to consider the implications of increased use of land capacity for housing on other land use requirements. The Mayor, in his draft Industrial Capacity SPG, had already indicated the land requirements needed to fulfil his employment projections, and had given targets at sub-regional level of hectares which could be released for other uses. The housing capacity included an analysis of the existing use of sites identified with housing potential:

- 23 per cent residential use;
- 23 per cent industrial use;
- 9 per cent retail use;
- 7 per cent office use;

- 5 per cent utility use;
- 33 per cent other uses.

The initial capacity study estimated that, over a ten-year period, some 828 hectares of industrial land might be lost to new housing development. This was in excess of the 490 hectares given in the Industrial Capacity SPG. The housing potential figure was therefore lowered to reduce the rate of assumed employment land release. The greatest protection was given to employment land in central London, with higher rates of release assumed in east London, where there was significant derelict and underused industrial land. These adjustments also took into account the space needed for additional waste management facilities, an issue which was to receive considerable attention in the consideration of the early alterations to the London Plan, where alterations on waste and housing were taken forward in parallel.

The estimated output from each supply category, compared with the previous study, is shown in Table 7.1.

The study produced a new estimated capacity of 31,533 homes a year for the period 2007/8 to 2016/17 (GLA 2005c). The new targets, following some minor adjustments between the completion of the study and the recommendations to the Examination in Public, were divided between sub-regions as shown in Table 7.2.

It is noticeable that the increased capacity was mainly in the East sub-region – the Thames Gateway growth area. There was also significant additional capacity in West and North London, with some capacity in South London, but with capacity in Central London reduced relative to the target based on the 1999 study.

Figures for individual boroughs are given in Table A.3 in the Appendix. The greatest increases in capacity relative to the pre-existing targets were in Newham, Greenwich, Barking and Dagenham, and Barnet.

Table 7.1 Sources of housing supply: annual figures – 2004 study compared with 1999 study

Source	2004 study	% of total	1999 study	% of total
Large sites	18,739	59.4	13,524	59.1
Small sites	9,815	31.9	5,524	24.4
Non-self-contained	1,828	5.8	2,611	11.4
Vacants returning to use	1,151	3.7	1,236	5.4
Total	31,533	100	22,895	100

Source: 2004 housing capacity study.

Table 7.2 New sub-regional housing targets

Sub-region	2004 target	Proposed new target	Change	% change
Central	7,010	6,285	–725	+12
East	7,140	13,795	+6,655	+93
North	2,970	3,595	+625	+21
West	3,000	3,795	+795	+27
South	2,805	2,980	+895	+32
Total	22,925	30,450	+7,525	+33

Source: GLA (2006i).

Identifying the capacity was only the first stage of the target-setting process. Following the 2004 Planning and Compulsory Purchase Act, and consequently after the completion of the London Plan Examination in Public considered in Chapter 4 above, the Planning Inspectorate, acting on behalf of the government, introduced new tests of soundness by which both Regional Spatial Strategies and Local Development Documents would be assessed (Planning Inspectorate 2006). PPS11 on Regional Spatial Strategies (ODPM 2004 para 2.49 (viii)) had stated that a plan was required to demonstrate 'whether it is realistic, including about the availability of resources, and is able to be implemented without jeopardising its objectives'.

The Mayor therefore had to demonstrate, not only that the development capacity existed, but that his proposed target was realistic and deliverable. In proposing the new target the Mayor stated that:

> the delivery of these targets is dependent on adequate funding for transport infrastructure, social infrastructure and affordable housing. This funding should ensure that development is sustainable and provides an appropriate mix of provision in terms of type and affordability and in accordance with the policies set out in this Plan. Delivery will also be affected by market factors.

(GLA 2005d)

The Mayor therefore published a further report in support of the new targets: *Delivering Increased Housing Output* (GLA 2006b).

This new report had to tackle some difficult issues, some of which were novel for a spatial planning report. The report gave further information about the assumptions behind the targets and the basis for the assumptions as to the phasing of completions across the full twenty-three-year period – the period for the new targets being in effect years 4 to 13. The report also drew attention to the scenario testing within the study report, which had been largely ignored. The study had assessed site capacity on a range of different options. The advantage of the GIS-based system was that assumptions could be changed, which would produce significantly different borough and aggregate figures. A number of alternative scenarios had been examined: different levels of employment site protection, transport access levels, small site intensification, density on large sites at the bottom or top of appropriate ranges rather than in the middle, stricter assumptions on impact of flood and noise constraints. The different scenarios had produced ten-year capacity assessments ranging from 273,000 to 413,000. In this context, the 305,000 figure selected as the basis for the new target was presented as cautious, being towards the lower end of the spectrum.

The report also reviewed assumptions on the relationship between housing capacity and the demand for other land uses and the need for social infrastructure to support new developments; the ownership and assembly of land for housing development; the planning decision process and the extent of outstanding planning permissions; development viability; the role of planning contributions and assumptions as to public sector subsidy towards affordable housing; whether the construction industry had the capacity for a 33 per cent increase in housing output; and how the new homes were to be marketed. Some components of the report were included to deal with contemporary controversies. There was a widespread debate over whether London boroughs were refusing more planning applications than they should be; the refusal rate in London had increased, but this in fact disguised a much more positive increase in the number of new homes given planning consents, with planning consents up from 20,000 a year in 1996 to over 50,000 in 2004/5. As at April 2006, there were 163,000 consented homes, of which 59,000 were under construction. The report, however, did not deal adequately with the issue of why the 104,000 consented homes had not yet started on site – and this at a time when the market was fairly buoyant.

The marketing issue was also problematic. Over half the identified capacity was in East London. Housing demand was generally greater in other sub-regions. This raised the issues of how to encourage people to move across London to buy homes and to rent new housing association homes, and how to integrate large numbers of new households into existing communities, or to establish sustainable new communities in areas with little social infrastructure and often inadequate transport connections. This debate arose at a time when the government was promoting housing choice, but not necessarily able to deal with people's aspirations, when existing communities and politicians in some parts of London, especially East London, were increasingly concerned about the impact of new arrivals, often households originating from outside the UK. Proposals by the Mayor and other Londonwide bodies such as the Housing Corporation, that access to social housing should be on a Londonwide needs basis, with no preferential treatment of existing residents in an area, were not popular with some councils who would rather not have more social housing in their areas than see it filled by 'outsiders'. The debate coincided with the right-wing anti-immigrant British National Party winning council seats in a number of East London boroughs and becoming the official opposition in Barking and Dagenham Council, the borough with the largest development site in London at Barking Reach. Some councils started to turn down the offer of housing grant from the Housing Corporation because it came with conditions. This was also linked to a concern that new homes were not necessarily followed by the new social infrastructure – schools and health facilities – necessary to support the new communities. These concerns were largely justified given existing deficiencies in provision and lack of funding either to improve existing facilities or to provide new ones. We will return to these issues in later chapters.

Given these controversies, it is perhaps surprising that, when the Examination in Public was held on the new housing targets, the substantive objections were limited to only two boroughs: Islington and Redbridge. The remaining thirty-one boroughs, including the City Corporation, either actively supported the new targets, or at least did not object to the Mayor setting them. This was perhaps attributable to the fact that all the boroughs had been involved in the capacity study from the beginning and were therefore party to the methodology. Moreover, as the capacity project steering group had also involved representatives from the Government Office for London, the House Builders Federation, the Association of London Government, the National Housing Federation and the three boroughs who had piloted the study, there was little room for argument on the overall approach. GLA officers had also been careful to make minor changes to some borough figures to ensure potential objections were not pursued. Officers from Redbridge and Islington tried to pursue their objections but were isolated; their objections were seen as political rather than of technical substance. The two objecting boroughs did reflect a wider concern as to the risk of overdevelopment but, given the government's pressure for higher housing output, supported by both private developers and housing associations as well as by the Mayor and the ALG, they received little sympathy.

This was to be in contrast with the experience of the Examinations in Public into the South East Regional Plan and the East of England Regional Plan, where proposals for much lower proportionate levels of increased output ran into objections from district and county councils, with the Panel imposing higher targets than the regional assemblies wanted, and the government insisting on higher targets still. Neither region had a comprehensive capacity study based on individual site assessment comparable with the London study.

Towards the London Plan review

With the increased housing target included in the London Plan, together with relatively minor changes to the policies on waste and minerals, the Mayor could focus on the further changes he wanted to make. The further alterations were driven mainly by the Mayor's increasing concerns as to the impact of climate change and his wish to get the proposals from his *Energy Strategy* (GLA 2004d) and the draft *Climate Change Action Plan* (final report: GLA 2007a) incorporated into the statutory planning framework. Before the early alterations EiP had commenced, he had published a *Statement of Intent* on further changes (GLA 2005a) (Box 7.1).

The statement selected ten areas on which the review would focus:

- Climate Change;
- London as a World City;
- The London Economy;
- Housing;
- Tackling Social Exclusion;
- Transport;
- London's Geography (including the sub-regions and inter-regional issues);
- London's Suburbs;
- Liveability (including safety, security and open spaces);
- The 2012 Olympic and Paralympic Games.

In the housing section of the document, it was stated that 'monitoring shows that there are concerns over the level of affordable housing being achieved in some areas, over the provision of family housing, internal space standards and the provision of related social and other infrastructure, especially transport and play space'.

Box 7.1 Mayor of London. *Statement of Intent* 2005

- include revisions to reflect the alterations to housing targets
- strengthen policies and review targets in relation to the provision of affordable housing
- consider the possibility of introducing internal and external space standards
- ensure that larger households including families, have access to appropriate housing in order to achieve sustainable communities and to avoid imposed out-migration by reviewing housing mix policies
- improve planning for infrastructure and related services, both to provide for

---

population growth and to deal with deficits in current provision, especially
of transport and provision for children, childcare facilities, play space and
healthcare provision
- clarify the need for additional housing in commercial and other non-residential
developments
- strengthen policies to ensure safety and security in housing developments
and the adjacent public realm whilst not restricting accessibility or resorting to
walled or gated developments
- include policies on affordable housing thresholds and off site provision

(GLA 2005d p. 30)

Given that the London Plan had been in effect for only eighteen months, and
that a significant rise in the housing target was about to be considered, this list
appears quite ambitious. The next four sections will consider the extent to which
these proposals were taken forward.

The new density policy

Chapter 6 presented some of the data relating to density of schemes granted consent
before and after the London Plan came into effect. Concerns had been expressed
by officers in the London Plan team and by other interested parties such as Peter
Eversden and Michael Bach of London Forum of Civic and Amenities Societies,
that the policy set out in the London Plan was not being applied correctly, with
the consequence that the principles of sustainable residential quality were being
abandoned in favour of maximizing unit output. The data presented above showed
a dramatic increase in the overall density of development. More problematically it
also showed that the majority of planning consents were being granted at densities
above the appropriate range, and that this was a contributing factor to the low
number of family-sized homes being built and the failure to achieve the targets for
larger homes set out in the Housing Supplementary Planning Guidance.

The GLA's London Plan team therefore commissioned the consultants URS,
together with the architects Patel Taylor, to examine the data and to propose
changes to the density policy to meet the objective set out in the Mayor's statement
of intent to increase the provision of family-sized homes.

The URS report (GLA 2006q), published in June 2006, proposed changes to
the density matrix, including:

- Removing the built form of the proposed development as a factor which
impacted on the density calculation.

- Removing car parking space assumptions as a contributing factor.
- Focusing the matrix ranges on habitable rooms per hectare and then exemplifying, for each range, the units generated if three different habitable rooms per dwelling were applied. This was to recognize that different sizes of units could be provided in similar locations.
- Completing the missing cells of the matrix – so ranges were given for family-sized homes in central London and for smaller homes in suburban areas, thereby removing the implication that the type of homes provided should be determined by public transport access and neighbourhood character.

The purpose of the changes was to remove the implied focus on built form which had encouraged the provision of dense developments comprising mainly smaller units and to refocus the guidance not just on density appropriate to an area but also on types of housing provision appropriate to meeting housing demand. The URS report also put forward a number of criteria which would support schemes with density either above or below the appropriate range – the intention being that this guidance would be included in updated Supplementary Planning Guidance. The purpose was to ensure that there was a rationale behind giving planning consent to high-density schemes, other than the common view included by planners in reporting to the Mayor that high-quality design was sufficient justification.

When the GLA proposals were presented to the further alterations examination in Public in June and July 2007, there was general support for the proposed change. It is possible that the change was seen as purely technical and that the significance was not fully understood by all participants. The Panel was in fact to include a key additional sentence in the explanation of the policy in the Plan – one not included in the Mayor's formal proposal: 'The form of housing output should be determined primarily by an assessment of housing requirements and not by any assumption as to the built form of the development' (GLA 2007s).

The revised matrix is set out in Table 7.3. This can be compared with the original matrix given in Chapter 4.

The review of affordable housing targets

This review was quickly concluded. ORS, the consultants who had undertaken the 2004 housing requirements study, were commissioned to update the study – partly to inform a review of both the affordable housing target and the guidance on mix and type in the Housing SPG, but also to inform the draft Mayor's Housing Strategy, which was to be prepared in anticipation of his being granted Regional Housing Strategy powers under a new Greater London Authority Bill

Table 7.3 Density matrix (habitable rooms and dwellings per hectare)

Setting	Public Transport Accessibility Level (PTAL)		
	0–1	*2–3*	*4–6*
Suburban	*150–200 hr/ha*	*150–200 hr/ha*	*200–350 hr/ha*
3.8–4.6 hr/u	35–55 u/ha	35–65 u/ha	45–90 u/ha
3.1–3.7 hr/u	40–65 u/ha	40–80 u/ha	55–115 u/ha
2.7–3.0 hr/u	50–75 u/ha	50–95 u/ha	70–130 u/ha
Urban	*150–250 hr/ha*	*200–450 hr/ha*	*200–700 hr/ha*
3.8–4.6 hr/u	35–65 u/ha	45–120 u/ha	45–185 u/ha
3.1–3.7 hr/u	40–80 u/ha	55–145 u/ha	55–225 u/ha
2.7–3.0 hr/u	50–95 u/ha	70–170 u/ha	70–260 u/ha
Central	*150–300 hr/ha*	*300–650 hr/ha*	*650–1100 hr/ha*
3.8–4.6 hr/u	35–80 u/ha	65–170 u/ha	140–290 u/ha
3.1–3.7 hr/u	40–100 u/ha	80–210 u/ha	175–355 u/ha
2.7–3.0 hr/u	50–110 u/ha	100–240 u/ha	215–405 u/ha

Source: GLA (2008m).

that was being introduced in parliament. The new study produced a slightly higher estimate of the overall housing requirement: 36,300 homes a year compared with the 35,400 in the 2004 study. However, there was a significant change in the affordability and bedroom size mix requirements. As house prices had increased, so the effective demand for market housing had fallen. As fewer households could afford market housing, this increased the demand for sub-market intermediate provision. Moreover this had an impact on the bedroom size requirements. The effective demand for family-sized market housing fell, but the demand for intermediate family-sized housing increased. However, the larger family-sized homes built by the market, which were generally penthouse flats in high-rise schemes in central London rather than suburban houses, would not generally be sold to families but were often underoccupied – used as second or third homes by international business people – so there was little policy benefit to be derived from the Mayor and boroughs encouraging developers to provide them. However in contrast with the findings of the 2004 study, the intermediate market demand was now substantially for family-sized accommodation. There was a difficulty in ensuring that intermediate housing, even that funded by Housing Corporation grant, was suitable for and affordable by family-size households.

The report was therefore problematic for the GLA. It could be used to justify an increase in the overall affordable housing target from 50 per cent to 65–70 per cent and an increase in the social rent target from 35 per cent to at least 50 per cent. GLA officers did consider the option of increasing the overall target to 65 per cent, and changing the 70:30 social rent–intermediate ratio to 80:20. This was, however, quickly rejected by mayoral advisors as undeliverable. As shown in Chapter 6, output was falling so far below existing targets that it was considered not only that higher targets would be challenged by the development industry, but that, in the absence of significant increases in public subsidy, they would be considered by the Examination in Public Panel to be undeliverable and consequently not meeting the new soundness test. There was also concern that revising the bedroom size mix guidance so soon after the Housing SPG had been published would be confusing to developers and local planning authorities alike.

This situation also led to the conclusion that it was not appropriate to include detailed guidance on size and mix in the plan policy itself, as application of any guidelines needed to be responsive to changes in both demographic pressures and market factors, and these changes were perhaps best dealt with through changes to the Housing SPG and the Mayor's Housing Strategy, which could be published later. The affordability thresholds for intermediate and market housing that were set out in the London Plan policy, which were being updated annually through an annex to the Annual Monitoring Report, could be updated in the reviewed plan, though they would remain subject to a continuing annual updating process beyond that.

There was little debate over this issue in the Examination in Public in June and July 2007. This was partly because there was no active representation from pressure groups such as Shelter and the National Housing Federation, representing housing associations, both of which had been active in the original 2003 Examination in Public. Representations were made by the London Tenants Federation, but these focused more on the affordability definition, which the Federation wanted extended to cover issues of cost in use, rather than the quantity of additional affordable housing needed. As the Mayor did not propose any changes to this specific policy, the issue was not actually scheduled for debate in the EiP and the tenants' representations were in effect set aside.

Affordable housing thresholds and off-site provision

These two issues had been identified in the Mayor's *Statement of Intent* (GLA 2005a). They were relatively minor matters of tidying up outstanding business from the original London Plan Examination. As discussed in Chapter 3 above, the Mayor had always opposed the idea that developers building on small sites should not be required to provide affordable housing. The government had set norm site thresholds of fifteen units in Inner London and twenty-five in Outer London before planning policy requirements for affordable housing applied. The Mayor had proposed a norm threshold of ten based on a research report (GLA 2003b). The government had then changed the national threshold to fifteen. This was despite the fact that in a number of boroughs the government had directed that a lower threshold of ten should apply. The Mayor used the opportunity in the London Plan review to introduce the ten threshold as Londonwide policy, to avoid the anomaly that in some boroughs developers providing fourteen homes had to provide affordable housing, while in other boroughs they did not. Despite the fact that the Mayor's proposal was technically in conflict with government guidance, the EiP Panel supported the Mayor's proposal and the Secretary of State did not object, so the new threshold was incorporated in the London Plan, overcoming the previous anomalous position.

The off-site provision issue was similar. The government had stopped the Mayor including policy in the original London Plan on whether affordable housing should be provided on or off site on the grounds that it was a matter for local determination. Subsequently in PPS3, the government had given national guidance on this matter. The Mayor argued that there was a case for a consistent approach to the issue across London and both the Panel and the government accepted that it was appropriate for the Mayor to set criteria. The criteria set were that (1) off-site provision should increase the quantity and quality of housing relative to what could be provided on site; (2) off-site provision should contribute to the development of mixed and balanced communities; (3) agreement to provision being made off site should not be of financial benefit to the developer; and (4) off-site provision had to be deliverable and the site should be identified so that the first three criteria could be assessed before consent for the primary sites was granted. This policy was not insignificant given that so many developments were high-density schemes and often high-rise schemes, where it was extremely difficult to provide affordable and good quality family housing *in situ*.

Children's playspace and space standards

The Mayor's *Statement of Intent* (GLA 2005a) also referred to external and internal space standards. In 2006, the GLA commissioned two consultants reports: one on playspace for children and young people from the consultants EDAW; the other on internal residential space standards from a consultancy consortium led by Andrew Drury of HATC, but also including the architects Levitt Bernstein and the planning consultants Oldfield King. The issue of playspace for children was taken up the Deputy Mayor, Nicky Gavron, and the GLA children's unit, and EDAW prepared Supplementary Planning Guidance (GLA 2006c) which put forward a new set of standards, of which the most critical was a requirement for external accessible playspace of 10 sq m per child likely to be housed within a new development. Local planning authorities were also required to develop play strategies which identified areas of deficient provision and proposed action to correct deficiencies. From the publication of the proposed standard, the Mayor and Deputy Mayor insisted that this standard was applied to planning applications referred under the Mayor's strategic planning powers, which was problematic in cases of high-density development. Developers who were not proposing to provide family-sized accommodation had less of a difficulty, and it was ironic that more critical attention was given to developers providing family-sized homes without playspace than to developers who were not providing family-sized homes at all. In some cases, schemes were accepted where the children's playspace was provided on roofs. Somewhat oddly, the fact that the Mayor was requiring a standard which did not at the time have a statutory basis was not challenged by developers. Once the relevant policy had been incorporated in the revised London Plan in February 2008, the draft guidance could be then published as final guidance and therefore the standard did become a material consideration for planning decisions (GLA 2008c).

The issue of internal housing space standards was even more of a problem. The HATC report, *Housing Space Standards*, published in August 2006 (GLA 2006d), had demonstrated that space standards in new development in the UK were below those in other European countries, and only a third of space standards in Australia. In Chapter 6 above, an analysis was made of space standards in a sample of schemes considered by the Mayor under his planning powers, which also demonstrated the variation in space standards between tenures, with the market sector providing both very small study flats and very large penthouse flats. The consultants proposed a set of standards for room sizes and dwellings as a whole, related to persons expected to occupy the home. The proposed standards were seen as absolute minima – a form of safety net:

- 1 person 37 sq m;
- 2 persons 44 sq m;
- 3 persons 57 sq m;
- 4 persons 67 sq m;
- 5 persons 81 sq m;
- 6 persons 92 sq m;
- 7 persons 105 sq m.

The proposal was that these standards be applied to all new development irrespective of tenure. The Housing Corporation already had a set of standards, *Housing Quality Indicators*, for affordable housing schemes it funded (Housing Corporation 2007a).

The London Plan already referred to the need to maximize internal space standards. However, proposals by GLA officers to incorporate the standards into the London Plan as policy, in line with the Mayor's *Statement of Intent*, met strong opposition from the developer lobby through the House Builders Federation. The proposal was therefore dropped. It was therefore somewhat surprising that a few months later the government's own regeneration agency, English Partnerships, announced its own set of space standards to apply to any development on land held by it. Despite the fact that these standards were somewhat higher than the 'safety net' minima proposed in the HATC report, they did not appear to meet the same level of hostility as the Mayor's proposal. However, as will be discussed further below, the issue has not gone away, with pressure from both the Royal Institute of British Architects (RIBA) and a set of standards published by the Building for Life best practice group (Building for Life 2007). Some form of new standard may yet be introduced through the London Plan, the Mayor's Housing Strategy, design guidance or the adoption of some new national standard by the new Homes and Communities Agency, which was established in December 2008 to replace both English Partnerships and the Housing Corporation.

The Mayor's draft Housing Strategy

One of the provisions of the 2007 Greater London Authority Bill, which was later to be enacted, was that the Mayor would take over responsibility from the Government Office for London for the publication of the London Housing Strategy. This would form the framework for the allocation of investment resources by the board of the new Homes and Communities Agency, which would be chaired by the Mayor. The draft Housing Strategy, published by the Mayor in September 2007 (GLA 2007b), was the first strategic housing document published by the Mayor since the Housing Commission report of 2000.

In the strategy, the Mayor set out his vision as follows:

Box 7.2 The Mayor's vision for housing in London

The Mayor will work with government, the boroughs, public and private investors, housing agencies, and community and voluntary organisations to improve the housing opportunities available to Londoners.

More homes, more family homes, more affordable homes:

We will drive up the supply of homes across all tenures, to ensure London remains a prosperous and successful city. We will maximise London's capacity to accommodate its growth within its boundaries, without encroaching on open space, tackling the barriers to development to provide more homes in all areas of London. We will increase the supply of family homes and affordable homes and give Londoners on low and moderate incomes more opportunity to share in the capital's growing prosperity.

Better design, greener homes, renewed homes, estates and areas:

We will raise standards for new homes and reduce the environmental impact of existing homes to make London an exemplary world city in mitigating and adapting to climate change. We will regenerate our poorer estates and communities and work towards a new Decent Environment standard for all existing homes. We will put design at the heart of housing to shape a more attractive, well designed city, to make London a healthier and better city for people to live in and to improve accessibility for all.

More choice and opportunity, less homelessness and overcrowding, more sustainable communities:

We will meet the challenges of extreme housing need, especially homelessness and overcrowding. We will embrace the diversity of London's communities and reflect this in meeting London's housing needs and aspirations. We will improve housing mobility and tenure choice. We will tackle work disincentives for tenants and those on high rents, such as people in temporary accommodation. We will create communities that are strong, inclusive, safe and sustainable and supported by excellent social, physical and economic infrastructure. We will help to empower residents and support high quality management of estates and neighbourhoods. We will ensure that the delivery of housing in London promotes social inclusion and tackles deprivation and discrimination.

(GLA 2007b p. 13)

In relation to housing supply, the Mayor stated the following policy objectives:

Box 7.3 The Mayor's objectives for housing supply

The Mayor will:

- seek to increase the overall supply of new homes, in particular new affordable housing, enabling the delivery of over 50,000 new affordable homes over the three years from 2008–2011 and almost doubling the supply of new social rented homes compared to 2003/04 and 2005/06
- boost the supply of homes with three or more bedrooms in the affordable sector
- ensure that more homes are built in each of London's sub regions in accordance with the spatial distribution set by the London Plan
- ensure appropriate supply of new supported housing and the provision of specialist forms of housing to meet specific needs
- align the housing and infrastructure investment programmes of public housing and regeneration agencies and prioritise key strategic sites

The Mayor will:

- encourage new forms of private investment and development to provide more homes for sale and for private rent
- improve public influence over development outcomes through innovative and collaborative use of public and private resources

- intervene to speed up land assembly and make more effective use of land already in public ownership
- encourage housing associations to take a lead role in development
- support councils and arms length management organisations wishing to build new homes
- promote a more consistent London wide approach to planning gain to achieve his housing and social objectives

The Mayor will:

- increase the number of low cost home ownership opportunities, especially for families
- set new priorities for intermediate housing, targeting it more closely as a route to home ownership for existing social tenants, key public service workers and others on moderate incomes
- simplify access to intermediate housing products and introduce new products along the lines of the popular Do It Yourself Shared Ownership
- encourage provision of additional homes for intermediate rent
- review the impact of social housing rent restructuring, seeking to improve affordability but also to encourage investment

(GLA 2007b pp. 15–16)

The intention was that following consultation on the document, and the enactment of the new Greater London Authority Bill, the document would be issued as a final strategy, which would set the framework for the 2008–11 London housing investment programme. Although the Bill became law in October 2007, the strategy was not finalized before Ken Livingstone's term of office ended, and he therefore was unable to take the opportunity to influence the distribution of the Housing Corporation's London three-year investment programme of £3.3 billion, or of the increased level of investment resources which was to fall under the control of the London board of the Homes and Communities Agency.

The housing situation in London in 2008

The most significant change was the dramatic increase in house prices. By June 2008, the average house price had risen to £345,136, an increase of 79 per cent over the June 2000 figure of £182,346. Between 2000 and 2007, the ratio between lower quartile house prices and lower quartile household income had increased from 4:1 to 7.25:1 – as compared with the standard safe lending mortgage–income multiplier of 3.5:1. In nineteen London boroughs the house price–income ratio was over 10:1 with the ratio in Kensington and Chelsea being over 20:1 (Table 7.4). This is significant as this was the measure of affordability used in the Barker review of housing supply, which will be considered in Chapter 8.

It is perhaps significant that in one of the poorest boroughs, Hackney, house purchase was less affordable for its residents than purchase in the City of London was for the residents of the latter.

Not surprisingly, there was a significant increase in households on waiting lists for council and housing association housing, from 196,995 households in 2000 to 331,230 households in 2006 – a 68 per cent increase. This latter figure represented 10.3 per cent of the total households in London. In three boroughs – Hackney, Newham and Haringey – the proportion was over 20 per cent.

Contrastingly, the number of households newly accepted as homeless had fallen from 30,000 in 2000/1 to 15,400 in 2006/7. The number of homeless households in temporary accommodation at the end of each financial year had, however, increased from 50,000 in March 2000 to nearly 60,000 in March 2007, though the number in bed and breakfast had fallen from over 7,000 to just over 2,000.

Local authority rents had increased from an average of £60.17 a week in 2000 to £72.79 a week in 2006, an increase of 21 per cent. Average housing association rents were slightly higher and went up from £62.60 to £78.07 over the same period, an increase of 25 per cent. Rent increases for both sectors were capped under the government's rent target regime, with increases capped at retail price index (RPI) + 1 per cent.

The sale of council homes had fallen from 11,331 in 1999/2000 to only 2,221 in 2006/7, reflecting the revision of the discount arrangements. In 2005/6, for the first time in twenty years, the figure for new social rented homes in London exceeded the loss through council house sales. Nevertheless the combined local authority and housing association stock in London fell from 912,000 homes to

Table 7.4 Boroughs with high house price–income ratios in 2007

Boroughs	House price–income ratio
Kensington and Chelsea	21:1
Westminster	13:1
Camden, Hammersmith and Fulham, Wandsworth	12:1
Barnet, Brent, Harrow, Kingston, Merton, Richmond, Waltham Forest	11:1
Bromley, City of London, Ealing, Hackney, Haringey, Hounslow, Islington	10:1

772,950, a loss of 139,000 affordable homes – 15 per cent of the supply. This was because the increase in housing association stock of 66,000 homes from new building and stock transfer was far less than the loss of 195,000 homes, through demolition, council house sales to occupants and transfer to housing associations.

Ken Livingstone's contribution

The impact of mayoral planning and housing policies was fairly marginal. Until 2008, when he became responsible for the London Housing Strategy, the Mayor had no control over the government's housing investment programme, and little influence over the Housing Corporation's investment decisions. Until 2008, the Mayor had no powers to approve specific development proposals, his powers being limited to the right to veto planning applications which did not comply with the London Plan. The Mayor had no land in his direct ownership; under government rules, the London Development Agency was not allowed to subsidize land disposal for affordable housing; and Transport for London needed receipts from sale of surplus land to fund transport investment. He had no control over the rents of housing association or local authority homes or over their lettings policies. Despite attempts to do so, Livingstone was unable to force local authorities to pool nomination rights so that councils with less housing pressure could help those with greater housing needs. Although his housing team established standards for use of temporary accommodation for homeless households, and monitored both the geographical distribution and standards of placements of homeless households, he had no powers of enforcement.

However, the Mayor's planning decisions in support of some higher-density schemes which breached his own sustainable residential quality criteria, and his support for schemes which maximized numerical output, often irrespective of the affordability of homes or the mix between family and non-family accommodation, acted both as an encouragement to developers and as a discouragement to local planning authorities seeking to modify such proposals.

Balancing quantity and quality is always a difficult judgment, but the fact that the London Plan's numerical housing output targets were generally met in the 2000 to 2008 period, while the targets for affordable housing, social rented housing and bedroom size mix were not, does imply that the balance was wrong and that a lower numerical output might have allowed for a better performance in relation to the qualitative targets. It could also be argued that, if more family rented homes had been provided during the period, there might have been a reduction in the number of homeless households in temporary accommodation rather than an increase, and that the dramatic increase in the number of households on waiting lists for council and housing association housing might have been mitigated.

It would however be wrong to put the blame for the worsening housing position in London primarily on Ken Livingstone. The main reason for the lack of affordable housing output in London was the lack of central government investment. The Mayor was fairly successful in obtaining subsidy from developers to affordable housing output. As will be considered further in Chapter 10, these contributions could not make up for deficits generated by the lack of adequate central government investment and the continuing pressures on the Housing Corporation from ministers and the Treasury to reduce the level of subsidy paid per home. This requirement was bound to have negative consequences at a time when both land costs and building costs were increasing, while rent income was capped, and when both the Mayor and the government were seeking higher standards especially in relation to energy efficiency and carbon emissions, all of which had significant cost impacts.

It was therefore a combination of the inappropriate application of planning policies, the lack of adequate government investment and external economic pressures that were together responsible for the lack of progress in meeting housing needs in the April 2000 to March 2008 period. It should be recognized that this was a period when the economy was strong and when many private developments were highly profitable. From the perspective of the market slowdown of autumn 2008 and the credit crunch, the earlier period can be seen as a golden age, in which, despite appropriate strategic planning policies, inappropriate policy application and lack of public investment led to opportunities being missed – opportunities which in the new economic context are no longer available, and which demonstrate that a new model for affordable housing provision is required. We will return to this issue in the concluding chapter.

The 2008 election and the new Mayor

The revised London Plan published by Ken Livingstone in February 2008, just before the end of his second term of office and his election defeat on 1 May 2008, had therefore only included some of the housing proposals set out in his earlier statement of intent. Of the major issues, density policy had been modified and a new children's playspace standard introduced, but the review of affordable housing targets and the introduction of internal space standards had not been introduced. The new Conservative Mayor, Boris Johnson, was to seek to deal with both of these outstanding issues.

In the run up to the May 2008 election, both Ken Livingstone and Boris Johnson published housing manifestos. The ensuing debate focused on Boris Johnson's wish to abolish Ken Livingstone's 50 per cent affordable housing target (Edwards and Isaby 2008).

Boris Johnson published a housing manifesto, *Building a Better London*, which made a number of pledges (Johnson 2008):

Box 7.4 The Johnson 2008 housing manifesto

- to help more Londoners afford their own home by
    - i) releasing £130m from the London housing budget to launch a 'First Steps Housing scheme' for first time buyers;
    - ii) work with the boroughs to build 50,000 more affordable homes by 2011;
    - iii) invest £60m to start renovating the capital's 84,205 empty properties;
    - iv) incentive the boroughs to release dormant housing;
    - v) work with local councils to deliver more family sized homes;
    - vi) increase shared ownership schemes for low income households by a third;
    - vii) protect private tenants from unscrupulous landlords by publishing a 'Fair Rents Guide';
    - viii) explore the possibility of a rent deposit scheme with a guaranteed arbitration panel.
- to design developments to combat crime by amending the London Plan
- to protect green spaces and historic views by
    - i) reinstating planning rules that protect the views of St Paul's cathedral and the Palace of Westminster;
    - ii) toughening up the London Plan to prevent development on domestic gardens;
    - iii) encourage builders to build more environmentally friendly homes in the private sector;
    - iv) protect the green belt by using the Mayor's powers to refuse applications to build on it.

Ken Livingstone's housing manifesto was titled *Why London Needs a 50% Affordable Housing Policy* (Livingstone 2008).

Box 7.5 The Livingstone 2008 housing manifesto

I shall:

- maintain the policy that 50 per cent of all new homes should be affordable
- ensure a much larger proportion of new affordable homes for rent are family sized (three bedrooms or more) to cut overcrowding
- deliver 50,000 new affordable homes over the next three years
- where necessary use the Mayor's powers to prevent councils letting down their local communities by not insisting that developers provide enough affordable housing
- work with councils and the government to ensure shared ownership schemes are genuinely affordable through rent free shared ownership and allowing purchasers to acquire smaller shares
- substantially increase the proportion of family-sized shared ownership homes to help young families stay in London and get on the property ladder
- help those on higher incomes who still cannot afford London house prices by promoting private sector and pension fund investment in new shared ownership schemes
- achieve the target of reducing the number of homeless households in temporary accommodation by half by 2012
- achieve further reductions in the number of empty homes, which are already the lowest since the 1970s
- support development of the Community Land Trust model, in particular through the proposed pilot in Tower Hamlets
- require the highest standards of design in new homes and maintain the London Plan requirement that all new homes meet the 'Lifetime Homes' standard and at least 10% are wheelchair accessible
- provide a comprehensive Green Homes Advice Service to help Londoners cut their carbon emissions and save money
- require all new homes receiving public subsidy to meet level 3 of the Code for Sustainable Homes and provide incentives to go further and faster to ensure there is a firm platform for moving to zero carbon by 2016
- develop and introduce a new Decent Environment standard for all social housing addressing carbon emission, energy efficiency, water use, internal sound insulation and recycling
- work with all social landlords to provide more personalised and neighbourhood-level employment support services to reduce the level of worklessness in social housing

- give social housing tenants much greater choice and mobility through working with councils to develop a London wide choice and mobility scheme, including a new register of accessible housing across London for disabled people
- work with councils to ensure they use their powers to enforce higher management standards in the private rented sector comprehensively and encourage them to provide landlord accreditation and tenancy deposit schemes
- work with pension funds and institutional investors to encourage them to invest in additional private rented housing, including considering how the planning system could encourage this.

In his first few weeks in power, the new Mayor, Boris Johnson, made it clear that as well as scrapping the 50 per cent affordable housing target he would increase the proportion of affordable housing which is intermediate provision, primarily shared ownership homes, and reduce the proportion which is social rented. He also made it clear that in his view planning is a matter which should generally be left to the boroughs.

In July 2008, Boris Johnson published *Planning for a Better London* (GLA 2008d), his statement of how he wished to change strategic planning policies and practice.

In his foreword to the document, the new Mayor set out five key objectives:

- All Londoners should have the homes, opportunities and services they need;
- London's businesses should have the opportunities they need to grow, to have access to markets and to attract the skilled workers they require;
- London's environment must improve and we must step up our efforts to tackle climate change;
- London's distinctive character, its diverse neighbourhoods and unique heritage must be cherished and protected;
- All Londoners should be able to share in their city's success, and enjoy an improving quality of life.

Much of the document focused on the need to support London's economic growth, the role of London's suburbs, the need to respond to climate change to protect London's historic and natural environment, and the need to plan for the new Crossrail rail line. In the housing section of the document, the new Mayor restated the objectives set out in his housing manifesto to deliver 50,000 affordable homes over three years and to remove the 50 per cent affordable housing target for new development, which was viewed as 'prescriptive and counter-productive'. He again stated his wish for a higher proportion of shared ownership and other 'intermediate' housing.

He also stated his intention to develop an evidence base on housing needs, capacity and markets. This referred to the updating of the 2004 housing capacity study and 2004 housing requirements study which had been planned by his predecessor, as well as a revision to his predecessor's draft Housing Strategy and to revise the Housing Supplementary Planning Guidance.

Although the London Plan remained the statutory plan for the capital, the new Mayor was in effect saying he would no longer impose some of the Plan policies on individual boroughs. So, just at the time the Mayor's powers had been significantly extended, a Mayor was elected who appeared reluctant to use them. It follows that there could be a shift from strategic Londonwide approaches to borough-led localism – the inverse of the justification for establishing the mayoralty and Greater London Authority in 2000. The extent to which the new Mayor will have an interest in influencing the distribution of housing investment through the Homes and Communities Agency regional board, which he will chair, is not as yet clear. The Assembly's Planning and Housing Committee together with some external commentators are concerned that he might argue for a switch of investment resources away from social rented provision to new home ownership initiatives (London Assembly 2008a, Bowie 2008b). Alternatively the Homes and Communities Agency national board may reject the Mayor's representations for changed priorities in London as being in conflict with national priorities and in fact overrule its London Board. There is precedent for ministers not allowing the London investment programme to vary too far from nationally determined objectives in that ministers overruled the London Housing Board priorities for the 2004/5 programme to impose a higher level of shared ownership programme. It was not insignificant that the new Mayor's first housing investment announcement in March 2008 was in fact criticized by the Housing Minister, Margaret Beckett, as being unauthorized and premature.

The new Mayor's more critical approach to high-rise development may encourage the promotion of lower-rise schemes more suitable for families, and relaxation of affordable housing targets may make development more attractive for house builders. However it is also possible that the new Mayor may support local opposition to development and be reluctant to impose higher housing output targets on local boroughs. This could mean a less adversarial relationship with boroughs but only by waiving one of the key responsibilities of the Mayor: to ensure resources across London are used to meet the needs of Londoners as a whole. What is less certain is whether this will lead to conflicts between the Mayor and the Labour central government, and whether the central government will seek to impose its housing targets and housing objectives on the Mayor. The government may well regret enhancing the Mayor's powers. Certainly having a Mayor who is sceptical of if not hostile to the concept of strategic regional government is not a positive result for those planning and housing professionals who see a strategic and interventionist regional government as being critical to meeting the long-term needs of the UK's capital city. After an era in which the Mayor, often for reasons outside his own control, failed to deliver his promised housing targets, we now have an experiment in regional governance based on a much more limited view of the importance of regional targets and objectives, with the focus shifting from strategic direction to voluntary collaboration between different tiers of governance. However, six months into his regime, Boris Johnson appeared to have moved away from the 'collaborationist' approach of his initial statements and in October 2008 proposed a set of affordable housing targets to boroughs which appeared to some to be tougher than those of his predecessor, if based on a different methodology (GLA 2008e). The tension between regionally determined planning and housing strategy and borough-led policies has not gone away. We will return to this issue in the concluding chapter.

Chapter 8

Challenges to the London planning regime

The Barker review of housing supply and the National Housing and Planning Advisory Unit

The implementation of the London Plan depended on a range of factors outside the Mayor's control. The central government had supported the overall objectives of the London Plan in that the government's representatives at the Examination in Public had not put forward substantive objections to the Mayor's policy and the Secretary of State had not used his powers to veto the Plan's adoption. However there was a degree of ambivalence in terms of the government's active support. In this context it should be remembered that Ken Livingstone was originally elected as an Independent and the adoption of the Plan in fact coincided with Ken Livingstone's adoption as the Labour candidate for the May 2004 election, despite opposition to his readmission to the Labour party from some leasing members of the government, including, so it is understood, the then Chancellor of the Exchequer, Gordon Brown.

It is therefore not insignificant that the main drive for changes in housing and planning strategy came from the Treasury rather than from the then Office of the Deputy Prime Minister, John Prescott, who was actually the responsible minister.

The government increasingly recognized that housing output, both in London and in the rest of the country, was falling well behind market demand. The Treasury therefore commissioned the economist Kate Barker to investigate the obstacles to increasing the supply of new housing. The review team had published an interim analysis report in December 2003. The final report was published in March 2004, just after the publication of the London Plan and a few weeks before Ken Livingstone had to seek re-election (Barker 2003, 2004).

The report was to focus on the objective of making market housing more affordable, or at least mitigating the worsening unaffordability, by seeking to reduce the rate of house price inflation. The report saw this objective as being achieved through the increase in the new supply of market housing.

The report recommended a number of reforms to the planning system:

Box 8.1 Barker report on housing supply: recommendations on planning

In setting housing targets and allocating land, planning bodies should take greater account of market signals, such as changes in house prices and levels of market affordability.

Stronger, more strategic regional strategies for housing and planning should be delivered through the bringing together of regional planning and housing boards and the establishment of new Regional Planning Executives to create a stronger evidence base for housing decisions. Regional Planning Executives should provide independent public advice on the scale and allocation of housing numbers within regions.

At a local level the allocation of land for housing should become more responsive to demand for housing. In drawing up local plans, planning authorities should allocate buffers of additional land, which would be released for development as triggered by indicators of unexpectedly high demand.

Action is also required to ensure that appropriate incentives are in place for local authorities to support development, and to ensure that development is not held up by the absence of necessary infrastructure:

- Local authority growth incentives should be introduced to address the costs of additional housing, allowing local authorities to 'keep' the council tax revenues from additional housing for a period of up to three years;
- More strategic use should be made of English Partnerships and area-based special purpose vehicles such as Urban Development Corporations to drive housing delivery;
- A Community Infrastructure Fund of £100–200 million should be created to overcome infrastructure blockages and facilitate development.

The focus of the Barker report on making market housing more affordable meant that it did not adequately consider the need for affordable housing of those unable to access the market – who in London were the main component of both outstanding and projected housing demand, as demonstrated in the Mayor's housing requirements study. In the London context, only a significant reduction in house prices would make market housing affordable by some of these households. The government target of reducing house price inflation to the European average, which was driven by the debate over conditions for entry into the European Monetary Union and single European currency, did not appear very relevant.

The Barker recommendation – that in setting housing targets, regional planning authorities should have regard to 'market signals' – appeared somewhat curious. Although the Mayor's housing requirements study had assessed house prices, effective market demand and affordability, housing targets were, in line with previous government guidance in Planning Policy Guidance 3, based on an assessment of housing capacity within the policy parameters set in the London Plan. This had been the basis for the new 2004 housing capacity study. It was recognized that these targets, and the sub-targets for social rent, intermediate and market housing within them, were insufficient to meet demand. Following the Barker review the government commissioned a macroeconomic model to demonstrate the linkage between housing supply and house price inflation. This led to the calculation of a number of new housing output targets relating to market housing, based on alternative assumptions as to the desired rate of house price inflation. The resulting report *Affordability Targets* was published in December 2005 (ODPM 2005a).

The organizational proposals in the Barker report also presented some difficulties in the London context. Although the Mayor supported bringing together strategic planning and housing functions, he was concerned at the proposal to set up a new regional planning executive, which appeared to imply the transfer of his strategic planning functions to another agency. Moreover since the mayoralty had the responsibility for setting borough housing targets through the London Plan, it was unclear why some new executive was required to give advice on these targets.

The decision by ministers to support GOL in having a role in ensuring boroughs delivered housing targets also impinged on the Plan's implementation. The borough housing targets proposed by the Mayor in the 2004 Plan were based on the 1999 housing capacity study. While the Mayor continued with his role of monitoring borough housing output relative to the proposed targets, a new housing delivery unit was established within GOL in April 2004, which required boroughs to develop action plans to deliver their London plan targets. The unit published a *Housing Delivery Plan* (GOL 2004). A new housing delivery grant was introduced and paid by the central government to the boroughs achieving targets. GOL then announced four boroughs – Islington, Brent, Barking and Barnet – that were to achieve significantly higher housing outputs. This process was carried out completely independently from the Mayor as the strategic planning authority responsible for housing capacity assessment and the setting of housing targets. Moreover GOL undertook this process while the new housing capacity study was under way. GLA officers were neither invited into GOL meetings with boroughs on housing supply nor copied into the borough action plans. Boroughs who already had a continuing relationship with the GLA on their performance on their targets found themselves subject to a completely different set of interventions by GOL.

Whereas the Mayor was as concerned as much with affordable housing proportions and bedroom size mix as with total numbers of homes, GOL's concern on behalf of the central government was only with the total numbers achieved and how many more homes above the then statutory target of 23,000 could be achieved – all at a time when London boroughs as a whole were significantly exceeding that target and while they were collaborating with the Mayor on a new capacity study.

Although the government did not proceed with the Barker recommendation for new Regional Planning Executive Boards, it did decide in 2006 to establish a new unit to advise both ministers and regional planning authorities on setting housing targets. The National Housing and Planning Advisory Unit (NHPAU) was launched in June 2007 (NHPAU 2007). The following month, in the Housing Green Paper, the government announced a new national housing target of 240,000 homes a year. Although not broken down to regional level, this total was 30,000 above the aggregate of Regional Strategy Statement proposals of 210,000, and was used by the government in challenging and then increasing the housing targets proposed in the South East England, South West England and East of England Regional Strategies. In its first year, NHPAU was to base its representations to regional planning bodies on its macroeconomic model, despite the fact that the regional assemblies all pointed out that the model had no or little regard to housing capacity, planning policy, demographic projections, housing type or location, and the fact that a significant component of unmet demand was for social rented and intermediate housing rather than market housing. Moreover the approach was completely at odds with the guidance in PPG3 and the government's Housing Market Assessment guidance. PPS3, published in December 2006, had a passing reference to advice from the NHPAU but did not require RSS targets to be based on the macroeconomic model. At the South East Region RSS Examination in Public in early 2007, government officials were required by the Planning Inspectorate to withdraw evidence based on a regionalized version of the modelling on the grounds that it had not been published. By 2008, when NHPAU published an update of the model, the original macroeconomic model was supplemented by demographic-based projections. The report (NHPAU 2008) summarized the two approaches as:

- The first utilises the Affordability Model, which integrates information about the labour and housing markets and demographic trends. The Model enables us to understand the effect of supply on affordability prospects.
- The second is a traditional demographic approach which draws on household projections and makes an allowance for constrained need and demand, vacancies in new supply and the demand for second homes.

It should be noted that the second approach was consistent with the government's own planning guidance but that the first approach was not.

The two methodologies produced London annual housing targets of 33,800 and 42,600. These compared with the London Plan housing target of 30,500 and the housing requirements study estimate of a requirement of 35,400 additional homes a year, and the 2006/7 outturn figure of 31,500. NHPAU's advice to the government is that the 33,800–42,600 range should be tested at the next review of the London Plan. As yet it is unclear how the figures are to be tested. Neither figure would appear to have any regard to housing capacity.

Some of the recommendations of the Barker report were taken up by the government in terms of additional guidance being inserted into the new Planning Policy Statement 3 on Housing and subsequently into the new PPS12 on Local Spatial Planning. The government introduced a requirement for all local planning authorities to include in their core strategies a trajectory for delivering their housing targets, showing how housing completions were to increase over a fifteen-year period. LPAs were required to identify all sites which would ensure achievement of this target over a five-year period and to make initial identification of sites for years 6–15. A minimum of five years' worth of sites were to be identified in the strategy. The Mayor successfully resisted pressure from the Government Office for London to include fifteen-year completion forecasts in the London Plan on the grounds that such projections would be spurious. The granting of planning consents did not automatically feed into completions in a predictable manner, as implementation of consents depend on both market factors and the availability of government support for affordable housing and transport and social infrastructure, which were uncertain in the short term, and more uncertain for the full fifteen-year plan period. The Mayor's officers pointed out that neither the Mayor or individual boroughs could be held responsible for delivery of housing when they were not themselves the implementation agencies, and had no control over either the level of government investment or the housing market or wider economic environment. Following the Barker review, the government was to pay grant under the Planning and Housing Delivery Grant regime (DCLG 2006b) to authorities as a reward for achieving increased housing output, whereas a more positive approach might be to provide grant to authorities that either were underperforming or faced the most serious external challenges, to help them enable increased output.

Other components of the Barker recommendations were not pursued by the government as vigorously as housing targets and trajectories. Although the government did set up a Community Infrastructure Fund as recommended, which is considered below, the government did not provide significant financial incentives to support growth or use English Partnerships or special purpose vehicles to promote housing supply in the way Barker had proposed. There were some limited new initiatives but, as far as London is concerned, EP's involvement in housing supply was quite limited, with progress on their two key sites, Greenwich Millennium and Barking Riverside, being slow and their Londonwide Key Workers Initiative dependent on top-up grant from the Housing Corporation.

The *Barker Review of Land Use Planning* and the 2008 Planning Act

The Barker report on housing supply identified planning as one of the key obstacles to housing output. This generated a debate on the extent to which local councillors blocked housing development, with ministers drawing attention to the increase in the proportion of planning applications refused. Kate Barker was then commissioned by the Treasury to investigate the planning regime. The government's prior assumption was that planning was acting not just as a constraint on housing supply but as a constraint on overall employment growth and the economic strength of the country as a whole. The Mayor was quick to use the criticism of boroughs to support his case that his own planning powers be increased, rather ignoring the fact that the increase in refusals in London was roughly proportionate to the increase in planning consents. The GLA housing team commissioned a special study of borough obstruction to development, but the report proved to be a very one-sided summary of developers' complaints about borough planners, without the views of the planning authorities being sought or the facts checked, and was not published.

When the Barker report on planning was published in December 2006, the initial critique of planning and planners had been moderated (Barker 2006a). The main recommendations are set out in Box 8.2.

Box 8.2 *Barker Review of Land Use Planning*: recommendations

- Streamlining policy and processes through reducing policy guidance, unifying consent regimes and reforming plan-making at the local level so that future development plan documents can be delivered in 18–24 months rather than three or more years;
- Updating national policy on planning for economic development (PPS4), to ensure that the benefits of development are fully taken into account in plan-making and decision-taking, with a more explicit role for market and price signals;

- Introducing a new system for dealing with major infrastructure projects, based around national Statements of Strategic Objectives and an independent Planning Commission to determine applications;
- Promoting a positive planning culture within the plan-led system so that when the plan is indeterminate, applications should be approved unless there is good reason to believe that the environmental, social and economic costs will exceed the respective benefits;
- In the context of the Lyons Inquiry into Local Government to consider enhancing fiscal incentives to ensure an efficient use of urban land, in particular reforming business rate relief for empty property, exploring the options for a charge on vacant and derelict previously developed land, and, separately consulting on reforms to Land Remediation Relief;
- Ensuring that new development beyond towns and cities occurs in the most sustainable way, by encouraging planning bodies to review their green belt boundaries and take a more positive approach to applications that will enhance the quality of their green belts;
- A more risk-based and proportionate approach to regulation, with a reduction in form filling, including the introduction of new proportionality thresholds, to reduce the transaction costs for business and to increase the speed of decision-making;
- Removing the need for minor commercial developments that have little wider impact to require planning permission (including commercial micro-generation);
- Supporting the 'town-centre first' policy, but removing the requirement to demonstrate the need for development;
- In the context of the findings of the Lyons Inquiry into Local Government, to consider how fiscal incentives can be better aligned so that local authorities are in a position to share the benefits of local economic growth;
- Ensuring that Secretary of State decisions focus on important, strategic issues, with a reduction by around 50 per cent in the volume of Secretary of State call-ins;
- Ensuring sufficient resources for planning, linked to improved performance, including consulting on raising the £50,000 fee cap and allowing firms to pay for additional resources;
- Enhancing efficiencies in processing applications via greater use of partnership working with the private sector, joint-working with other local authorities to achieve efficiencies of scale and scope, and an expanded role of the central support function ATLAS (the Advisory Team for Large Sites);

- Speeding up the appeals system, through the introduction of a Planning Mediation Service, better resourcing, and allowing Inspectors to determine the appeal route. From 2008–09 appeals should be completed in 6 months; and
- Improving skills, including through raising the status of the Chief Planner, training for members and officers, and wider use of business process reviews.

The recommendations were to feed into a new government planning bill. The report acknowledged that the problems of delivery were not solely caused by local 'nimbyism' but that the government shared some responsibility. Although the government did not publicly recognize that mistakes had been made in establishing the new national planning regime in the 2004 Planning and Compulsory Purchase Act, it did take steps to speed up some of the lengthy processes established by the Act, conscious of the lack of progress made by local planning authorities in adopting core strategies to replace the outdated Unitary Development Plans. Five years after the passage of the legislation, only seventy or so core strategies had been adopted across the country, with only two of the thirty-three London planning authorities, Havering and Redbridge, having core strategies in place by the autumn of 2008. The government therefore allowed authorities to speed up the plan-making process by removing the need to undertake a consultation exercise on alternative options before moving to a preferred option proposal. Moreover, in July 2008, a new Planning Policy Guidance (PPS12) (DCLG 2008a) on Local Spatial Planning was issued, which for the first time set out an explicit purpose for local planning, with a much clearer focus on infrastructure and delivery, with explicit new requirements on supporting housing delivery.

The planning bill had a difficult passage through parliament. The main point of dispute was the proposal, originating in the Barker review, that planning decisions for major infrastructure projects be taken by an independent planning commission, rather than by parliament or by the local planning authority. This arose from the lengthy inquiry process for projects such as Terminal 5 at Heathrow airport and nuclear power stations. The proposal generated objections both from local government and from campaigning groups, especially those campaigning against airports, nuclear power stations or new motorways. However, that element of the bill raised less concern in London, as major infrastructure projects of this kind are rarely located within the London boundary. The bill was eventually enacted in November 2008. Possibly of greater significance was a clause in the 2007 Housing and Regeneration Bill, also now enacted, that the government could designate the new Housing and Communities Agency, established in December 2008 based on bringing together English Partnerships and the investment functions of the Housing Corporation, as the local planning authority for growth areas and growth points, providing a mechanism for the central government to overcome opposition to development by the local planning authority. In contrast with the furore over the independent planning commission, this clause was put through parliament with very little debate. It is unclear to what extent the government will use this new power.

The government also sought to streamline the planning application process by introducing a standard application form for all planning applications – previously each local authority had its own form, which was clearly troublesome for developers working in different areas. Additionally the government recognized that delays were also due to the extent to which the Secretary of State intervened in planning cases and the long delays in considering cases at inquiry, caused mainly by the lack of resources in the Planning Inspectorate, which handled inquiries and whose workload had increased as a result of the requirements of the 2004 Act that all substantive local planning documents had to go through the public inquiry process. Such delays led to GOL officials advising boroughs not to prepare area plans other than the core strategy as there were insufficient planning inspectors to consider them. The government was to maintain its interest in speeding up the planning decision-making process by commissioning in March 2008 David Pretty, former chief executive of the house builder Barratt, and Joanna Killian, chief executive of Essex County Council, to carry out a further review of the process. This reported in November 2008 (DCLG 2008b).

The Thames Gateway, the growth areas and the Olympics

The government's 2003 Sustainable Communities Plan identified the Thames Gateway, including a wide area of east London both north and south of the Thames, as a growth area (Map 8.1). This was not a new idea, as in fact the government had issued specific Regional Planning Guidance for the area as early as 1995 (DoE 1995). This report had identified a capacity for 98,400 homes in the whole area, of which 30,600 were within London. This Guidance had estimated that, of these, 24,300 homes or 80 per cent could be completed by 2006.

The 2003 Plan (ODPM 2003) estimated a potential for 120,000 homes by 2016, which the report stated was 40,000 more than the existing target. The three main London sites were stated as Stratford with 4,500 homes, Greenwich with 20,000 and Barking Reach with 10,000. The key sites outside London were Thurrock in Essex and Ebbsfleet in Kent. The report was silent on how many of these homes should be affordable. Although the proposal clearly represented an increase on the 1995 target, it was unclear, as far as any of the London part of

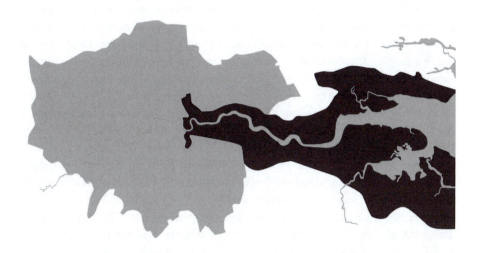

Map 8.1 Thames Gateway growth area. Source: GLA (2007f).

the Gateway was concerned, whether the new estimate represented any increase on the provisions put forward in the draft London Plan, which were based on the 1999 housing capacity study, and were, once adopted in February 2004, the new statutory targets. A key difficulty with the Thames Gateway figures is that the area was not coterminous with local authority boundaries and that capacity was quantified on a different statistical basis. It discounted supply from small sites and conversions as well as discounting supply from non-self-contained accommodation and vacant property returning to use, all components of the London Plan target. It was also unclear whether the new estimate discounted losses from demolition. The Thames Gateway boundary was also somewhat fluid, with both Barking and Lewisham town centres included later, both areas of significant preplanned redevelopment activity.

The new initiative created a plethora of new management structures. The central government set a new Thames Gateway unit. A London Thames Gateway steering group was established between the minister and the Mayor, supported by an officer group. There were parallel structures for the south Essex and north Kent areas. The Mayor then delegated a monitoring function to the London Development Agency, while Richard Rogers and his architecture and urbanism unit took on design advisory and masterplanning functions. The GLA itself set up a small Thames Gateway coordination unit, though its ability to coordinate agencies outside the GLA was limited. The government then established a new London Thames Gateway Development Corporation with development control powers for the main development sites within the London element of the gateway: Lower Lea and the Barking Riverside area (though not the Royal Docks area of Newham). The Corporation had a similar role and constitution to the former London Docklands Development Corporation, having an appointed board, with no accountability to the boroughs and no representative of the Mayor. The Mayor nevertheless retained his strategic planning powers in relation to applications where the Development Corporation was the local planning authority. The Development Corporation was not a plan-making body, but nevertheless sought to establish development control policies, including a standard planning contributions tariff, across its area, which included parts of the boroughs of Tower Hamlets, Newham, and Barking and Dagenham (LTGDC 2008).

There was a succession of Thames Gateway strategy and delivery documents. The LDA and the GLA published in April 2004 the *Thames Gateway Delivery and Investment Framework* (LDA with GLA 2004), which increased the London Thames Gateway housing target to 91,000 homes, arguing that this was achievable through development at higher densities than previously assumed. This document referred to the London Plan 50 per cent affordable housing requirement. In November 2006, the government published a *Thames Gateway Interim Plan* (DCLG 2006c). This increased the target to 160,000 homes across the Gateway by 2016 – a further 40,000 above the earlier target, though the figure was not disaggregated between the London, Essex and Kent sub-areas. Whereas by this time the Mayor had published the 2004 housing capacity study, the new Gateway target appeared somewhat optimistic as to the likely build-out rate of identified large sites, especially since the plan implied that most of the 40,000 increase would be within London. The Gateway plan also set a target that across the area 35 per cent of homes should be affordable – a target not consistent with the 50 per cent target in the London Plan. Moreover no distinction was made between social rented and intermediate housing. In November 2007, the government published a *Thames Gateway Delivery Plan* (DCLG 2007a). This showed that housing completions in the Thames Gateway had actually fallen from 6,000 in 2003/4 to 3,000 in 2006/7. The plan nevertheless sought to increase the output up to 10,000 a year by 2009/2010.

The selection of London as the site for the 2012 Olympics added another dimension. The main Stratford housing development site for 4,500 homes had in fact already been granted planning permission by Newham Council, with the support of the Mayor, before the Olympic location decision was made. The proposal had then to be incorporated within the Olympic plan as the main village for athletes, while proposals for neighbouring residential developments had to be reconfigured to meet the Olympics' requirements. Although the Mayor emphasized the regenerative legacy of the Olympic development, the focus soon shifted to the extent to which proposals, including housing schemes, met the Olympic brief rather than the longer-term housing needs of London. At the same time there remained some uncertainty whether or not there were special funding arrangements for the Olympic housing or whether the affordable element was to be financed solely from the Housing Corporation's mainstream budget. The fact that a new Olympic Delivery Authority headed by David Higgins, the former Chief Executive of English Partnerships, was established to deliver the Olympic plan, and that the new agency was given its own planning powers for Olympic-related schemes, complicated the arrangements as it clearly has very different priorities from the longer-term regeneration and development strategy set out in the London Plan. By the autumn of 2008, it was clear that the athletes' village needed significant additional government funding if it was to proceed.

Work was also undertaken on implementing a development programme in the London sections of the London–Stansted–Cambridge growth area. In October 2004, the GLA published an initial housing capacity assessment by Roger Tym consultants (GLA 2004e).

Sustainable communities and social infrastructure planning

The London Plan (GLA 2004a) set out a number of policies for the planning of social infrastructure including health and education facilities:

Policy 3A.15 Protection and enhancement of social infrastructure and community facilities

UDP policies should assess the need for social infrastructure and community facilities in their area, including children's play and recreation facilities, services for young people, older people and disabled people, as well as libraries, community halls, meeting rooms, places of worship and public toilets. Adequate provision for these facilities is particularly important in major areas of new development and regeneration. Policies should seek to ensure that appropriate facilities are provided within easy reach by walking and public transport of the population that use them. The net loss of such facilities should be resisted.

Policy 3A.17 Health objectives

UDP policies should promote the objectives of the NHS Plan, Local Delivery Plans and Modernisation Programmes and the organisation and delivery of health care in the borough. This should be in partnership with the strategic health authorities, primary care trusts and Local Strategic Partnerships and with voluntary and community organisations involved in delivering health services.

Policy 3A.18 Locations for health care

UDP policies should support the provision of additional healthcare within the borough as identified by the strategic health authorities and primary care trusts. The preferred locations for hospitals, primary healthcare centres, GP practices and dentists should be identified in appropriate locations accessible by public transport.

Policy 3A.21 Education facilities

UDP policies should reflect the demands for pre-school, school and community learning facilities, taking into account GLA demographic projections, and should ensure adequate provision in partnership with the local education authority, local strategic partnership and users. Boroughs should provide a criteria based approach to the provision of different types of educational facilities and the expansion of existing facilities, taking into account:

- the need for new facilities
- the potential for expansion of existing provision
- the possibility of inter-borough provision
- safe and convenient access by pedestrians, cyclists and by public transport users
- the other policies in this plan, including safety, sustainable design and construction, inclusive design, enhancement of the public realm and the protection of the green belt, Metropolitan Open Land and other open spaces in London.

The Mayor will continue to work with the government and boroughs to assess and review strategic educational needs and the land use implications of these.

Policy 3A.22 Higher and further education

The Mayor will and boroughs should work with the London Development Agency and the higher and further education sectors to ensure that the needs of the education sectors are addressed in Sub-Regional Development Frameworks and in UDPs. This will include:

- promoting policies aimed at supporting and maintaining London's international reputation as a centre of excellence in higher education
- taking account of the future development needs of the sector, including the provision of new facilities and potential for expansion of existing provision
- recognising the particular requirements of Higher Education Institutions for key locations with good public transport access, and having regard to their sub-regional and regional sphere of operation
- recognising the distinctive locational and access needs of Further Education establishments
- supporting the provision of student accommodation.

Provision for the education sector must take account of the other policies in this plan, including mixed use, safety, sustainable design and construction, inclusive design, enhancement of the public realm and the protection of Green Belt, Metropolitan Open Land and other open spaces in London.

The London Plan (GLA 2004a) also included a policy on the inclusion of infrastructure in area planning briefs for major new developments:

Policy 3A.5 Large residential developments

Boroughs should encourage proposals for large residential developments in areas of high public transport accessibility, including the provision of suitable non-residential uses within such schemes.

Boroughs should prepare planning frameworks for all large residential sites of 10 hectares or more, or that will accommodate more than 500 dwellings.

In the further alterations of 2008, the planning framework threshold was reduced to 5 ha, to reflect the fact that average development densities were now over 100 dwellings a hectare.

None of these policy requirements have in fact been implemented in any systematic manner, either in relation to mayoral scrutiny of borough Unitary Development Plans and core strategies, or in consideration of major residential development schemes referred to the Mayor. Although GLA officers generally requested an assessment of the number of children likely to live in a new scheme in order to assess compliance with the 10 sq m external playspace standard, the issue of the accessibility of school places and health facilities was rarely raised. Moreover when the Mayor considered a housing scheme for 500 or more homes, the local planning authority was not required to produce an area planning framework or demonstrate that such a framework was under preparation.

As discussed above, one of the purposes of the Sub-regional Development Frameworks (SRDFs) and the Opportunity Area (OA) and Area for Intensification (AI) Frameworks was to carry out an assessment of social infrastructure requirements. The SRDFs did this only in the most general of terms and those OA and AI frameworks which have been prepared are also largely deficient in this respect. The fundamental reason is that the responsible agencies, boroughs, the Government Office for London, the Department for Children, Schools and Families and the National Health Service, cannot agree on assessments of surpluses and deficits in existing provision or requirements to meet population growth, irrespective of the fact that the GLA provides regularly updated detailed demographic projections which incorporate the projected population moves arising from the provision of new housing consistent with the capacity identified in the 2004 housing capacity study.

Considerable work on social infrastructure requirements was undertaken for the Thames Gateway and the *Thames Gateway Delivery Plan* (DCLG 2007a) does now include some quantifications of planned social infrastructure provision by area linked to estimates of housing provision and employment growth. These are shown in Table 8.1.

It could be argued that, when related to the housing, employment and community facilities projections, the planned provision of education and health facilities appears to be at a fairly early stage. The government did, however, fund consultants to undertake social infrastructure planning for London Thames Gateway, which produced the Social Infrastructure Framework, which included a model for assessing social infrastructure requirements at a local level, based on a set of population-based standards for provision of different types of social infrastructure.

Following this methodology, and taking the GLA demographic projections for 2006–26, it is possible to estimate future requirements assuming that there are no surpluses or deficits as at 2006. The following population-based standards were taken:

- nursery day care: 25 per cent zero- to one-year-olds, 25 per cent one-year-olds, 45 per cent two- to three-year-olds, 80 per cent four-year-olds;

Table 8.1 Housing, jobs and social infrastructure in London Thames Gateway

Area	New homes	New jobs	Higher education places	Schools	Community facilities (sq m)	Healthcare facilities	Completion date
Barking Riverside and Town Centre	10,491	4,135			200		2018
Bromley by Bow and Three Mills	4,871	2,401	2,000 places		400	1	2018
Canning Town	9,920	3,573			8,900		2016
Lower Lea Valley	8,957	256		1	12,500		2016
Olympic Arc	5,483	3,354		1	2,934		2018
South Dagenham	2,900	2,908		2			2016
Belvedere	250	8,000					2014
Crayford	0	30		1	1,300		2016
Erith	806	3,400			704		2025
Deptford and New Cross	2,981						2021
Northern Royals	2,000				5,340		2014
Southern Royals	7,000			1	23,000	1	2025
Charlton	No figure			1			2016
East Greenwich and Peninsula	13,172	9,971					2021
Woolwich Town Centre	6,068	4,182					2018
Total	74,899	42,210	2,000	7	55,278	2	

Source: *Thames Gateway Delivery Plan* (DCLG 2007a).

- one primary school per 420 five- to ten-year-olds;
- one secondary school per 900 eleven- to fifteen-year-olds;
- sixth form places/vocational training places: all sixteen- to seventeen-year-olds;
- higher education places: 50 per cent of eighteen- to twenty-four-year-olds;
- open space: playing pitches 12 sq m per person;
- informal open space: 4 sq m per person;
- children's playspace: 10 sq m per child (GLA standard);
- allotments: 2.5 sq m per person;
- swimming pools: 11.24 sq m per 1,000 persons;
- leisure centres: 0.31 courts per 1,000 persons;
- community space: 61 sq m per 1,000 persons;
- library space: 26.5 sq m per 1,000 persons;
- one doctor per 1,700 persons;
- one dentist per 2,000 persons;
- 0.31 police officers per 1,000 persons;
- three-appliance fire station per 64,000 persons;
- ambulance service: 125 emergency calls p.a. per 1,000 persons;
- water requirements: 110 litres per day per person.

Applying the demographic projections produced the following Londonwide requirements to 2026:

- 24,000 more child day care places;
- 196 more primary schools;
- 52 more secondary schools;
- 679 more GPs;
- 570 more dentists;
- 14 sq m of playing field;
- 353 leisure centre courts;
- 30,200 sq m of library space;
- 353 more police officers;
- 18 more fire stations.

These data were also calibrated at sub-regional level and borough level. The demographic composition of projected population change varied between sub-regions. The projected population growth was concentrated in the East and Central sub-regions.

Public investment

Kate Barker in her housing supply report had pointed to the importance of infrastructure and proposed a Community Infrastructure Fund of £100m–£200m. In 2005 the government established a fund of £200m for projects in the South East, some of which was to support projects in the London parts of the two growth areas and in the growth boroughs identified by GOL. By 2008/9, the budget had increased to a three-year programme of £732m, but this was now spread between growth points across the whole country as well as the initial four growth areas. £40m of the 2008/9 growth area allocation of £135m was distributed between the London boroughs of Hackney, Redbridge, Enfield, Haringey, Waltham Forest, Brent, Barnet and Islington, with a further indicative allocation of £24m from the £169m allocation for the subsequent two years, but limited to the first five boroughs. The remaining £256m growth points allocation went to areas beyond the South East, so London's share of this new infrastructure budget is falling, reflecting a shift of focus away from the capital. The £24m allocation for London for a two-year period is a relatively insignificant contribution to the infrastructure requirements of the region.

The main source of public investment in new affordable housing remained the Housing Corporation. The Housing Corporation's national programme increased from £1.4 billion in 2001/2 to £1.7 billion in 2002/3, fell to £1.4 billion in 2003/4, then increased to £3.3 billion for the two-year period 2004 to 2006, then to £3.9 billion for the two-year period 2006 to 2008 and then to £8.43 billion for the three-year period 2008 to 2011. In terms of annual budget, there has therefore been a doubling from £1.4 billion to £2.8 billion, though the impact of this is reduced by inflation in land cost and build cost. Despite this, in recent years the Housing Corporation has been required by the Treasury to achieve an 'efficiency' saving of 7 per cent each year in terms of grant per home.

Because of its high level of housing need relative to the rest of the country, London has generally received between 40 per cent and 45 per cent of the national budget. In 2006, the Housing Corporation stated that it had spent £4,875 million in London in the previous nine years – 1997/8 to 2005/6 – equivalent to £542m a year, with a further £1,762 million allocated for the two-year period 2006/7 to 2007/8 (Housing Corporation 2006). The Housing Corporation's outturn statement for 2006/7 gave an expenditure figure of £890.9m (Housing Corporation 2007b).

In the Housing Corporation's 2006 factsheet, it is stated that some 52,871 social rented homes had been funded in the previous nine years (or an average of 5,875 a year), and 29,577 low-cost home ownership homes (or an average of 3,286 a year). These figures combine to 9,161 a year, falling slightly short of the original draft London Plan target of 10,000 a year. The target following the London Plan alterations became 15,250 – 50 per cent of the new housing capacity-based target of 30,500 a year. These targets can also be related to the original housing needs requirement estimate of 23,300 referred to in Chapter 5. The new Mayor has now adopted a target of 50,000 affordable homes over three years – equivalent to 16,665 a year, though it should be noted that this target is based on a different definition from that in the London Plan, as it is gross rather than net completions and also includes grants to households to buy market homes through the open market homebuy scheme.

Although the level of Housing Corporation investment did increase significantly in the period after 2006/7, the level of investment has still been below the level required. Moreover the balance of investment between social rented homes and intermediate homes has not met the London Plan target. The unit output stated by the Housing Corporation has been 64:36 in favour of social rent, compared with the London Plan 70:30 ratio and the housing requirements study ratio, which was actually 89:11. These figures also discount the Housing Corporation's key worker initiative, which provided funding to support house purchase – 5,115 homes in 2004–6. Although the London Housing Board, which included the London region of the Housing Corporation, as well as the Government Office for London were in agreement with the 70:30 ratio in the London Plan, which was incorporated into the London Housing Strategy published by the Government Office for London, the national targets set by the government led to funds being diverted from the social rented programme to support the key workers initiative. In fact the minister overruled the London Housing Board's recommendations for the London housing budget.

Planning obligations, Planning Gain Supplement and the Community Infrastructure Levy

In the wish to keep public subsidy for affordable housing to a minimum, the government, and the Housing Corporation as its agency, increasingly looked to the private sector, and specifically to the profit from private residential development, to support affordable housing.

Between 2000 and 2008, the government considered a number of options for reforming the system of planning obligations which operate under section 106 of the 1990 Town and Country Planning Act. This was the process by which local planning authorities could seek wider community benefits from development. The process is covered by Government circular 5/05 (ODPM 2005b), which specifies that planning obligations must relate to the specific development in terms of being necessary to make a development acceptable:

Planning obligations (or 's106 agreements') are private agreements negotiated, usually in the context of planning applications, between local planning authorities and persons with an interest in a piece of land (or 'developers'), and **intended to make acceptable development which would otherwise be unacceptable in planning terms**. Obligations can also be secured through unilateral undertakings by developers. For example, planning obligations might be used to **prescribe** the nature of a development (e.g. by requiring that a given proportion of housing is affordable); or to secure a contribution from a developer to **compensate** for loss or damage created by a development (e.g. loss of open space); or to **mitigate** a development's impact (e.g. through increased public transport provision). The outcome of all three of these uses of planning obligations should be that the proposed development concerned is made to accord with published local, regional or national planning policies.

The circular also states that:

A planning obligation must be:

(i)   relevant to planning;
(ii) necessary to make the proposed development acceptable in planning terms;
(iii) directly related to the proposed development;
(iv) fairly and reasonably related in scale and kind to the proposed development; and
(v)   reasonable in all other respects.

Section 106 contributions have made an important contribution to supporting the provision of affordable housing in London. However, in practice, most affordable housing in London has been provided through a combination of planning obligations, social housing grant and private finance rather than solely through planning obligations.

This is demonstrated by an analysis of units completed in London in 2006/7 under planning obligation agreements (Table 8.2). This analysis demonstrates that only 20 per cent of affordable homes provided through planning obligations in London were provided without some form of direct public subsidy. It also demonstrates that the majority of affordable homes completed in London did rely on planning obligations to supplement public subsidy from either the Housing Corporation or the local authority. The London Housing Corporation's 2006/7 outturn report shows 5,889 social rented completions, which compares with the 3,199 completed s106 social rent schemes with Housing Corporation funding in the above table; so 54 per cent of the Housing Corporation funded output was dependent on s106 contributions. The Housing Corporation intermediate rent output was 833 units, of which 617 or 74 per cent were dependent on planning

Table 8.2 Housing output from planning obligations in London 2006/7

Tenure	Units with Housing Corporation funding	Units with local authority funding	Units with Housing Corporation and other public funding	Units provided by developers with no public funding	Total	No grant units as % of total
HA social rented	2,416	93	783	692	3,984	17
HA intermediate rented	329	0	258	28	615	5
HA shared ownership	1,571	43	645	737	2,996	25
Private 'affordable' units	0	0	0	38	38	100
Total	4,316	136	1,686	1,495	7,633	20

Source: Analysis of 2007 Housing Strategy Statistical Appendix, Section N (http://www.communities.gov.uk/documents/housing/xls/sectionn.xls).

HA, housing association.

contributions. The Housing Corporation shared ownership output was 3,491 of which 2,216 or 65 per cent were dependent on planning contributions. This analysis confirms the findings of earlier research reports that affordable housing generally relies on a combination of government subsidy and planning contributions from private developments (Monk *et al.* 2000, 2005a,b, 2006).

Planning contributions are of course used to support services other than affordable housing. As is shown in the analysis of major London development schemes in Chapter 10 below, s106 contributions for purposes other than for on-site affordable housing were generally under £20,000 a unit, with most schemes in the range of £5,000–£10,000 a unit. However, there were three schemes where, instead of affordable housing provision being made on site, a significant s106 contribution was made to affordable housing off site, amounting to between £40,000 and £160,000 for each on-site unit.

Following the 2001 Planning Green Paper (DTLR 2001), in its 2002 statement *Sustainable Communities: Delivering through Planning* (ODPM 2002) the government proposed replacing the planning obligations system by a regime of locally set planning tariffs. In the 2004 Planning and Compulsory Purchase Act, the government introduced a modified provision for a new system of Optional Planning Charges. The principle was that a developer could decide whether to negotiate a section 106 agreement specific to the development scheme or instead opt in to a planning charge set by the local authority as a fixed rate per home built. However, Kate Barker's review of housing supply, referred to above, came forward with a proposal for an alternative system: the Planning Gain Supplement (DCLG 2006d). Each local planning authority would set a standard rate for a development to contribute to social infrastructure across the authority's area (thus removing the necessity to relate the charge to services relating to a specific scheme) while a section 106 contribution would still be levied in relation to site-specific matters, including any contribution to a requirement to provide affordable housing on site.

In order to test the potential impact of the proposed Planning Gain Supplement, an exercise which the government did not itself carry out satisfactorily, the Association of London Government, representing the thirty-three London local planning authorities, analysed the s106 contributions agreed by London boroughs in relation to planning consents granted in 2005/6 to identify the potential division between contributions which would be covered by the PGS system and funds which would fall under the residual site-specific s106 arrangements. They identified a total of £232m contributions, of which £151m would in future be treated as Planning Gain Supplement charges with only £81m relating to site-specific matters (ALG 2006).

Although the government had rushed a Planning Gain Supplement Preparation Bill through parliament in April 2007, in October 2007 the Chancellor of the

Exchequer announced he was not going to proceed with the proposal. The government then developed an alternative approach which was called the Community Infrastructure Levy. The government included provisions for the new levy in a new Planning Bill introduced into parliament in August 2008.

The statement outlining the proposal (DCLG 2008c) stated that:

> The Community Infrastructure Levy (CIL) will be a new charge which local authorities in England and Wales will be empowered, but not required, to charge on most types of new development in their area. CIL charges will be based on simple formulae which relate the size of the charge to the size and character of the development paying it. The proceeds of the levy will be spent on local and sub-regional infrastructure to support the development of the area.

As in the case of the proposed Planning Gain Supplement, the levy would supplement s106-based planning obligations rather than replace them, as site-specific matters, including affordable housing requirements, would still be dealt with under planning obligations. Although the Bill was enacted in December 2008, the government did not publish the draft regulations until July 2009.

The failure of the government to introduce any of its new proposals for revising the planning obligations regime has added to uncertainty in the property development market as developers and local authorities assess the potential implications of each new proposal for their schemes. Even if the CIL proposals are brought into effect, the introduction by a specific local planning authority of a CIL regime depends on the adoption of a core strategy which includes a CIL rate. In the interim a number of planning authorities, such as the City Corporation and the London Thames Gateway Development Corporation, have sought to introduce localized standard charge regimes. One of the difficulties with a fixed charge regime is that it is predicated on the value increment arising from planning consent being the same per unit for all schemes within a local authority area, though the CIL would allow planning authorities to vary rates by sub-area. The concept, however, ignores the fact that scheme viability varies widely between different schemes, even within the same neighbourhood. All the government's proposals have ignored the fact that value may appreciate both before and after planning consent, and therefore would not deliver funding for infrastructure from this longer-term value appreciation. In a context when values are now falling, the government's belief that ether PGS or CIL would raise significant funding for infrastructure now appears misplaced.

Sustainable development and the climate change agenda

In 2002, in the middle of his first term, Ken Livingstone established the London Sustainable Development Commission. The Commission, which was independently chaired and comprised a range of external experts, both promotes sustainable development and had a role in assessing the range of mayoral strategies and initiatives to ensure they complied with sustainable development principles, following the approach of the 1987 UN Brundtland report, *Our Common Future* (United Nations 1987).

The Commission's terms of reference were:

Box 8.3 London Sustainable Development Commission terms of reference

The London Sustainable Development Commission (LSDC) works to develop a coherent approach to sustainable development throughout London, not only to improve the quality of life for people living, working and visiting London today and for generations to come but also to reduce London's footprint on the rest of the UK and the world. The LSDC recognises that this requires co-ordinated action to identify key priorities for London and to focus on unsustainable trends, policies and practice that will not be reversed on the basis of current or planned action. In particular, the Commission will:

- Develop and drive a London Sustainable Development Framework for action and monitor progress.
- Promote the integration of sustainable development into all strategic decision-making in London, and provide commentary on the sustainable development dimensions of key London-wide strategies, policies and practice to the Mayor, the Assembly, London bodies and the public.
- Stimulate and encourage research, programmes, or action plans to further the purpose of the Commission and the implementation of the London Framework for action.
- Provide an independent London voice on matters that relate to sustainable development, and take responsibility for advocating, encouraging, supporting and promoting best practice on sustainable development to all sectors.

(LSDC 2003)

This body was to take the lead in developing new policies on sustainable development and construction. The Commission published a Sustainable Development Framework (LSDC 2003), and then in June 2005 an Implementation Guide (LSDC 2005).

The Commission was to take a keen interest in the review of the London Plan and the development of the Mayor's Housing Strategy, especially following the appointment as Commission chair in 2007 of June Barnes, the Chief Executive of the East Thames Housing Group, which was one of London's leading housing associations, and had itself published research reports and implementation guides on sustainable housing and density policy.

Following commitments given in his 2004 election manifesto, Ken Livingstone in his second term of office (commencing in May 2004) gave increasing priority to the issue of climate change. In March 2006, in partnership with EDF Energy, he established a Climate Change Agency. The new agency was established as a municipally owned company. It was to enter into partnerships with private sector firms to deliver low- and zero-carbon energy projects and services. This would be through a combination of combined cooling, heat and power, energy efficiency, renewables and other innovative technology in new developments and retrofit projects. The agency, directed by Alan Jones, who had pioneered this approach in Woking, was to seek to catalyse markets for renewable energy and energy service in London. Projects might be waste, water or transport related.

In his *Statement of Intent* for the review of the London Plan, published in December 2005 (GLA 2005a), climate change was the first key issue for plan review:

Box 8.4 Mayor's *Statement of Intent*

In reviewing the London Plan the Mayor proposes to:

- make London an exemplary world city in tackling and adapting to climate change
- set challenging energy targets – including the use of renewable and sustainable energy; to clarify the basis upon which energy assessments will be made; to require electricity, heating and cooling systems to demonstrate that they minimise emissions of greenhouse gases
- encourage development of the hydrogen economy
- support potential for appropriate renewables development and decentralised community energy provision
- reduce the need for active cooling systems
- promote security of energy supply
- strengthen the existing policy on climate change with targets from the SPG on sustainable design and construction, including the requirement that the location and design of new development and infrastructure is considered in the context of the climate change that they will experience in their lifetime
- require developments to mitigate flood risk by sustainable urban drainage

---

principles and to be appropriately flood resilient and to resist some flood sensitive uses in high flood risk areas

- ensure sufficient water supply by introducing water efficiency/consumption targets and enabling sustainable additional resources
- ensure more sustainable wastewater management by improving existing sewerage systems and encouraging more local wastewater plants
- recognise the potential threat from summer hotspots and identify heat sensitive land uses and to address adverse effects by promoting heat tolerant building construction and design, including recognising the role of green infrastructure for flood mitigation, and respite from higher temperature, and supporting 'green roofs'.

This priority was reaffirmed in the preamble to the draft further alterations to the London Plan published in September 2006 (GLA 2006e):

The most substantial changes I am proposing to make to the London Plan relate to tackling climate change. If the world does not take rapid and sustained action to reduce greenhouse gas emissions then we risk leaving our children and grandchildren to cope with potentially catastrophic global warming. The majority of the world's population will soon live in cities so the cities of the world must confront climate change. To deliver my vision for London we must lead the way in showing how one of the world's greatest cities is planning for and adapting to already inevitable warming, and even more importantly achieve very substantial reductions in our emissions of carbon dioxide.

The Mayor proposed a new set of policies:

- Policy 4A.15   Tackling climate change;
- Policy 4A.2ii   Mitigating climate change;
- Policy 4A.2i   Sustainable design and construction;
- Policy 4A.8   Energy assessment;
- Policy 4A.5i   Decentralised energy – heating and cooling;
- Policy 4A.7   Energy efficiency and renewable energy;
- Policy 4A.5ii   Hydrogen economy;
- Policy 4A.5iii Adaptation to climate change;
- Policy 4A.5iv   Overheating;
- Policy 4A.5vii Sustainable drainage.

The overall framework was set out in proposed policy 4A.15 on tackling climate change:

Policy 4A.15 Tackling climate change

The Mayor will and boroughs should in their DPDs require developments to make the fullest contribution to the mitigation of and adaptation to climate change and, in particular to: minimise emissions of carbon dioxide, adopt sustainable design and construction measures, prioritise decentralised energy generation, including renewables.

These contributions should most effectively reflect the context of each development – for example, its nature, size, location, accessibility and operation. The Mayor will and boroughs should ensure that development is located, designed and built for the climate that it will experience over its intended lifetime.

The Mayor will work with all relevant bodies, including the Government, Environment Agency, London Regional Resilience Forum, neighbouring regions, boroughs and water and energy authorities and companies to achieve an holistic approach to climate change, to promote changes in behaviour and to improve the operation of existing buildings, infrastructure, services and facilities. He will support the strengthening of regulatory mechanisms, such as Building Control, to achieve this. He will encourage co-ordination of spatial planning and emergency planning to deal with weather related incidents.

The Mayor will work with other agencies to promote measures to increase the cost-effectiveness of, and incentives to use, technologies and applications that support mitigation of and adaptation to climate change.

A new target was established for the reduction of carbon emissions:

Policy 4A.2ii Mitigating climate change

The Mayor will work towards the long-term reduction of carbon dioxide emissions by 60 per cent by 2050. The Mayor will and boroughs and other agencies should seek to achieve the following minimum reduction targets for London against a 1990 base; these will be monitored and kept under review:

- 15% by 2010
- 20% by 2015

- 25% by 2020
- 30% by 2025.

In May 2006, the Mayor had issued the final version of his *Sustainable Design and Construction Supplementary Planning Guidance* (GLA 2006f). This had previously been issued as a consultative draft. It was to prove contentious as it proposed a set of preferred standards which went further than the policies set out in the adopted London Plan. For each standard, there were two levels: an Essential Standard, based on the plan policy, which could be required through the Mayor's use of his development control powers, and a Preferred Standard, which could be encouraged but not enforced. The further alterations therefore provided a opportunity to put higher standards on sustainable design and construction on a statutory basis:

Policy 4A.2i Sustainable design and construction

The Mayor will, and boroughs should, ensure future developments meet the highest standards of sustainable design and construction and reflect this principle in DPD policies. These will include measures to:

- make most effective use of land and existing buildings
- reduce carbon and other emissions that contribute to climate change
- design new buildings for flexible uses throughout their lifetime
- manage overheating
- make most effective and sustainable use of water, aggregates and other resources
- minimise energy use, including by passive solar design, natural ventilation, and vegetation on buildings
- supply energy efficiently and incorporate decentralised energy systems (Policy 4A.5i), and use renewable energy where feasible (Policy 4A.7)
- minimising [sic] light lost to the sky, particularly from street lights
- procure materials sustainably
- ensure designs make the most of natural systems both within and around the building

- reduce air and water pollution
- manage flood risk, including through flood resilient design
- ensure developments are comfortable and secure for users
- conserve and enhance the natural environment, particularly in relation to biodiversity and enable easy access to open spaces
- avoid creation of adverse local climate conditions
- promote sustainable waste behaviour in new and existing developments, including support for local integrated recycling schemes, CHP and CCHP schemes and other treatment options.
- encourage major developments to incorporate living roofs and walls where feasible
- reduce adverse noise impacts.

The Mayor will and the boroughs should require all applications for major developments to include a statement on the potential implications of the development on sustainable design and construction principles. This statement should address demolition, construction and long-term management. Boroughs should ensure that the same sustainability principles are used to assess other planning applications.

The Mayor will and boroughs should ensure that developments minimise the use of new aggregates and do not use insulating and other materials containing substances which contribute to climate change through ozone depletion.

Developers should use best practice and appropriate mitigation measures to reduce the environmental impact of demolition and construction.

The new policy focus was to have a significant impact on housing development in London. This was further enhanced by the publication by the government in December 2006 of the *Code for Sustainable Homes* (DCLG 2006e), which introduced a new set of national guidelines, though it should be recognized that these guidelines were less ambitious than those put forward by the Mayor.

Even before the new standards were incorporated in the revised London Plan in February 2008, the Mayor sought to apply his preferred standards to planning applications referred to him under his strategic powers. His focus was initially on renewable energy, an issue pursued vigorously by his Deputy Mayor Nicky Gavron, but by 2007 he was also focusing on the proposed targets for reductions in carbon emissions. There developed a competition between the Mayor and central government ministers as to who could set the most ambitious targets. Ken Livingstone argued for faster progress towards carbon neutrality than ministers considered practical. He supported the development of carbon-neutral schemes such as the Bedzed project developed by Bill Dunster for Peabody Trust in Sutton, and wanted to see that project replicated elsewhere. While the government was requiring all new development to meet level 3 in the *Code for Sustainable Homes*, the Mayor wanted all new development to meet level 4 in the medium term, moving to level 5 as soon as possible. This had major cost implications for developers as well as implications for affordable housing output.

When schemes were presented to the Mayor at his fortnightly planning decision meetings, considerable attention was given by both Ken Livingstone and Nicky Gavron to renewable energy and carbon emissions, with affordable housing issues often being seen as secondary considerations. Not surprisingly developers aware of this policy shift concentrated on demonstrating that their proposals were as 'green' as possible rather than focusing on maximizing affordable housing output, as had been the case in the 2002 to 2006 period. Financial appraisals were used to demonstrate the additional cost of meeting the Mayor's energy and carbon emission targets, which were then used to justify lower affordable housing outputs than would otherwise be achievable. A report published by the Housing Corporation and English Partnerships in February 2007, based on research by the consultants Cyril Sweett (Housing Corporation 2007c), assessed the additional costs of complying with the *Code*. This conclusion was that, whereas level 3 of the code could be met at a cost of £5,000 a home, meeting level 4 or 5 could cost up to £30,000 a home. No attempt was made to cost compliance with level 6: full carbon neutrality.

The Housing Corporation did not, however, increase the level of grant available per home to support these additional costs and in fact the targets to reduce grant per unit required by the Treasury were not relaxed. The Mayor nevertheless exerted pressure to increase the code level requirement for Housing Corporation-supported social housing in London. The Corporation had proposed level 4 as a minimum requirement from 2012, with an objective of achieving carbon-neutral development by 2015 (Housing Corporation 2007a). English Partnerships had a slightly different trajectory: level 3 from April 2007, level 4 from April 2010 and level 5 from April 2014. With Bedzed as the only example of a carbon-neutral level 6 scheme, though admittedly a project that was not always fully operational in terms of this intention, and a scheme for a similar scheme in Merton not having progressed, the LDA supported a new housing scheme at Gallions Park in Newham, which was expected to achieve level 5.

The agreement reached with the London Housing Corporation through the Housing Investment Panel of the London Housing Board was that level 3 would be required for the 2008/9 Housing Corporation programme, but that level 4 would be required from 2010/11. The Mayor also wanted an innovation programme that would support projects which achieved higher levels ahead of this timescale and a special funding pot was included in the London targeted 2008–11 investment programme (GLA 2007b, GLA 2008f). Following the new powers granted to the Mayor under the GLA 2007 Act, this programme was the responsibility of the Mayor, though when these powers came into effect the Mayor was no longer Ken Livingstone but Boris Johnson. To support this proposal, the Mayor then set up a Zero Carbon Housing Group, chaired by his sustainable development adviser and supported by the London Development Agency.

Developers were generally supportive of the Mayor's push for higher-quality environmental standards. With the government also supporting Ecohomes initiatives, and promoting a new network of so-called 'EcoTowns', developers who were innovative in this arena got favourable publicity as well as the prospect of winning contracts for projects. The likelihood that without more Housing Corporation subsidy higher environmental quality would be achieved at the expense of qualitative affordable housing outputs was not a problem for developers – in fact it could be a benefit in terms of increasing sales values on mixed tenure schemes given that social housing proportions were likely to be lower. It is unlikely to be entirely coincidental that, in the last year of Ken Livingstone's second term, as shown in Chapter 6, affordable housing proportions for schemes referred to the Mayor fell significantly.

London and the wider metropolitan region

The relationship between London and the wider metropolitan region was largely ignored in the original London Plan. As discussed in Chapter 3, this was a conscious decision by the Mayor to focus on the compact city vision, to a large extent ignoring the case put forward by the chair of his external advisory group, Sir Peter Hall. Although the issue was raised again at both the early alterations and further alterations examinations, the representatives of the South East and East of England Regional Assemblies were reluctant to expose the housing supply deficit still assumed in the revised London Plan, as to do so would only draw attention to the more serious levels of underprovision in their own Regional Plans. Moreover government planners, by focusing on the discredited Barker macroeconomic model in their representations for higher targets at the SEERA and EERA Examinations in Public, led to a diversion of attention from the real issues of inter-regional deficits and the implications for commuting and transport planning. The Inter-Regional Forum was not an effective body in terms of coordinating cross-regional planning. Although it commissioned the inter-regional report from Robin Thompson referred to above, it did not then develop an adequate programme of cross-regional evidence collection and planning coordination to deal with these inter-regional relationships and deficits. SEERA and EERA were embroiled in disputes with the central government, first on housing targets, then on the lack of infrastructure funding, then the EcoTowns programme, which involved development of some greenfield sites, and then with the government's plans to transfer the regional planning functions to the Regional Development Agencies. In February 2007, the then Deputy Mayor, Nicky Gavron, took over chairing the Inter-Regional Planning Forum, with her main priority for the Forum being wider climate change issues.

Although the new Mayor's statement *Planning for a Better London* (GLA 2008d) focused to a large extent on the needs of the suburban boroughs, it also included a recognition of an increase in outward commuting from London and that 'it is impossible to address the issues of Outer London without considering what is happening in adjoining places outside the city's boundaries'. The report recognized that the challenges of accommodating growth and providing housing and infrastructure are shared across the wider metropolitan region. The new Mayor, as a former Oxfordshire Member of Parliament and sharing more of the politics of his Home Counties colleagues than his predecessor, clearly wished to have a more constructive engagement with the Inter-Regional Planning Forum, recognizing that the body has not been very effective. Whereas this may mean some return to some joint thinking and even research at a cross-regional level, the government's proposals to abolish the regional assemblies outside London are clearly not going to assist collaboration if the Mayor and his officers then have to collaborate with 100 or so separate local planning authorities. This would be a return to a position similar to that of the joint planning committee set up within the fragmented local government structure for the 1929 Unwin plan.

Chapter 9

Planning for growth in a globalized transient world

Changes in London's demography

London's population has been increasing since the 1980s and is projected to grow to 8.7 million by 2026.

Recent population growth has, however, been uneven with growth concentrated in inner East London boroughs such as Hackney, Tower Hamlets and Newham and Inner London boroughs such as Westminster, Lambeth and Southwark and the outer northwest London borough of Barnet. There has not been a depopulation of the central area like that found in other cities such as Paris, Berlin or Venice, nor has there been increasing suburbanization in recent years. In fact there has been some revitalization of residential use in the central areas. The population growth in both east and northwest London has been driven both by indigenous population growth and by increased international in-migration – though in some locations concentrations of new housing have also made a contribution.

Projections of future population growth are based on projections of indigenous population change and migration, but also reflect the anticipation of the potential location of new housing supply, based on the assessment of potential housing sites and their capacity in the 2004 London housing capacity study.

It is projected that 59 per cent of population growth between 2006 and 2026 will be in Inner London boroughs, and that population growth in each sub-region will be as shown in Table 9.1.

Converting population projections into estimates of housing requirements is a difficult science, as assumptions have to be made as to average household size, a factor which may itself be affected by the availability of housing supply. The revised London Plan includes a higher range estimate of 778,000 additional households, taking the total to 3.92 million by 2026. This is equivalent to a rate of 36,000 a year. This figure ignores any requirement for additional homes to meet the historic backlog of overcrowded households, previously estimated at 11,200 a year over ten years. Reference has already been made in Chapter 6 to revised household projections which led to the National Housing and Planning Unit proposing a London annual housing requirement of 42,600 a year. Government projections of population change have proved to be both unreliable and subject

Table 9.1 Projected population growth by sub-region

Sub-region	Population growth 2006–26
Central	297,000
East	476,000
North	127,000
South	93,000
West	145,000
London	1,138,000

to significant correction. The 2001 census failed to improve the projections, as in 2005 the government accepted that there had been significant undercounting in some central London boroughs, an issue that became highly contentious as funding for local authorities from central government was based to a large extent on population estimates.

Migration and transience

Planning for a transient population has become increasingly uncertain. Transience relates to both international and internal UK migration, but there is also significant migration between London boroughs for both employment and residential reasons. Large numbers of homeless households are placed in temporary accommodation outside their home borough. Many children cross borough and Greater London boundaries to go to school, a trend which has been augmented by differential educational quality between schools and areas and the application in school entry procedures of the principle of parental choice.

Transfer across borough and regional boundaries at secondary school level was analysed in a report, *Secondary Schools Places Planning in London*, prepared by a team led by Christine Whatford for the Department for Education and Science London Challenge project (DfES 2005). The travel of children to school is generally from Inner London to Outer London and from Outer London to schools outside London. In some cases up to 20 per cent of school-aged children resident within a borough will travel to a school in another borough. It is not insignificant that a study by GLA Economics of the factors influencing house prices in London, *London's Housing Submarkets*, showed a significant correlation with school test results (GLA 2004f).

The net international in-migration into England is estimated by the government's Office for National Statistics (ONS) at 153,500 in 2006/7, rising to 210,000 in 2007/8 (GLA 2008g). The most recent estimates for London for 2006/7 show international in-migration to London of 199,600 (31 per cent of the England total), with out-migration of 136,500 (28 per cent of the England total) giving a net figure of 63,100 (41 per cent of the England total). However, this figure is more than balanced by net migration from London to other UK regions of 93,600 (with in-migration at 145,500 and out-migration at 239,100). The net annual increase in London's population from international migration is less than 1 per cent of London's total population, whereas net out-migration to other UK regions is over 1 per cent of London's population. Nevertheless, these figures represent a significant turnover in London's population with 345,100 people arriving and 375,600 leaving in a year. The boroughs with the highest net international in-migrants are Camden, Westminster, Newham, Brent, Kensington and Chelsea, and Haringey. The boroughs with the highest numbers of net out-migrants to other UK regions are Newham, Brent, Ealing, Lambeth, Haringey and Southwark.

In addition there are moves between boroughs (GLA 2008h). According to the 2001 census, some 349,000 Londoners had moved between boroughs in the previous year – about 5 per cent of the total population. Total moves between areas therefore represented about 18 per cent of London's population. The highest transience rates were generally in Inner London boroughs such as Westminster, Camden and Wandsworth, while the lower levels were in suburban boroughs such as Havering, Bexley, Bromley and Sutton.

The government's records of migration relate to persons staying, or stating that they would stay, for a minimum of one year. Consequently population estimates have not included short-term migrants. ONS, however, in November 2007 published an assessment of short-term migrants, based on analysing data for 2005 (Tables 9.2–9.4 below; ONS 2007).

This degree of transience means that the concept of a stable community is not relevant to a significant proportion of London's population. What is more uncertain is the extent to which moves, whether between countries, regions or London boroughs, are driven by active choice or are an enforced response to circumstances outside the individual's control. Some moves will arise from a welcome job change, other from loss of a job; some will arise from a positive choice to move to a different, perhaps better, area, others in order to find somewhere cheaper to live. Some moves will be to live near family; others will arise from household dissolution. The figures nevertheless show that there are more moves into London for employment reasons or to become a student than moves out, whereas most out-migrants are moving for other reasons – perhaps to find more affordable housing (but without changing job so probably taking a longer commute to work) or to retire. Transience and the reason and characteristics of movers, short-term and longer-term, all have implications for planning and service delivery.

This issue was considered in a report by Tony Travers, Christine Whitehead and colleagues from the London School of Economics for London Councils in 2007

Table 9.2 Short-term in-migrants

	1–2 months	3–12 months	Total
Employment/student	54,000	36,000	90,000
Other	241,000	62,000	303,000
Total	295,000	98,000	393,000

Table 9.3 Short-term out-migrants

	1–2 months	3–12 months	Total
Employment/student	13,000	10,000	23,000
Other	641,000	78,000	719,000
Total	654,000	88,000	742,000

Table 9.4 Stock of short-term residents with average length of stay

	Total	Length of stay
Employment/student	25,000	3.5 months
Other	56,000	2.4 months
Total	81,000	2.7 months

Source: ONS (2007).

(Travers *et al.* 2007). This study concluded that the level of population mobility was greater in London than in the rest of the UK and that this put additional demand on services. The authors pointed out that, under the local government funding regime, rural authorities benefited from a 'sparsity' factor in the grant formula and that a factor should be introduced to reflect population mobility and turnover.

Employment and residential dispersal

One of the main criticisms of the 2004 London Plan was that it was a Zone 1 Plan and that Ken Livingstone as Mayor was only interested in Central London. This was primarily because the employment growth projection was concentrated in the Central and East London sub-regions, the latter including the City of London and Canary Wharf (Table 9.5). Some Outer London boroughs were concerned that with significant residential growth expected in Outer London boroughs that the Inner/Outer London housing/jobs supply mismatch would be increased rather than reduced.

The Association of London Government, advised by Martin Simmons, who had been the chief strategic planner at LPAC, argued for a more polycentric approach.

Table 9.5 Indicative annual sub-regional growth 2006–16

	Population growth	2004 annual housing target	Employment growth	% population growth	% housing growth	% employment growth
Central	14,200	7,100	15,900	26	31	38
East	18,100	6,900	16,600	34	30	39
West	9,300	3,000	5,700	17	13	13
North	9,000	3,100	1,700	17	13	4
South	3,400	2,800	2,400	6	12	6
London	53,900	23,000	42,400	100	100	100

Source: London Plan (Mayor of London 2004).

The concern was that the suburban boroughs would increasingly become residential dormitories with limited economic activity. This concern was partly generated by a study of projected employment growth between 2001 and 2016 of 17.6 per cent in Inner London, 3.9 per cent in Outer London and 12.7 per cent in the London periphery (Gordon 2006). The South London Partnership published a set of reports on South London town centres and their potential in October 2005 (South London Partnership 2005).

The GLA undertook reviews of office demand and capacity (GLA 2004g, 2007c). These followed on from reviews carried out by LPAC in 1996 and 1999. The second study, in 2007, gave special attention to the problems of limited demand for and the low quality of office accommodation in some suburban centres, notably Croydon. The report, by the consultants Ramidus Consulting and Roger Tym, concluded that:

> In summary, our view is that office demand will focus on certain centres within the London suburbs. These centres are predominantly to the West and include Chiswick, Uxbridge, Ealing and premier business parks. We also believe that certain other centres can capture substantial demand, but only with policy support (for example, Stratford) or substantial private sector investment in quality office stock (e.g. Croydon).
>
> It is entirely possible to encourage demand in a particular location by providing the right sort of sites and buildings, as well as other locational attractors such as communications, amenities and a quality public realm. But, putting organic growth to one side for a moment, it is also important to recognise that this is a zero sum game: one location's increase in demand is another's empty buildings. Planning policies aimed at 'directing' office activity to certain locations by creating capacity are unlikely to succeed without a whole raft of other things – some which policy can influence, and others that it cannot – happening alongside, and with public and private initiatives complementing one another.

For London's suburbs, these considerations emphasise the importance of policy in terms of encouraging offices in those centres with the greatest potential for growth: where public transport is already good; where access to central London is good; where there is an opportunity to reinforce identity through a mix of residential, retail and leisure buildings; and where there are opportunities to provide good quality office space through mid-urban business parks and town centre schemes.

(GLA 2007c pp. 64–5)

The GLA also carried out a series of town centre 'health checks' to assess how each town centre was performing (GLA 2007d). This also enabled the town centre categories in the London Plan – International centres (the West End and Knightsbridge), Metropolitan centres, Major centres and District centres – to be reviewed.

The early alterations in 2006 increased the housing targets in some, though not all, suburban boroughs. As shown in Chapter 7, the increases were concentrated mainly in East and North West London, with targets for most South and West London suburban boroughs actually falling. The role of the suburbs was, however, to be a key issue in the further alterations to the London Plan. The Mayor first published a report *Tomorrow's Suburbs: Tools for Making London More Sustainable* (GLA 2006g), and then a report on *Outer London: Issues for the London Plan* (GLA 2007e).

The London Plan Alterations (GLA 2008m) introduced a new set of policies on suburban development:

Policy 2A.9 The Suburbs: supporting sustainable communities

The Mayor will and boroughs should support sustainable communities in suburban areas of both inner and outer London. Development Plan Documents, Community Strategies and other relevant policies for these areas should seek to enhance the quality of life, economy and environment of suburban London by:

• realising job opportunities that can be generated by population increase associated with new housing; addressing structural economic challenges, including changes in the office market, facing some areas (particularly outer London); promoting and rigorously managing strategic and local industrial locations; improving provision for small and medium sized enterprises; refreshing the local skills base; increasing childcare provision; developing the

---

contribution of the public sector to the wider economy; realising scope for home based working and providing better access to the wider opportunities of the city region

- maintaining and improving the features that make London's suburbs attractive, including improving the public realm, conserving open space and providing spatial policies that support improvement of services, including health facilities, schools, community facilities and policing
- focusing retail, leisure, key commercial activity and community services in town centres; increasing housing provision within them; improving their safety and security and where necessary promoting public transport accessibility and capacity improvements
- supporting and enhancing the role of district and more local centres for 'walk to' services and meeting day to day needs, especially for convenience goods
- promoting and making more efficient use of land in areas around town centres that have good access by public transport and on foot to the town centre as appropriate for higher-density and mixed-use development including housing
- where appropriate, modernising or redeveloping the housing stock and providing a mix of housing types, sizes and tenures, including affordable housing, that can meet the full range of residents' needs
- encouraging a low carbon dioxide emission approach across London's suburbs, including lower density areas, taking into account the need to foster more sustainable approaches to the re-use, recycling and management of waste and the use of water, energy and land by Londoners themselves through changing lifestyles; within the existing stock of buildings; in the design and construction of new development, and in transport use and
- The Mayor will support [sic] the continued improvement of services which enhance the quality of life in London's suburbs such as health centres, hospitals, care centres, schools and nurseries and community facilities. He will continue to invest in public transport and take measures to improve the quality of policing and crime prevention.

The Further Alterations (GLA 2008m) also included a specific commitment to supporting a polycentric approach to London's development:

Policy 2A.8 Town Centres

The Mayor will and boroughs should use the network of Town Centres as the basis for policy development and delivery within them. Whilst recognising the key economic importance of the Central Activities Zone, the Mayor will work with sub-regional partnerships and other agencies to implement a polycentric strategy for London's development by:

- sustaining and enhancing the vitality and viability of town centres including community and civic activities and facilities
- accommodating economic and housing growth through intensification and selective expansion
- reducing delivery, servicing and road user conflict
- meeting the needs of Londoners and improving the sustainability of London's development

Account should be taken of the relationship with town centres in adjoining sub-regions and in the regions adjoining London, to provide strategic direction for the development of the network of centres.

Neither set of policies set specific targets or land use allocations for individual town centres or suburban areas. The intention was to establish a framework which supported the boroughs as local planning authorities in developing area frameworks for their town centres. There were only a few changes made to the London Plan town centre hierarchy in the 2008 revisions, for example the promotion of the Canary Wharf shopping centre. Little progress was made with the planning frameworks for town centres or suburban areas identified as Opportunity Areas or Areas for Intensification in the original plan, such as Croydon town centre or the South Wimbledon area, and GLA officers, concentrating on the growth areas and key central London Opportunity Areas such as Waterloo or White City, tended to leave the suburban boroughs to make progress at their own speed. Nevertheless interest in the economic potential of Outer London has not waned, with the North London Strategic Alliance and the West London Alliance publishing a new report by the consultants URBED in October 2008 (URBED 2008) and New London Architecture running a series of seminars on *London's Towns: Shaping the Polycentric City* in the same month.

Some of the outer boroughs, while supporting individual higher-rise commercial or residential blocks in town centres, were reluctant to progress area plans. The

Mayor chose not to intervene. Boroughs such as Sutton and Redbridge, which were quite keen on some town centre intensification, actually received little support from the Mayor's officers, though in some cases they received design advice from Design for London or were included in a pilot to test the Sustainable Suburbs toolkit approach, for example in the case of Mitcham in Merton. One of the more innovative suburban intensification projects was the TEN project initiated by the North London Alliance of boroughs with support from the central government, which published a study on designs for the intensification of ten town centre sites in North and Northeast London, most of which were within the London–Stansted–Cambridge–Peterborough growth area. After May 2008, the new Mayor, Boris Johnson, considered that contentious issues of suburban densification and competing town centres were best left to the boroughs as local planning authorities to deal with.

The issue of the potential for wider residential and employment dispersal beyond London has received surprisingly little attention. Although the government has a target to seek to reduce the differential between regional rates of employment growth, there is little evidence that the central government has taken significant action to steer inward investment and employment generation; it appears to have generally left the location of housing and employment investment to the market to determine. The fact that employment has not shifted from West London to East London and that private sector investment in outer Thames Gateway remains low (with the exception of Dubai Ports investment in the London Gateway port at Thurrock outside the London boundary) demonstrates the weakness of government interventions in the market. The government also recognizes how important London's economy is to that of the UK and how steering inward investment away from London to other regions is unlikely to be successful and would just lose investment to continental cities, New York, Tokyo or India. This was the argument of the report *Growing Together,* published by GLA Economics in January 2005 (GLA 2005e).

Similarly, the issue of planned residential dispersal was not widely debated. As shown in the migration figures above, there was considerable 'voluntary' dispersal of households to the Home Counties and beyond. In fact there was a net migration from London to every other UK region. At one time the government introduced a programme of compulsory dispersal of newly arrived asylum seekers from London to areas of lower housing demand – mainly in Scotland and the North of England. This was contentious and any suggestion of compulsory dispersal of London's 30,000 homeless applicants a year is probably politically unacceptable. The government had supported a number of voluntary mobility schemes in the social housing sector, including the HOMES national scheme and a scheme set up by the London boroughs called LAWN. The national mobility scheme, however, collapsed in 2006 when the government transferred the contract from HOMES to a private contractor who then failed to deliver. At one stage the Housing Corporation held back some of London's housing investment budget for out-of-London schemes but the take-up was limited. A suggestion that some of the housing development in the growth areas outside London might be made available to Londoners was also not pursued. Attempts to reactivate the former Greater London Council's Seaside and Country Homes scheme were also unsuccessful. The main issue was that the out-of-London authorities were unenthusiastic at the idea of receiving social housing tenants from London, and most London boroughs were not prepared to be seen to be pushing dispersal. The exception was a proposal from Westminster City Council in 2001 for out-of-London councils to be given quotas for rehousing London households. This was not supported by either the central government or the Association of London Government representing London borough councils. The focus of both the Housing Corporation and the Mayor remained to share London's development and investment resources to meet the needs of Londoners within London rather than pursue the dispersal option.

The conflict between growth and the environmental agenda

Perhaps the most surprising fact of the debates in the 2000 to 2008 period was how the conflict between growth and the environment became hidden in the sense that it was rarely raised explicitly.

This is primarily because Ken Livingstone, in convincing himself that the 'compact city' approach resolved this conflict, also convinced others. London's growth in terms of population, jobs and homes was regarded as not just critical to London's world city role, but also somehow inevitable and to that extent irresistible. The Mayor, however, by taking a position of opposing the development of protected open space and supporting higher densities and generally more intensive use of previously developed land for both homes and employment uses, managed to satisfy most of the environmental lobby. Amongst his strongest supporters were the Campaign for the Protection of Rural England (CPRE), for whom densification of London was the best way to protect the Green Belt and the far less intensive development in the Home Counties (CPRE 2007, CPRE London 2006, 2008).

One environmental issue which began to get some attention towards the end of the Mayor's term of office was the development of housing on land that was at risk of flooding. This became a significant issue with greater awareness of climate change, the flooding of New Orleans by Hurricane Katrina in 2005 and lower-level flooding on the English coast. The 2004 housing capacity study had assumed a relatively low level of flood risk, though one scenario had assumed a higher risk level, thus producing a lower estimate of capacity. The higher estimate had been used. The approach of the Mayor and his advisors to the Thames Gateway and other sites at risk was to plan flood relief areas into the landscape rather than restrict development. The advice from the Environment Agency was not to put residential accommodation on ground floors, so, for flood risk areas, the capacity study reduced residential capacity by 10 per cent. Government figures show a relatively high proportion of new dwellings in London being built in areas of high flood risk: 22 per cent in 2000, rising to 26 per cent in 2004, with a provisional figure of 18 per cent for 2006. Ken Livingstone as Mayor, despite his wider concern on climate change issues, was relaxed on the issue of development in flood risk areas, and was supportive of higher housing output targets for Thames Gateway, which were predicated on more development in flood risk areas. This assumption may need to be revisited in the light of renewed concerns and stronger advice from the Environment Agency. Developers may also be increasingly nervous of investing in flood risk areas, given the reluctance of the insurance companies to provide flood risk insurance.

With the emphasis of the environmental debate shifting from the protection of open space to energy efficiency, green roofs and reducing carbon emissions, there was little debate over the negative impacts of higher-density development on the quality of life of residents. Ken Livingstone appeared convinced by the combination of Richard Rogers's arguments for higher-density living, the positive impacts on cultural regeneration and 24-hour lifestyles in the city centre, and the arguments of his chief economist, Bridget Rosewell, on the positive 'agglomeration' effects of intensifying residential and economic activity (Ormerod and Rosewell 2007). Ken Livingstone and his advisors were effective in suppressing any debate or analysis on the impacts of the compact city policies. The case was presented as self-evident: a compact city would reduce the need for commuting; car dependency would be minimized; people would be nearer to social infrastructure and shops. These were rightly regarded as positive environmental benefits. Negative environmental considerations such as the noise on transport routes and in city centres set out in the Mayor's *Ambient Noise Strategy* (GLA 2004h) or the 'heat island' effect of agglomeration of activity in a report on *London's Urban Heat Island* (GLA 2006h) were ignored when proposals for high-density development were considered. All these matters were seen as resolvable by improved urban design, and designers and architects were seen as the new urban magicians and saviours.

Chapter 10
Planning and the market

Land values

One of the critical determinants of the property market in London has been the cost of land. The analysis below is taken from London Development Research's dataset of pipeline schemes in 2007/8 – that is before the impact of the slowdown in the property market. This showed average land cost was £19m a hectare. Values were highest in Westminster at £349m a hectare, followed by the City of London at £161m a hectare and Kensington and Chelsea at £82m a hectare. Although some of these values reflected the hope value arising from a site being allocated for housing in an adopted plan, or from planning consent being granted for a residential development, they also took into account the value of a site in its existing use or in potential alternative use. In London 98 per cent of residential development takes place on previously developed land, which therefore has a value other than as agricultural land or as protected open space.

The only boroughs with land costs under £5m a hectare were Sutton at £2.1m a hectare, Bexley at £2.8m, Greenwich at £3.5m and Barking and Dagenham at £4.8m. Borough data are given in Table A.5 in the Appendix.

Development densities varied between boroughs, so it is important to consider the impact of land on unit costs. Average land costs across London were £89,000 a home.

Land costs remained highest in Westminster at just under £1m a unit. The next most costly boroughs were the City at £270,000 a unit, Hammersmith and Fulham at £253,000, Camden at £209,000 and Kensington and Chelsea at £204,000. Land costs in the majority of boroughs were between £35,000 and £90,000 a unit. The high cost in Westminster significantly increased the Londonwide average. It should be noted that the schemes in the analysis included the two Candy and Candy prestige developments at Noho Square in Fitzrovia (the former Middlesex Hospital) and at One Hyde Park.

The Government's Valuation Office publishes data on residential land values.

Table 10.1, given in the January 2008 residential property market report, compares residential land values for developments of flats and maisonettes in Inner and Outer London with other regions. The analysis, however, explicitly excludes land values in the central area of Westminster and Kensington and Chelsea, which

Table 10.1 Residential land costs by region as at January 2008

Region	Cost per hectare, sites for flats or maisonettes
Inner London	£14,130,000
Outer London	£9,140,000
South East	£4,600,000
South West	£3,710,000
Eastern	£5,030,000
West Midlands	£2,830,000
East Midlands	£2,390,000
Yorkshire and Humberside	£3,060,000
Merseyside	£1,750,000
North East	£3,110,000
North West	£3,370,000
Wales	£2,780,000
Scotland	£4,320,000
Northern Ireland	£3,800,000

Source: Valuation Office Agency. Property Market Report January 2008.

as Table A.5 shows are much higher than in other London boroughs. Nevertheless the Valuation Office report shows that land values in the rest of Inner London are several times higher than in other regions. This differential cost is clearly not reflected in the Housing Corporation grant rate for schemes in London relative to other regions.

The Valuation Office report also gives a trend analysis of residential land costs in London as a whole, by three categories of development. For London as a whole, excluding central London, average land costs are shown as increasing from £759,000 a hectare in autumn 1983, when records started, to £2,770,000 a hectare in spring 2000, when Ken Livingstone came into office, to £8,590,000 in January 2008, a few months before his term of office ended (Table 10.2). This therefore shows a 264 per cent increase in the seventeen-year period before 2000, but a further 210 per cent increase in the following eight years. Before 2000 the average annual increase in land value was 16 per cent; in the subsequent eight years, the figure was 26 per cent. It should be stressed that these figures exclude the most expensive central London land.

The Valuation Office also publishes land costs for selected areas. Table 10.3 compares 2001 and 2008 figures for selected London locations, again taking data for sites for flats and maisonettes.

Information on acquisition cost and existing use value in relation to specific schemes is also available from the analysis of development appraisal for development schemes referred to the Mayor between July 2006 and June 2007, which was

Table 10.2 London residential land values

Date	Cost per hectare
Spring 2000	£2,770,000
Spring 2001	£3,965,000
Spring 2002	£4,907,000
Spring 2003	£6,000,000
January 2004	£6,262,500
January 2005	£6,895,000
January 2006	£7,265,000
January 2007	£7,715,000
January 2008	£8,590,000

Source: Valuation Office Agency. Property Market Report January 2008.

Table 10.3 Residential land values: 2001 and 2008 specific locations

Area	Spring 2001	January 2008	% increase
Inner London			
Tower Hamlets (E2–E3 postal codes)	£3,700,000	£10,000,000	170
Camden	£16,000,000	£24,159,000	51
Hackney	£5,000,000	£10,500,000	110
Lewisham	£4,500,000	£10,000,000	120
Southwark (SE15)	£3,000,000	£16,000,000	433
Outer London			
Romford, Havering	£3,500,000	£8,440,000	141
Redbridge	£3,500,000	£7,630,000	118
Barnet	£7,000,000	£11,400,000	63
Hanwell, Ealing	£7,500,000	£11,935,000	59
Ruislip, Hillingdon	£7,000,000	£9,500,000	36
Greenwich/Bexley	£3,500,000	£8,000,000	128
Sutton	£4,400,000	£7,250,000	65
Wimbledon, Merton	£4,200,000	£9,000,000	114

Source: Valuation Office Agency. Property Market Reports. Spring 2001 and January 2008.

referred to in Chapter 6. This is given in the section on financial viability below. The land cost per hectare varies widely. In some cases there was no land cost, as development was within a site acquired historically by the developer. In one extreme case, land cost was over £500m a hectare. It should be noted that, whereas in most cases the cost related to a purchase price, in a few cases the land cost was based on an existing use value.

Development viability

An analysis of development appraisal for development schemes referred to the Mayor between July 2006 and June 2007 enables a detailed analysis of scheme cost, value and development viability. These appraisals were all carried out using the Three Dragons/Nottingham Trent University development control toolkit used by the GLA for strategic housing projects referred to the Mayor. The purpose and practice of the appraisal system was considered in Chapter 4. Schemes cannot be identified, as the appraisals included data which were treated as commercially confidential. It should be noted that the appraisals related to scheme information provided either prior to planning application or as part of the application process, and did not necessarily relate to the final consented scheme. In fact a few of the schemes appraised were not consented. It should also be emphasized that the appraisals included developers' profit for market housing, normally at 15 per cent of value (this was later increased to 17 per cent), and builders' profit on affordable housing, normally set at 10 per cent of cost, so references to gross residual value relate to value of completed scheme net of these two components of profit. Net residual value is any surplus once costs of land have also been taken into account. Guidance notes on the methodology used in the appraisal system are published by the GLA with benchmarks updated annually (see GLA 2008i for 2008/9 update).

Schemes have been categorized by sub-region and split between Inner and Outer London boroughs (Table 10.4). The high number of schemes in the East sub-region reflects the balance of the development programme.

The schemes can also be categorized by scheme size as in Table 10.5.

Table 10.6 shows the density ranges. The majority of schemes appraised were over the average consented scheme density of 137 dph in 2006/7. This reflects the fact that, because of the height and size referral thresholds, schemes referred to the Mayor were generally at densities above the London average.

The land cost per hectare varied widely. In some cases there was no land cost as development was within a site acquired historically by the developer. In one extreme case, land cost was over £500m a hectare. It should be noted that,

Table 10.4 Categorization of appraised schemes by location

	Inner London	Outer London	Total
South West	3	3	6
South East	5	3	8
West	5	5	10
North	2	0	2
East	10	4	14
Total	25	15	40

Table 10.5 Categorization of appraised schemes by size

Scheme size	Number of schemes
Fewer than 100 units	7
100–249	8
250–499	11
500–999	7
1,000+	7

Table 10.6 Categorization of appraised schemes by density

Density in dwellings per hectare	Number of schemes
Fewer than 100 dph	2
100–249 dph	12
250–499 dph	17
500–999 dph	7
Over 1,000 dph	2

although in most cases the cost related to a purchase price, in a few cases the land cost was based on an existing use value.

For the forty schemes appraised, build costs were generally between £250,000 and £400,000 a unit. There were, however, four schemes with build costs alone (i.e. excluding land costs) at over £500,000 a unit, including one at £1m a unit and two schemes over £2m a unit. These were all prestige projects in Central London, including two relatively small developments.

There was a relationship between build cost and height of dwellings. The appraisal toolkit has benchmark build costs in pounds per square metre set for different types of built form. The model used in 2006/7 for these appraisals had benchmark costs as in Table 10.7.

An analysis was also undertaken on the relationship between height of development (taking the highest storey) and the build cost per unit. There was some limited correlation between height and unit cost.

These costs varied widely between schemes. Some schemes had no exceptional costs. In other cases, the build cost included significant physical or social infrastructure costs, in three cases amounting to over £300,000 a unit. In one case this was because the full costs of a mixed-use development were included in the appraisal, as the housing was enabling the development of a non-residential project.

Most schemes included some element of non-residential use. In the majority of cases this was commercial or retail space, or in some cases income from rental of car

Table 10.7 Benchmark built costs (£ per sq m) 2006/7 according to Development Appraisal Toolkit by area cost group

Built form	A1	A2	A3	A4	B1	B3
Flats 40+ storeys	2,783	2,783	2,783	2,783	2,783	2,650
Flats 16–39 storeys	2,589	2,507	2,403	2,258	2,341	2,091
Flats 6–15 storeys	2,096	2,029	1,945	1,827	1,894	1,692
Flats up to 5 storeys	1.585	1,515	1,453	1,365	1,415	1,264
Houses under 75 sq m	1,335	1,292	1,238	1,164	1,206	1,078
Houses over 75 sq m	1,169	1,131	1,085	1,019	1,056	944

Source: 2006/7 Toolkit Defaults.

Cost groups are Housing Corporation cost groups.

parking space, which provided a cross-subsidy to the residential component of the project. In most schemes this was under £10,000 per residential unit. In four cases this was equivalent to £100,000 or more per residential unit. In three schemes there was a cross-subsidy from the residential component to non-residential components, in one case equivalent to £200,000 per residential unit – in effect the housing being an enabling development for the non-residential component. There has been increasing use of residential development value to support employment generation or leisure uses which are not self-financing.

The analysis showed that, in the majority of schemes, s106 contributions for purposes other than for on-site affordable housing were generally under £20,000 a unit, with most schemes in the range of £5,000–£10,000 a unit.

However, there were three schemes where, instead of affordable housing provision being made on site, a significant s106 contribution was made to affordable housing off site, amounting to between £40,000 and £160,000 for each on-site unit.

The affordable housing (social rent and intermediate) proportion in the appraised schemes ranged from 0 per cent in three cases to 52 per cent. The proportion of social rent housing varied from 0 per cent in eight cases to 35 per cent.

Not all schemes appraised proposing to provide social rented or intermediate housing assumed the availability of social housing grant and in some cases grant was assumed at a low level per unit relative to average grant rates at the time.

Grant assumed per unit would reflect the balance between social rented and intermediate homes.

The term 'net residual value' is used to reflect residual value (RV) less land costs. Land cost could be either acquisition cost or an existing use value. Gross residual value ranged from £158m to a negative RV of –£36m. Once land costs had been taken into account, net RV ranged from £138m to a negative RV of –£50m. Gross RV per unit ranged from £944,000 to a negative RV of –£268,000.

Once land costs were taken into account, net RV per unit ranged from £163,000 to a negative RV of –£268,000.

Clearly schemes with significant negative residual values were not viable unless costs were reduced, values were increased or more public subsidy was made available. Where a significant positive RV was shown, the developer would normally be expected to increase affordable housing provision, either on or off site, or make a greater contribution to other planning policy objectives through enhanced s106 contributions. This process is considered in the next section.

Since the beginning of 2008, there has been a significant fall in the value of residential property in London. This has led to a significant weakening of the viability of many of the larger development schemes in London, including some of the projects included in this analysis. Some schemes are no longer proceeding to start on site, while in a few cases, as at early 2009, construction of schemes has been put on hold. This is, however, outside the timespan covered by this study, the period of Ken Livingstone's mayoralty, which terminated in April 2008. The impact of the credit crunch on scheme viability in London has been subject to a separate published analysis (Bowie 2009a).

Negotiating with developers, Housing Corporation funding and cascade agreements

The government's circular 5/05 (DCLG 2005) on planning obligations includes the following statement:

> In some instances, perhaps arising from different regional or site-specific circumstances, it may not be feasible for the proposed development to meet all the requirements set out in local, regional and national planning policies and still be economically viable.

London Plan policy on negotiating affordable housing on individual sites was consistent with this approach:

> Boroughs should seek the maximum reasonable amount of affordable housing when negotiating on individual private residential and mixed-use schemes . . . and the need to encourage rather than restrain residential development and the individual circumstances of the site. Targets should be applied flexibly, taking account of individual site costs, the availability of public subsidy and other scheme requirements.
>
> (GLA 2004a Policy 3A.8)

As set out in Chapter 5, the GLA developed a model by which the impact on a specific development proposal of different planning policy requirements could be assessed. Although the focus of the Mayor was on the 50 per cent affordable housing target, and the 70:30 social rent–intermediate target within this, the assessment could also consider bedroom size mix in terms of the guidance in the Housing Supplementary Planning Guidance, the wheelchair homes target of 10 per cent of development, the density of a scheme and compliance with broader policies on planning obligations.

As is evident both from the analysis in Chapter 6 of strategic housing schemes referred to the Mayor and from the analysis of forty schemes in the previous section, very few planning applications as submitted met the 50 per cent affordable housing and 35 per cent social rented housing targets, and few included the proportions of family-size homes sought by the guidance in the Housing SPG. The reason for requiring the applicant to provide a full scheme appraisal using the GLA/Housing Corporation development control toolkit, known as the 'Three Dragons model', was to check the assumptions made by the applicant and to examine whether the scheme could be adjusted to get closer to the Mayor's planning policy objectives while still being viable. Part of the assessment was to examine the potential for Housing Corporation social housing grant or other public subsidy to be made available to support an enhanced affordable housing output.

Some schemes did not include the provision of any affordable housing, whereas other schemes, although including some affordable housing, generally at low proportions, had not made any assumption as to the availability of Housing Corporation grant. As set out in the protocol agreed between the GLA and the London Housing Corporation (GLA 2005b appendix) affordable housing output could be optimized in quantitative and qualitative terms only if the planning and investment processes were undertaken in parallel.

Planning applications for strategic developments should be first submitted to the London borough (or the City of London) as the local planning authority, which would then refer the application to the Mayor. In some cases, however, the developer would initiate discussions with GLA officers independently, sometimes prior to the application being discussed with the local planning authority. There were cases in which a developer would seek to reach an agreement with the Mayor's planning decisions unit and then present this as a fait accompli to the local planning authority. GLA officers, however, generally took the view that a tripartite discussion was the best approach. Some London boroughs sought to apply a predetermined affordable housing proportion to an individual scheme, a proportion that was often lower than the 50 per cent set by the Mayor, without undertaking an appraisal of whether this was viable in terms of the requirements quoted above from both circular 5/05 and the London Plan. Some boroughs either were not interested in scheme-specific appraisals or did not have the staff capacity either to undertake appraisals or assess appraisals prepared by developers or their consultants. The GLA and Three Dragons provided an extensive training programme for both borough planning and housing policy officers and for London Housing Corporation investment staff over a three-year period, but staff turnover and pressure of work meant that only a few boroughs carried out appraisals on a regular basis, and in fact some boroughs contracted out the work to private consultants, while other boroughs relied on the GLA officers. At the same time, a number of private planning and affordable housing consultants developed considerable expertise on the use of the appraisal model and how to present data to minimize the potential affordable housing outturn. Ironically, a tool developed in the interests of optimizing community benefit from development value could be manipulated to achieve the opposite effect if local planning authorities, or for that matter GLA officers, were not in a position to undertake a comprehensive assessment of the assumptions put into the model.

A further complication of the negotiation process was that the Housing Corporation investment process largely worked on an annual or biannual bidding round basis. Planning applications were submitted to the local planning authority and referred to the Mayor on a continuing basis. Many developers at the stage of submitting a planning application had not entered into any partnership with a housing association or other affordable housing provider and had not had discussions with with or made a formal bid to the Housing Corporation for funding. Consequently the appraisal either assumed that no grant would be available or had made a rough assumption of grant based on funding levels for other schemes. GLA staff on receiving the appraisal had both to check published Housing Corporation data on grant levels but also to check with the Housing Corporation whether they were aware of the proposal, and whether or not it might be fundable. In the majority of cases, the Housing Corporation was unaware of the development proposal or, if it had been approached, had made no funding commitment.

The failure of the developer to consider subsidized development options was sometimes due to a lack of knowledge of both the London Plan requirements and the guidance, or of the funding regime, but was sometimes intentional. Boroughs with affordable housing targets lower than the London Plan 50 per cent requirement would often discourage a developer from considering a grant-supported option if the development proposal the developer had made already met their local policy target. For many years this was the normal practice in Tower Hamlets and Southwark, for example. A further complication was also introduced by the Housing Corporation's requirement that households in housing need should be nominated to major new schemes either across a sub-regional group of boroughs or across all London's thirty-three housing authorities. A borough was less likely to be supportive of a scheme in its area if a significant proportion of lettings were made to households from other areas. Where a borough had 100 per cent nomination rights to a scheme, a saving on a borough's homelessness costs would be significant; if less, not only would the savings be limited but the council might incur increased homelessness and education costs if lower-income households moved in from other areas. The pooling requirement, though necessary in terms of reducing the spatial imbalance between supply and demand, was not supported by revenue transfer mechanisms, and therefore acted as a disincentive for new provision to both high-stress and low-stress boroughs. Boroughs that had been contributing positively to new affordable housing provision looked at neighbouring boroughs and concluded that they were doing more than their fair share, while lower-stress boroughs did not see how they and their existing residents benefited from helping other boroughs. In some cases these issues had racial dimensions, as the majority of households in need were ethnic minority households. The less stressed boroughs with significant development capacity were generally boroughs with historically low ethnic minority populations, but where internal and international migration was already having an impact on ethnic mix in the owner-occupied and private rented sectors.

Affordable housing targets were only one of numerous policy objectives set out in the London Plan, and boroughs as local planning authorities would have their own more localized policy objectives. The Mayor, encouraged by Transport for London, increasingly gave priority to public transport provision – public transport and affordable housing being coequal as top priorities for use of planning obligations in terms of London Plan policy. Employment generation was often prioritized, especially in areas with little market-led employment activity, and the use of planning obligations for employment and training was often promoted by the London Development Agency. The Mayor increasingly promoted the provision of large leisure facilities as well as supporting the use of planning obligations to meet climate change-related policy objectives. Boroughs and the National Health Service made increasing use of residential development value to fund schools and health facilities, and some boroughs used formulae to calculate impact fees. Planning obligation requirements varied significantly between boroughs and became increasingly onerous on private developers. As is shown in the analysis of the forty schemes above, although in most cases planning obligations were equivalent to between £5,000 and £10,000 a unit, in a few cases they were significantly higher. Higher levels of planning obligations inevitably reduced the proportional level of affordable housing which could be cross-subsidised from development value.

Many schemes had high exceptional costs. Given that over 95 per cent of new development was on previously developed land, with a significant number of the larger developments on former industrial sites, site preparation costs, including site decontamination and demolition, were often significant. In some cases major transport infrastructure was essential given that some sites were isolated, so new road junctions or bridges feature in some projects. For major new communities, schools, education and leisure facilities were required. In one case a developer included in its costs the provision of a private primary school, regarded as essential if family housing was to be marketed.

The financial appraisal system allowed for the modelling of alternative development options. An applicant would often be asked to prepare a revised appraisal with a higher output of affordable housing; the GLA priority was normally to increase the number of family-size social rented homes. The applicant would then be encouraged to discuss options with an affordable housing provider and approach the Housing Corporation for grant. As set out in the Mayor's Housing SPG, affordable housing proportions could be calculated in habitable rooms, not units (GLA 2005b para 18.10), to allow for social rented homes to be targeted at larger households than private homes; so schemes were often adjusted to include social rented homes, which were predominantly three bedrooms or larger, whereas market homes would often be studios and one- and two-bedroom flats. Shared-ownership homes were generally a mix of one-bedroom and two-bedroom units. The GLA tended to argue for family-sized market units only in lower-density schemes where these would be in the form of houses or maisonettes, recognizing that larger flats in higher-density schemes would rarely be sold to family households, as they would be regarded as neither affordable nor suitable. The guidance in the Housing SPG also allowed for flexibility on the balance between social rented and intermediate housing, in relation to the existing tenure mix within a neighbourhood (ibid. paras 18.8–18.9).

The fundamental problem that GLA officers had in improving the affordable housing outcome of development proposals was the difficulty in negotiating an improved scheme output which was economically viable. This tended to be dependent on Housing Corporation investment decisions being taken within the relatively short timescale of the planning decision process. Moreover the Mayor and his advisors were reluctant to block a scheme which fell short of mayoral policy targets, once it had been demonstrated by the developer, on the basis of validated information on costs and values and in the absence of guaranteed Housing Corporation subsidy, that the proposal had the maximum affordable housing achievable and consequently complied with the London Plan policy requirement. One option considered in some cases was a cascade agreement. This was an arrangement by which the affordable housing output could be varied depending on the extent of subsidy available. The option of a cascade agreement was allowed for in the Mayor's guidance (ibid. para 18.16), though the government's Planning Policy Statement 3 had been silent on the issue. Developers often welcomed this approach, as it meant that, if subsidy was not forthcoming, they could retain scheme viability by reducing, or changing the nature of, the affordable housing output. From the perspective of the GLA and the local planning authority, a cascade agreement, if drafted appropriately, could allow for an increase in affordable housing if more grant became available. This approach was later supported in a research report: *Cascades: Improving Certainty in the Delivery of Affordable Housing for Large Site Development* (ATLAS 2007). Given that the Housing Corporation normally committed allocations for only a two- or three-year period, agreements were essential for large schemes, with much more extensive build-out periods; the largest schemes in London assumed development timescales of ten to twenty-five years.

An alternative approach to determining affordable housing output for a large scheme, which was referred to in the joint GLA/Housing Corporation protocol, was the idea of reviewing the housing output at the end of each phase of the scheme (GLA 2005b appendix para 13). This was essential where a scheme was subject to a single planning consent, and where the market demand for different types of housing output and the relationship between cost and value were likely to change over time. Such reviews would be based on full financial appraisals which would also take into account the availability of subsidy at a point in time. To be legally enforceable, arrangements for the review needed to be included as a condition of the original planning consent. This review arrangement was agreed, for example, for the Barking Riverside project, at 10,822 homes the largest consented scheme in London's development pipeline, with an assumed twenty-five-year build-out period. The arrangement also ensured that the Mayor of London would be party to the process rather than the review being solely a matter for the borough as local planning authority.

Both PPS3 and the Mayor's Housing SPG allowed for agreements on off-site provision of affordable housing in specific circumstances. Whereas the PPS3 criteria relate in very general terms to mixed and balanced communities, the London Plan (as amended in 2008) and the Mayor's Housing SPG are much more specific, and require an applicant to demonstrate (a) that the output is both quantitatively and qualitatively better than could be provided on site; (b) that off-site provision will contribute to the provision of mixed and balanced neighbourhoods; (c) that off-site provision is deliverable; and (d) that the developer does not benefit financially from a planning policy requirement to provide affordable housing being transferred off site.

Where a developer was proposing a high-rise development on a constrained site, there was little point in arguing that the scheme should include a significant proportion of family-sized social rented units, as not only would the amenities be poor with limited or no external playspace for children but also, even if rents were at target rents and therefore affordable by lower-income households, service charges would be so high as to breach the London Plan affordability guidance, which referred to service charges as well as rents (GLA 2005a para 15.2). In the 2006/7 update of the appraisal toolkit, the GLA introduced a new component which enabled the affordability of units within a development proposal to be assessed.

In such cases the main GLA objective in negotiations was to ensure appropriate off-site provision. By allowing the transfer of affordable housing off site, the value of on-site market provision would normally be enhanced. Applying the financial neutrality argument, the contribution to affordable housing could therefore be increased by comparing appraisals for on-site provision with or without affordable housing; the difference was the basis for the contribution. So a 100-unit scheme, which would normally be expected to provide fifty affordable units on site, could actually support a much higher number of affordable units off site. Moreover, through the choice of an appropriate location and built form, off-site provision could provide good-quality low- and medium-rise family homes in a location with both open space and social infrastructure. The main challenge was to ensure that an off-site package was actually deliverable. Developers were often reluctant to identify and acquire other sites, and boroughs were sometimes unable or unwilling to identify other sites, or established such limited areas of search that finding an appropriate site was very difficult. GLA officers wanted to avoid the repeat of previous practice in some boroughs of taking planning contributions from developers and then not knowing what to do with them. Nevertheless there were a number of schemes in London in the 2005 to 2008 period in which appropriate and deliverable off-site schemes were negotiated, though in a couple of cases intervention was necessary to stop the off-site affordable housing being located in areas which would have increased rather than reduced social polarization.

The use of development viability appraisal models did lead to better-informed negotiations. An appraisal system cannot in itself produce a right or wrong output, but depends on the data input into the model and the policy parameters applied. The process allows for the testing of different options and allows for explicit identification of trade-offs. Data in appraisals are to a large extent commercially confidential – the term sometimes used of 'open book' appraisals is misleading, and consequently it is important that developers have the confidence that commercial data will not be released. Some toolkit appraisals have nevertheless been debated in detail in planning inquiries, which implies that the appraisal system is treated as a material consideration, whereas it is the policy application which is the fundamental issue in dispute. An appraisal will show only whether a proposal is or is not economically viable and not whether or not it is acceptable in policy terms. A development proposal should not be accepted just because it has demonstrated it will produce the maximum viable affordable housing output, if it still fails substantially to meet critical components of a planning policy. The

London experience has generally been a positive one, with appraisal methods being adopted by authorities outside London, and is now advocated as best practice by central government agencies. The impact on affordable housing outputs is relatively marginal; unless the appraisal process leads to a reduction in costs or a more positive assessment of sales value or facilitates an increase in public subsidy, impacts will be limited. In practice, interventions by the London Mayor following appraisals sometimes led to an increase in affordable housing output or social rented homes by up to 5 per cent, as can be seen by comparing planning reports on specific development schemes at stage 1 and stage 2 of the process, but rarely led to a substantive reconfiguration of a development scheme.

The Mayor, the Central Activities Zone and the city fringe

The Central Activities Zone had been set out in the 2004 Plan as the area in which the expansion of central area activities including government functions and office development would be supported and encouraged. Although the zone was only an indicative boundary, the Mayor supported the growth of London's role as a world financial centre and encouraged the expansion of the CAZ area. It should also be recognized that the Canary Wharf area of Tower Hamlets was also supported as an additional area in which office provision would be encouraged. The 2008 CAZ map expanded the boundary to cover a number of additional areas: the western end of Wapping in Tower Hamlets including the News International site, Bishopsgate Goodsyard on the City/Tower Hamlets/Hackney boundary, and part of the Borough North Southwark. At one stage, the extension was to include the Chelsea Barracks site on the Westminster boundary with Kensington and Chelsea, but this was excluded. The Mayor recognized that it was inappropriate to provide housing on site in parts of the CAZ, as this would constrain employment growth, and off-site provision was supported. The CAZ designation was, however, to become more significant when in 2006 the central government directed Westminster on its Unitary Development Plan to set a separate affordable housing requirement for areas outside the CAZ at 50 per cent, with a requirement for sites within the CAZ at 30 per cent whether the provision was on or off site. This meant that the exclusion of the Chelsea Barracks site from the CAZ was critical, as it left the affordable housing requirement at 50 per cent rather than the lower figure of 30 per cent.

The Mayor's support for the expansion of CAZ functions was part of his belief that this growth was central to London's economic future. This had spatial and social policy implications, as it meant the expansion of office and office-related functions into areas that had been previously of a mixed-use or predominantly residential character. This was in contrast to his policy in the Greater London

Council up to 1986, when together with his Planning Committee chair, George Nicholson, he had established a Community Areas policy, which protected those residential communities threatened by the expansion of market-led commercial development in areas such as Waterloo and Coin Street, Wapping, Spitalfields, Pimlico, Paddington, Euston, Soho and Covent Garden. In his mayoral role, Livingstone explicitly encouraged commercial and private residential developments in many of these city fringe locations and actively promoted high-rise development; in some cases, such as the Doon Street development by Coin Street Community Builders, he waived any requirement for a contribution to affordable housing either on site or off site.

Conclusion: planning as promoting private investment or managing the market?

The analysis of development viability has demonstrated the extent to which housing outputs have been driven primarily by market factors – the relationship between cost, including land cost, and value – rather than by planning policy requirements. It is clear from the analysis in Chapter 6 that the London Plan adoption of the 50 per cent target and its adoption by an increasing number of boroughs did not lead to an increase in the overall proportion of housing output in London that was social rent or intermediate housing. In fact there is evidence that for larger strategic projects – those considered by the Mayor – the proportion which was affordable actually declined in 2006/7 and 2007/8. The failure of the government and the Housing Corporation to increase grant as costs increased and the pressure from the Treasury to achieve efficiency savings put increasing pressure on housing associations to apply for lower levels of grant. The Corporation's move from 2005/6 onwards away from a grant regime which related to costs and rent income to a competitive approach, in which grant went to the cheapest bidder, also forced housing associations to depend on cross-subsidy from development value and cross-subsidy from their own reserves, including receipts from shareowners buying equity or from their own asset disposals.

Clearly the use of planning obligations did generate some cross-subsidy to affordable housing output, but the level of this subsidy was fairly limited even when the private housing market was strong. Moreover the market largely determined the built form and bedroom size mix of housing output in London. Developers largely relied on values continuing to increase at a rate faster than cost inflation, which is why so many developers were prepared to proceed with developments which appraisals demonstrated were at the best only marginally profitable. The market, especially for the high-rise, high-density small flat product on which developers were focusing, has, however, proved to be more of a short-term nature than developers had foreseen. This has meant that the deficits developers now face by proceeding with schemes are in some cases acute.

The Mayor and boroughs have had fairly limited impact in steering the market. Both Mayor and boroughs have supported development schemes which fall far short of the policy guidance on density, tenure mix or bedroom size composition, on the basis that, given cost–value relationships as demonstrated by financial appraisals, these are the only developments which are viable. In some cases, mayoral or borough intervention has led to minor improvements in scheme composition. In other cases, mayoral prioritization of policy objectives such as public transport. employment growth, leisure provision or mitigating the impact of climate change have reduced both the quantity and quality of affordable housing outputs. Ironically the main contribution of Ken Livingstone as Mayor to steering the market has been to encourage higher-density and often high-rise schemes, often in breach of his own published planning policy. This is clearly evidenced by the analysis of scheme density and output in Chapter 6.

Intervention by the Housing Corporation in terms of higher grant levels to support social rented housing for families has countered some of this trend. However, with high-density schemes being encouraged, Housing Corporation grant would have been needed not just to cover the cost of larger family units but also to contribute to funding the opportunity costs for developers of not building the smaller market units that the market appeared to demand at the time. Although the appraisal system made explicit the opportunity cost issue, the Housing Corporation, even though it was prepared to move from a grant per unit to a grant per person basis to correct the bias in favour of smaller units, was never prepared to consider the opportunity cost issue: the cost to developers of building something other than what was most profitable for them. Moreover, with planning consents given for hyperdense schemes, there was a bidding up of land values based on the assumption that requirements on density, bedroom size and tenure could be breached. A stricter application of strategic planning policy would have gone some way to controlling this growth of excessive hope value. However, in London, the ability of planning to contain land value increases will always be limited, as 98 per cent of development is on previously developed land, with most sites allocated for a mix of uses. The bottom line in land value is often set by existing use value, or in some cases by alternative use value. As the analysis of land acquisition costs earlier in this chapter showed, land in London rarely comes cheap, and the cheapest land comes only with massive site preparation or infrastructure costs. Moreover the public sector no longer gives land away for affordable housing.

The conclusion of this analysis, in terms of the question posed, is that not only has planning policy as set out in the London Plan had limited impact on steering the market, but also planning practice has had relatively limited success in managing the market in terms of achieving the best public sector benefit. By pushing higher density above and beyond his own published policy, the Mayor's planning practice has actually given greater support to the market to go in what in the short term was the most profitable direction. This has not only seriously damaged the overall balance of housing outcomes relative to housing requirements but, as the market has changed, left many developers with an unsaleable product.

Chapter 11

The management of land and space

Strategic planning and the allocation of land uses

As a strategic plan, the London Plan is not able to determine specific land uses on specific sites. This is strictly a matter for the borough as local planning authority. It is through the borough's core strategy and other development plan documents that sites are allocated or zoned for specific land uses. With the new emphasis on mixed use, many sites are zoned for mixed-use development. This normally comprises a housing component and a non-residential component, which might be offices, retail, industrial, leisure, hotel or other land use. Although the London Plan may through its policies encourage change of land use, the Mayor's only direct role in this process is when a strategic application involving change of use from a site allocation in an adopted plan is referred to him.

Housing growth and other land uses

In the section on the 2004 housing capacity study in Chapter 7, it was indicated that a high proportion of land identified as having some potential for housing development was in employment use: 23 per cent as industrial, 9 per cent as retail, 7 per cent as offices and 5 per cent as utilities. Mixed-use development on an intensified basis would in some cases allow for residential-led development which retained some of the pre-existing use. There was nevertheless a critical issue: given the demand for additional homes and, at least up till the 2008 downturn in the property market, the potential return to landowner and developer, how land for less profitable uses could be retained. The report on *Mixed Use Development and Affordable Housing* (GLA 2004c), referred to in Chapter 7, had sought to inform the development of mayoral policy on this issue. Government land use change statistics showed that some 220–240 hectares of land in London was changing from non-residential use to residential use each year. This dataset also showed that, for the 2003 to 2006 period, 95 per cent of residential development was on previously developed land (compared with the England average of 61 per cent and the national target of 60 per cent), with 42 per cent of the total being vacant or derelict, 33 per cent in residential use, and 20 per cent other previously developed uses.

The GLA therefore sought to assess the demand for other land uses. Studies were therefore commissioned into demand for open space, offices, industrial and warehouse land, comparison retail floorspace, wharves, convenience goods floorspace, strategic parks, hotels, land for transport facilities, waste recycling facilities, logistics, boatyard facilities, wholesale markets, children's playspace and places of worship (GLA 2004g,i,j,k, 2005f,g, 2006j,k, 2007f,g,h,i,j, 2008c,j).

The key issue for the Mayor was to protect land for employment. There was a specific issue in East London with the Olympics development requiring use of significant former industrial land in the Lower Lea Valley. The GLA therefore undertook a specific study of the potential for release of surplus industrial land in North East and South East London, the areas where the surplus was considered to be most significant (GLA 2007k). This led to a revision of the benchmarks for the release of industrial land for residential use which had previously been incorporated in the 2004 housing capacity study and the new borough housing targets (GLA 2007k). The new study recommended a monitoring benchmark of 814 hectares of industrial land release in London over the period 2006–2026 or 41 ha per annum. It was suggested that with rigorous management of vacancy rates the annual average release was likely to be higher at 48 ha in the earlier phase, 2006–2016, reducing to 31 ha per annum in the later phase, 2016–2026. Whereas the previous land release targets had been set at a sub-regional level, the new quantitative benchmarks together with qualitative indicators for the management of industrial land were set for all London boroughs. The report was an attempt to reconcile the fact that release of industrial land had been running at a higher rate than had been assumed in the targets in the earlier draft Industrial Provision SPG. The setting of borough-level targets allowed the Mayor to monitor loss of industrial land at borough level. He could not direct specific land use, though the information could be used to inform his planning interventions in the case of strategic planning applications.

The GLA was unable to adequately identify land use requirements for a range of social infrastructure, notably schools and health and leisure facilities. In Chapter 8, we discussed the various attempts to identify these requirements. It was not, however, possible to quantify the land use take for such provision or consequently to adjust the borough housing targets. Where land for a new school or health facility had been identified by a borough, this had been excluded from the residential capacity assessed in the housing capacity study. The published Housing Capacity Study report (GLA 2005c) had also included a rough estimate that 15 ha a year might be needed for educational provision, of which 8 ha would be for school playing fields, which in some cases might be provided on existing open space. However, in some cases boroughs were only to identify need for extra schools after the study had been completed and the housing targets set. It will be important for the Mayor in the next housing capacity study, which must now follow new government guidance for strategic housing land availability assessments (DCLG 2007b), to have a fuller reconciliation with other land uses, especially those critical to ensuring the development of sustainable new communities.

Strategic planning and strategic development control

The Mayor's strategic development control functions do give him authority to intervene on land use decisions – a power which is not held by other regional planning bodies outside London. Given that the Mayor is not himself able to allocate sites for specific uses, his view on whether to support a local authority wishing to vary a land use for a specific site from its published plan, or to support a developer seeking to vary a land use allocation against the wishes of the local planning authority, must be justified by reference to policies adopted in the London Plan. The requirement to refer applications to the Mayor as strategic relates to any development which departs from an adopted Borough Unitary Development Plan or subsequent Local Development Document which provides 150 homes or 2,500 sq m of non-residential use. The referral requirement also applies to any development involving the loss of four or more hectares of industrial land, any development of 1,000 sq m or more in the Green Belt or Metropolitan Open Land, or any development which involves the loss of two or more hectares of playing fields. These referral requirements give the Mayor significant power to impact on land use allocations, a power which was extended under the 2007 GLA Act to enable the Mayor to grant planning applications as well as veto them.

Ken Livingstone used his power to veto any proposals to develop on the Green Belt or Metropolitan Open Land. In the case of proposals by Bromley to develop two schools on Green Belt land, the Mayor objected to the proposals at public inquiry, only to be overruled by the Secretary of State, who put the need for new schools before the planning policy of protecting the Green Belt. Livingstone was, however, more relaxed on the issue of protection of employment land, and was generally supportive of proposals to develop housing on employment land, even where the sites were Strategic Employment Locations and supposed to be protected for continued employment use. He was, however, insistent on protecting safeguarded wharves, going to public inquiry to defend Peruvian Wharf in Newham from residential development – a position that appeared at odds with his support for a residential-led scheme designed by his urbanism adviser, Richard Rogers, on

Convoys Wharf in Lewisham, part of which also had safeguarded status. As has been mentioned earlier, Livingstone also used his development control powers to support high-rise residential developments, opposed by English Heritage, or by the local planning authority, even where the proposals were not in residential areas. In some cases the Mayor was selective in the use of London Plan policies to support his interventions and in some cases no adequate assessment was undertaken of competing land use demands. Given his overall position in promoting maximum housing output, it is perhaps not surprising that the rate of release of employment land was higher than originally envisaged. The Mayor was, however, as stressed above, generally responding to market forces, and he was generally not interested in steering developments on specific sites towards specific land uses.

Chapter 12

Planning for diversity

Combating social polarization

Planning for diversity

The increase in the proportion of black and other ethnic minority households in London's population has been one of the more significant changes in London's demography. In some parts of East, West and South London, increases between 1991 and 2001 have been up to 25 per cent, though in many suburban areas increases have been less than 5 per cent.

Ken Livingstone as Mayor of London had a long-established reputation for being concerned with the interests of different ethnic minority groups from his time as leader of the former Greater London Council, when he had established an ethnic minorities committee. There were to be more controversies over his race policies in his mayoral role. The Mayor paid considerable attention to working with the representatives or self-appointed leaders of the main ethnic groups, especially the Irish, Orthodox Jewish and different Muslim groups. Some of these relationships were mediated through his Race Advisor, Lee Jasper, whose enforced resignation in early 2008 was to be a contributing factor to Livingstone's defeat in the May 2008 election. The Mayor was therefore acutely sensitive to the need to demonstrate that his strategic planning policies and his strategic planning decisions had regard to the needs of the wide range of different ethnic, national and faith-based groups, as well as to the needs of other diversity categories, such as disabled persons, young and old people, one-parent households and persons of different sexuality. Demonstrating that this was the case was to prove an extremely difficult task.

The original London Plan dealt with the issue of planning for diversity in very general terms. There were three policies:

Policy 3A.14 Addressing the needs of London's diverse population

DPD policies should identify the needs of the diverse groups in their area. They should address the spatial needs of these groups, and ensure that they are not disadvantaged both through general policies for development and specific policies relating to the provision of social infrastructure, the public realm, inclusive design and local distinctiveness. Existing facilities that meet the needs of particular groups should be protected and where shortfalls have been identified, policies should seek measures to address them proactively.

Policy 3A.15 Protection and enhancement of social infrastructure and community facilities

DPD policies should assess the need for social infrastructure and community facilities in their area, including children's play and recreation facilities, services for young people, older people and disabled people, as well as libraries, community halls, meeting rooms, places of worship and public toilets. Adequate provision for these facilities is particularly important in major areas of new development and regeneration. Policies should seek to ensure that appropriate facilities are provided within easy reach by walking and public transport of the population that use them. The net loss of such facilities should be resisted.

Policy 4B.7 Respect local context and communities

The Mayor will, and boroughs should, work with local communities to recognise and manage local distinctiveness ensuring proposed developments preserve or enhance local, physical, cultural, historical, environmental and economic characteristics

---

By the time of drafting of the further alterations in 2006, this aspect received greater attention. The Mayor commissioned an Equalities Appraisal of the proposed alterations (GLA 2006l). In parallel, GLA officers were drafting a Supplementary Planning Guidance on Planning for Equality and Diversity in London. A draft of this SPG was published for consultation in December 2006, though the final document was not approved until the following October (GLA 2007l).

The Equalities Appraisal considered in turn each of the 'equalities groups' and in each case concluded that the further alterations would have beneficial impacts. The groups were as follows:

- women;
- black and minority ethnic people;
- gypsies and travellers;
- refugees and asylum seekers;
- disabled people;
- older people;
- children and young people;
- lesbians, gay men, bisexuals and transsexual people;
- faith groups.

In aggregate these 'minority' groups comprised the vast majority of London's population.

The assessment of benefit to the different 'minority' groups was not systematic, and in effect asserted that these groups would all benefit from an increase in the availability of affordable housing, increased employment opportunities, improved quality of the environment, improved community safety and public transport, and affordable childcare. Reference was also made to the assessment of the need for additional permanent sites for gypsies and travellers, which was the subject of a separate study, and the existing policies on lifetime homes and wheelchair homes, which as stated above were not as yet monitored. Reference was also made to the need for faith schools and places of worship, though not to the need for faith-specific burial facilities, which had become a contentious issue. Both the Equalities Impact Assessment and the SPG were in fact lists of issues raised by different groups through the consultation process, rather than a systematic analysis of whether different groups had specific different needs, or whether there were differential impacts of either existing or proposed policies on different 'equalities' groups. Neither document dealt with the fundamental dilemma of planning – that, whereas it can enable development to meet different needs, it cannot explicitly positively discriminate in favour of one group against another. There has been a failure to recognize that planning policies can in fact have negative impacts as well as positive impacts, and that a market-led implementation of development will inevitably disadvantage those persons, many of whom are members of the 'equalities categories' listed above, who cannot afford access to facilities provided at 'market value'. All the work on planning for diversity ignores that the most fundamental barrier to access to good-quality environment and services is lack of wealth and lack of income.

Social polarization

While there was an overall net increase in London's housing stock of 166,000 homes over the seven-year period, there was a loss of social housing of over

27,000 homes. In effect demolitions of local authority housing and sales through the right to buy exceeded new housing association supply. However, this varied between sub-regions and there were actually increases in social housing supply in the West and South sub-regions (Table 12.1). There were significant increases in private sector supply in all sub-regions, with the greatest increases in the East and Central sub-regions, the two sub-regions where the increase in overall supply was concentrated.

The shifts are summarized in Table 12.2. It is in the sub-regions with the greatest proportions of social sector housing in 2001 that the proportionate shifts to the private sector are greatest, thus producing a small narrowing of the differentiation between tenures across London.

Table A.6 in the Appendix gives borough figures for social sector and private sector housing stock in 2001 and 2008. There were in fact a few boroughs where there was a marginal shift in the tenure balance towards the social sector: Kensington and Chelsea, Redbridge, Ealing, Hammersmith and Fulham, Harrow, Bromley and Richmond. With the exception of Hammersmith and Fulham, all these boroughs had had social housing proportions in 2001 below the London average of 26.5 per cent.

Table 12.1 Additions and losses to stock by tenure by sub-region 2001–8

	Public sector 2001–8	Private sector 2001–8	Total change
Central	−17,288	+67,739	+50,451
East	−13,148	+69,943	+56,795
West	+3,604	+21,455	+25,059
North	−1,442	+16,731	+15,289
South	+718	+18,124	+18,842
London	−27,556	+193,992	+166,436

Table 12.2 Tenure shifts by sub-region

	Social sector 2001	Public sector 2007	Change
Central	36.6%	32.0%	−4.6%
East	32.2%	28.6%	−3.6%
West	21.5%	21.2%	−0.3%
North	20.1%	19.1%	−1.0%
South	14.7%	14.3%	−0.4%
London	26.5%	24.3%	−2.2%

The boroughs with the largest shifts in tenure balance towards private housing were Tower Hamlets (12 per cent), Southwark (9 per cent), Islington (9 per cent), Lambeth (7 per cent), Hackney (7 per cent) and Greenwich (6 per cent) – all boroughs which had had above-norm proportions of social housing in 2001.

Stock change figures are the product of a number of factors: differential rates of new social and market sector output, differential rates of demolition by tenure, individual council house sales, bulk disposals of social housing and acquisitions of private housing for social use. The figures are not effected by transfers of stock from councils to housing associations, as both categories are included within the social sector category.

It is also interesting to analyse recent output of affordable housing by borough with the tenure mix as at 2001, to see if at borough level the new social housing programme has changed or reinforced the previous public/private tenure balance. This produces Tables 12.3–12.6, with boroughs grouped into different categories.

In two boroughs, social housing output at 11 per cent was the same as the 2001 social housing proportion: Kensington and Chelsea at 20 per cent and Harrow at 11 per cent.

This analysis is summarized in Table 12.7. This would appear to demonstrate that the new social rented housing programme has contributed to some equalization of tenure mix between boroughs with the majority of boroughs with high existing social housing proportions having lower levels of social rent output, and the majority of boroughs with low historic levels having increasing output. However there is some reinforcement of high levels of social housing in three boroughs – Hammersmith and Fulham, Brent and, to a lesser extent, Haringey – and a reinforcement of low levels in six boroughs, notably Wandsworth and the City of London, but also in Westminster, Hounslow and Havering, with the position being static in two other low social housing boroughs: Harrow and Kensington and Chelsea.

Table 12.3 Boroughs with high proportions of social housing at 2001 and higher proportions of social rent output in 2003/4 to 2007/8 (%)

Borough	Social housing at 2001	Social housing as % of 2003/4 to 2007/8 output	Difference
Hammersmith and Fulham	33	41	+8
Haringey	29	30	+1
Brent	25	35	+10

Table 12.4 Boroughs with low proportions of social housing at 2001 and higher proportions of social rent output in 2003/4 to 2007/8 (%)

Borough	Social housing at 2001	Social housing as % of 2003/4 to 2007/8 output	Difference
Waltham Forest	24	29	+5
Hillingdon	19	24	+5
Ealing	19	24	+5
Croydon	17	32	+15
Sutton	17	30	+13
Enfield	17	29	+12
Merton	15	19	+4
Bexley	15	16	+1
Barnet	14	15	+1
Bromley	13	18	+5
Richmond	12	18	+6
Kingston	12	14	+2
Redbridge	9	13	+4

Table 12.5 Boroughs with high proportions of social housing at 2001 and lower proportions of social rent output in 2003/4 to 2007/8 (%)

Borough	Social housing at 2001	Social housing as % of 2003/4 to 2007/8 output	Difference
Hackney	55	25	−30
Southwark	55	23	−32
Tower Hamlets	53	24	−29
Islington	50	23	−27
Lambeth	44	16	−28
Greenwich	41	12	−29
Camden	39	24	−15
Barking and Dagenham	37	26	−11
Newham	36	25	−11
Lewisham	35	28	−7

Table 12.6 Boroughs with low proportions of social housing at 2001 and lower proportions of social rent output in 2003/4 to 2007/8 (%)

Borough	Social housing at 2001	Social housing as % of 2003/4 to 2007/8 output	Difference
Westminster	25	20	−5
Hounslow	24	18	−6
Wandsworth	23	3	−20
City of London	19	9	−10
Havering	15	14	−1

Table 12.7 Tenure changes as relating to pre-existing tenure mix

	Social rent output higher	Social rent output lower	Social rent output as 2001 proportion	Total
Boroughs with high proportions of social housing	3	10	0	13
Boroughs with low proportions of social housing	13	5	2	20
Total	16	15	2	33

The impact of new development on social mix may be more significant at a local level rather than at borough level. In 2007, the GLA undertook an exercise to look at the concentrations of new affordable housing (incorporating social rent and intermediate housing) at ward level, relative to the tenure mix in 2001 demonstrated by the census. A chart was published in the evidence report for the draft London Mayor's Housing Strategy (GLA 2007b).

This showed that the areas with high levels of existing housing got high proportions of new development but higher proportions of new affordable housing: the 10 per cent of wards with most social housing in 2001 received 18 per cent of all new development in 2004/5 and 2005/6 and 21 per cent of new affordable housing. Unfortunately the published analysis does not disaggregate between the concentration of new social rented housing and new intermediate housing. The analysis does, however, demonstrate that there was significant affordable housing being built in wards which had previously had low proportions of social housing.

The Housing Corporation's investment programme was opportunity led. Although, as described in Chapter 3, the London Plan policy and guidance has regard to the existing neighbourhood tenure mix in the application of the overall policy targets of 50 per cent market, 35 per cent social rent and 15 per cent intermediate housing and the broader objective of achieving mixed neighbourhoods, this was perhaps less of a consideration for the Housing Corporation in responding to individual development proposals. The Housing Corporation no longer had targets for the level of investment for an individual borough, in terms of either relative housing need or an assessment of development capacity which could be taken from the London housing capacity study, whereas in the regional investment statements of the 1990s investment parameters, in terms of total investment level, balance between social rent and intermediate housing and between different bedroom size mixes were agreed with each of the thirty-three local housing authorities. With the focus on achieving a unit target and a social rent/intermediate mix across London as a whole, borough targets were no longer regarded as necessary.

Although the Housing Corporation encouraged all significant development proposals to include a mix of tenures, it is unclear whether there has been any practice of negotiating different mixes for different locations. The outcome of Housing Corporation investment decisions in terms of spatial distribution of investment and location of individual schemes is therefore an aggregate of the consideration of individual development proposals in terms of their ability to contribute to Londonwide targets, with the focus being primarily on the unit output in relation to grant paid and the competence and development capacity of the developing housing association. In contrast with the regime operated by the London Housing Corporation in the 1990s, with the focus on the delivery of Londonwide targets, the borough's perspective on the appropriate development for a specific site was now less central to the investment decision-making process. Clearly, where a borough had published a planning brief for a site, the borough could specify its housing requirements and how a development should relate to the wider neighbourhood and transport and social infrastructure, but this was generally not the case; even where masterplans are provided for large sites, there is often little attention paid to the type and form of housing to be developed and the needs of the potential occupants.

The end of social planning?

This does raise the issue of whether, despite the fact that the vision of the London Plan includes a focus on equity objectives, the third 'E' of the framework for spatial planning established in the European Spatial Development Perspective has been disregarded both in the Plan's implementation and in the decisions made both by funding agencies such as the Housing Corporation and by the boroughs as local planning authorities in terms of location for affordable housing schemes.

The evidence considered here would lead to a conclusion that, in a context in which development proposals are determined primarily by market-led interests, the funding authorities' decisions are driven by relatively narrow definitions of value for money, site-planning briefs are either non-existent or urban design based, and inadequate provision is made for social infrastructure, the broader social policy or equity objectives, which should be a core element of spatial planning, have been given insufficient consideration.

It could be argued that the Sustainability Appraisal process should have considered the social equity implications of both the Plan and its implementation. The Sustainability Appraisals undertaken for the original London Plan and the early alterations and further alterations to the London Plan were all inadequate in this respect. These appraisals all tended to focus on environmental aspects of the proposed planning policies, rather than giving adequate consideration to the wider range of preconditions for sustainable communities and to the broader social policy objectives. They could have considered, for example, the need to provide affordable housing to low- and middle-income households, the need to reduce social polarization and the need to ensure that lower-income and other disadvantaged households, including ethnic minority households, had access to employment opportunities and basic amenities.

Although the London Plan has a set of policies on the provision of health, education and leisure services, these are generally not quantified and lack performance indicator targets; consequently their implementation cannot be monitored. Whereas there is monitoring of loss of open space, there has been no monitoring of the provision of new school places, health facilities or leisure facilities in relation to new residential communities developed since the London Plan was adopted. It could be argued that this is a matter primarily for the thirty-three boroughs as local planning authorities, but the Mayor could and should have set up a framework for such social planning implementation and monitoring, through quantifying requirements in the Plan and the Sub-regional Development Frameworks, setting key indicator targets, promoting a social planning framework for the Opportunity Areas and Areas for Intensification identified in the London Plan, and establishing Londonwide monitoring systems. The Mayor does have information on non-residential development consents within the London Development Database, but has to date used this comprehensive dataset only for monitoring residential development. The proposed approach would also enable the Mayor as strategic planning authority to identify deficiencies in borough core strategies in relation to social planning objectives as well as to have regard to such policy requirements in his consideration of strategic development proposals referred to him. There is some indication that planning for social infrastructure may be given higher priority by the new Mayor.

Chapter 13

Planning and new approaches to metropolitan governance

The Mayor and central government

When Ken Livingstone was elected Mayor of London, he faced considerable hostility from the central government. Although Labour ministers, led by the Minister for London, Nick Raynsford MP, had created the new governance structure, they had campaigned against Livingstone, who had been expelled from the Labour party and stood as an independent candidate. Ministers instead supported the Labour candidate, Frank Dobson, who had been Minister of Health and previously leader of Camden Council. In supporting Dobson, Labour ministers, including the then Prime Minister, Tony Blair, and the Chancellor of the Exchequer, Gordon Brown, had attacked Ken Livingstone, holding him responsible for the abolition of the Greater London Council by Margaret Thatcher in 1986.

When Livingstone was elected, relationships were inevitably frosty. The government was relieved that the Mayor's powers were fairly limited. The Government Office for London was not just maintained but expanded and the government maintained the post of Minister for London, though this was held by a junior minister who was not a member of the cabinet and, relative to the Mayor, was to have a low profile. The first Minister for London under the new arrangements was Keith Hill, the MP for Streatham.

The central government however soon learnt to live with Ken Livingstone as Mayor, and the Mayor's performance provided them with reassurance that Livingstone was less of a loose cannon than he had been as leader of the Greater London Council. Only two of Livingstone's former colleagues in the GLC leadership were given jobs: Mike Ward, who had been GLC deputy leader in 1985–6, as chief executive of the London Development Agency, and Dave Wetzel, who was the last chair of the GLC transport committee, as deputy chair of Transport for London. Another former GLC member, Paul Moore, also joined the board of TfL. Four other members of Livingstone's GLC leadership team had become MPs: John McDonnell, Tony Banks, Paul Boateng and Valerie Wise. Boateng and Banks were critical of Livingstone. Two of Livingstone's Labour party rivals, who had both had aspirations to be mayoral candidates, also had jobs at City Hall: Nicky Gavron, the former chair of the London Planning Advisory Committee, was appointed by Livingstone as Deputy Mayor, while the broadcaster Trevor Phillips, who had fronted London Weekend Television's *The London Programme*, as an elected member of the Assembly, became chair of the Assembly. Both Ward and Phillips, however, soon moved on: Ward in January 2004 'to pursue policy and research interests', later in 2008 to be chief executive of the British Urban Regeneration Agency (BURA), and Phillips to become chair of the Commission for Racial Equality in 2003.

Government seemed to have welcomed Livingstone's initial 'big tent' approach. Livingstone announced a cabinet of advisors, which included such diverse figures as Glenda Jackson MP, who became adviser on homelessness, and Judith Mayhew, who was leader of the City Corporation, as adviser on business and the city. A later example of the Mayor's ambitious recruitment strategy was his appointment of the Boston transport manager and former CIA operative, Bob Kiley, as London's Commissioner for Transport and head of Transport for London, on an attractive salary with a £2m house thrown in. The GLA's chief executive, or head of professional staff, was Anthony Mayer, a career civil servant who had been chief executive of the Housing Corporation. It was, however, Livingstone's political advisors who were to be his main supporters and negotiators with ministers and political bodies: Neale Coleman, a former Westminster Labour councillor, became his link to the London boroughs, representing him on the leaders' committee of the Association of London Government, while John Ross, his long-term economic advisor and co-writer of his published books, took on the role of developing the Mayor's economic and international relationships and building up an economics team under the former Trades Union Congress economist Bridget Rosewell. This was a strong team and was to have a much higher profile than the relatively anonymous civil servants of the Government Office for London.

Ken Livingstone made it clear that he was not going to be constrained by his limited powers. As a directly elected independent Mayor, with the largest personal vote of any politician in the United Kingdom, he saw himself, and was soon seen by the electorate and the media, as the advocate of Londoners' interests. As discussed in Chapter 3, despite having no housing powers, one of his first actions was to set up a Housing Commission under Chris Holmes of Shelter to carry out an investigation into London's housing needs, the most comprehensive study since the Milner Holland report of 1965.

The first two years of Livingstone's administration were dominated by a dispute with the central government on the funding arrangements for upgrading the London Underground network – the Public Private Partnership or PPP – a funding framework which was imposed by the Treasury on the Mayor and Kiley. However, the Mayor had first-term successes in three other policy areas: the London Plan, which has been described in detail above and was published in February 2004; the introduction of a congestion charge for cars and other private vehicles using roads in central London on weekdays, which came into effect in February 2003; and his decision to bid to hold the Olympic Games in London in 2012, with London being announced by the International Olympic Committee as on the final shortlist a few days after Livingstone's re-election in May 2004.

These were all to prove successful initiatives, in which the government had no choice but to follow the lead taken by the Mayor. Ministers, although recognizing that much of the London Plan was innovative, were to endorse the Plan. Ministers who had generally thought the congestion charge was suicidal and would lose Livingstone the election had to admit they were wrong. Ministers also initially thought the Olympics bid was unrealistic but, when London had a chance of winning, both Tessa Jowell, the sports minister, and Tony Blair, as prime minister, were quick to be seen to be enthusiastic and were later to be even quicker in claiming their share of the credit for London's success. Appointing Sebastian Coe, Conservative member of the House of Lords and sporting hero, as bid organizer was another example of Livingstone's 'big tent' approach.

So, when it came to the run up to the May 2004 election, ministers were struggling to find a strong Labour candidate to stand against Livingstone. The Deputy Mayor, Nicky Gavron, was adopted as Labour candidate, but stood down in Livingstone's favour when Livingstone was readmitted to the Labour party, despite the strong opposition of Gordon Brown. In the Mayor's second term, cooperation between the Mayor and central government became closer, with considerable focus on progressing the Olympics plans and security issues following the London bombings in July 2005. The Mayor worked well with the new Minister for Housing and Planning, Yvette Cooper, who shared Livingstone's ambitions to increase housing output; the minister and the Government Office for London were supportive of the London Plan Early Alterations, which increased London's annual housing target from 23,000 homes a year to 30,500 homes a year. Livingstone and the minister also collaborated on plans for the London Thames Gateway, sharing the chair of the project steering group. The Mayor was no doubt frustrated by the insistence of the government on setting up new structures including a London Thames Gateway Development Corporation, which was given development control powers, and a new central government Thames Gateway unit headed up, somewhat briefly, by Judith Armitt, rather than letting the GLA and the London Development Agency take the lead. London Thames Gateway delivery was to prove slow, and the housing targets appeared to have been overambitious.

Livingstone focused his attention on getting support for Crossrail, the new east–west rail line, which he considered to be essential to the development of Thames Gateway. The government ensured the enabling legislation went through parliament and committed some funding but implementation was nevertheless delayed, with the project still being dependent on private funding contributions. Livingstone had proposed to amend the London Plan to include levying contributions through planning powers to part fund Crossrail, but lost power before he was able to pursue this. In October 2008, with the ability to raise funds from the market and from development value being limited by the slowdown in the property market and new construction, the Chancellor, Alistair Darling, gave a commitment that Crossrail would still proceed.

The government also appeared to welcome Livingstone's enthusiasm for tackling climate change, although it must have found his international profile, with his world city mayors' initiative, a little galling. The Mayor's increasingly close relationship with the radical President Chavez of Venezuela and his oil-for-advisers agreement also annoyed ministers, who did not consider that the Mayor of London should pursue his own foreign policy and trade deals. Livingstone's improved relationship with the central government was reflected in ministers proposing to extend the Mayor's powers. In 2007, the government issued consultation proposals and steered a bill through parliament in the same year. As set out below, this both strengthened the Mayor's planning powers and gave him strategic housing powers which the mayoralty had been denied in the 1999 Act. In the May 2008 election campaign, both Tony Blair and other ministers were to support Livingstone's candidacy, pointing out how much he had achieved for London and Londoners.

The Mayor and the boroughs

In 2000, the majority of the boroughs were Labour controlled and the Labour party controlled their representative body, the Association of London Government (Table 13.1).

The Mayor initially joined the Association of London Government, sending his advisor Neale Coleman to represent him at the ALG's leaders committee. However,

Table 13.1 Borough party political control summary

Party political control	1998	2002	2006
Labour	23	17	8
Conservative	7	9	16
Liberal Democrat	1	6	4
Labour/ Liberal Democrat	1	0	1
Conservative/ Liberal Democrat	0	0	3
Non-party	1	1	1

Source: GLA: London Borough Elections May 2006.

this arrangement soon terminated, to be replaced by bilateral negotiations, by which the Mayor would occasionally meet borough council leaders. The GLA also set up a structure by which GLA officers, together with representatives with the GLA functional bodies – the London Development Agency, Transport for London, the Metropolitan Police and the Fire and Emergency Planning Authority (LFEPA) – met individual borough chief executives and their senior officers. These meetings were generally led from the GLA side by either Anthony Mayer as chief executive or Neale Coleman. The GLA, however, soon replaced these meetings by meetings with sub-regional groupings of boroughs. These round-up meetings were not very useful for either party. LDA, TfL, LFEPA and the Metropolitan Police all had their own borough liaison arrangements, and the GLA's Spatial Development Strategy team also maintained a sub-regional consultation framework.

In practice, higher-level liaison between the Mayor, senior GLA advisers and officers and boroughs was fairly limited. Ken Livingstone concluded fairly quickly that he could deal directly with government ministers and did not really need the support of the boroughs. Livingstone was perceived by the government and by the electorate generally as the key figure in London government, and the boroughs, despite retaining most key local government functions, were soon sidelined in debates over London's future. The Association of London Government, as the representative organization for the London boroughs, also found itself having a more limited role. This was partly because some of the leading figures in borough politics, such as Toby Harris, former ALG leader and leader of Haringey Council, John Biggs, former leader of Tower Hamlets, Len Duvall of Greenwich, and Graham Tope, former Sutton leader, all abandoned their council roles for the London Assembly or, in the case of Harris and Tope, for seats in the House of Lords as well. The ALG leadership was taken by Robin Wales, the directly elected Mayor of Newham, whose interests were local rather than Londonwide. Then, in 2002, Labour lost control of the ALG, which had no party in overall control till 2006 and then became controlled by the Conservatives, with the leadership taken by Cllr Merrick Cockell, the leader of Kensington and Chelsea. So, with Livingstone rejoining the Labour party in 2003, the relationships between the Mayor and the Labour government became closer, while the government increasingly saw the ALG as the opposition.

Representing such a diverse group of boroughs, in terms of both political control and interests, the ALG, which was renamed as London Councils in 2006, was unable to put forward a strong position. In effect the ALG saw its main role as facilitating the defence of local interests by individual boroughs, rather than attempting to put forward its own regional agenda. Although the ALG undertook some useful research work and lobbied primarily on local government finance issues, after 2002 it abandoned any attempt to put together a Londonwide policy position on housing and planning issues. It was unable to resist the Mayor's takeover of the London Housing Forum, which, having been established as a joint ALG/mayoral initiative, was transformed into the Mayor's Housing Forum. On planning issues, the ALG's main role was to be negotiating places at the table for borough representatives at the three Examinations in Public in 2003, 2006 and 2007, so that boroughs could pursue their own individual agendas. The housing team at the ALG, which had comprised over ten staff and was initially larger than the GLA's own housing and homelessness team, had limited output and impact and was slimmed down, while the ALG was slow to appoint its own planning officers after LPAC's abolition in 2000. The two experienced planning staff it did appoint soon moved on to other organizations. The ALG therefore became increasingly dependent for its planning advice on Martin Simmons, the former LPAC chief planner, who after a short time at the GLA had become a private consultant. As Simmons also acted as adviser to most of the sub-regional borough partnerships, he was often advocating sub-regional interests rather than the wider Londonwide perspective. On the housing front, the main role of the ALG/London Councils was to resist pressure from both the Housing Corporation and the Mayor for greater Londonwide collaboration on social housing lettings, borough politicians generally not being sympathetic to housing other areas' homeless households within their own borough. The Mayor was to become very successful in persuading ministers, especially Yvette Cooper in her term as housing and planning minister between 2005 and January 2008, that the boroughs were the main obstacles to getting housing and that, if he were given more housing and planning powers, the obstacles could be overcome.

The Mayor and the London Assembly

Livingstone was quick to give jobs to Assembly members from all parties other than the Conservatives. This was clearly intended to ensure Livingstone had majority support for his budget, the one real power the Assembly had. Lord Toby Harris, former leader of the London Borough of Haringey and chair of the Association of London Government, became chair of the Metropolitan Police Authority. The Liberal Democrat Lord Tope became adviser on equalities. Darren Johnson, a Green Party Assembly member, became adviser on the environment. Livingstone also transferred £1.65m of his budget to the Assembly, to fund two assistants per Assembly member and one additional assistant per party group. Assembly members, with limited powers, immediately had more direct staff support than most Members of Parliament.

In appointing Nicky Gavron, Assembly member and former chair of LPAC, as Deputy Mayor and planning adviser, Livingstone weakened the Assembly's ability to intervene in planning matters. The Assembly established a planning committee under the Conservative Assembly member Tony Arbour. In its first two years of existence the committee was consulted by the Mayor before the Mayor made determinations in relation to borough plans. Livingstone soon found that this slowed down the process; given that the planning powers were his rather than delegated, by 2003 the arrangement had been changed so that the Mayor just reported his decisions to the Assembly as a whole as part of his monthly mayoral report. The Mayor's planning decisions on cases referred to him were made in a fortnightly confidential meeting, attended by GLA officers and Nicky Gavron, but with neither applicant nor borough representatives present. There was, however, a procedure by which developers could make a presentation to the Mayor in advance of making an application. In such cases, borough planning officers might be invited to attend. Reports submitted to the Mayor, in terms of both initial consultation by the borough, known as stage 1, and final decision, known as stage 2, were published on the website and copied to the constituency Assembly member, but only after the decision had been made.

Assembly members were not satisfied with this arrangement and in June 2002 published a report *Behind Closed Doors* (London Assembly 2002b), which was critical of the fact that the Mayor held meetings in private and met selected developers. The Mayor ignored the Assembly criticism. In January 2006, the Assembly published a further report on the Mayor's planning decisions (London Assembly 2006a), which analysed a number of individual cases, concluding this time that the Mayor's intervention was generally consistent and productive, though raising the need for further clarifications of processes and policy requirements.

In 2001, the Assembly had set up a separate committee to review the development of the London Plan, chaired by the Conservative Assembly member Bob Neill, who later became a Member of Parliament. The committee and its successor committees made a number of responses to the different stages of the Plan consultation – the reports were generally supportive of the Mayor's overall approach, though they did question some of the Mayor's assumptions about the rate of growth and whether sustainability could be achieved (London Assembly 2002a,c). The Assembly committee was represented at the Examination in Public in 2003 and was generally supportive of the Mayor. The Assembly did not intervene significantly in the debate over the early alterations in 2006; their focus was on increasing the housing target, and individual party groups made separate representations to the Panel; but the Assembly committee did participate more fully in the debate over the further alterations with their emphasis on climate change in 2007 (London Assembly 2006b). This was primarily because of the intervention of the Green Assembly member, Darren Johnson, who chaired the Assembly's environment committee.

It should be stressed that the Assembly committee had very limited professional resources. Although it could request the Mayor, his advisors or senior staff to attend meetings to answer questions, it had to commission independent reports as it was not entitled to receive briefings from staff who reported to the Mayor. Its work therefore operated independently from the work of the GLA London Plan team, the planning decisions team, the housing team and other GLA staff. The committee had access to one scrutiny officer as well as a committee administrator so any substantive research depended on external consultants. The planning committee, chaired by either Tony Arbour or Bob Neill for most of the 2000 to 2008 period (apart from the year 2004–5, when its role was subsumed within the Economic Development and Planning committee chaired by the Liberal Democrat Assembly member Dee Doocey), did commission a wide range of investigations, for example on access to the Thames river, London's urban renaissance, London's waterways, Heathrow airport expansion and listed buildings (London Assembly 2003, 2004a, 2006c,d, 2007c). The committee also undertook investigations into two of the more problematic issues raised in the London Plan review: the relationship of London to the wider metropolitan region and the role of London's suburbs. In the first report (London Assembly 2004b), the Assembly concluded that the London Plan needed to give fuller consideration to the relationship between London and the wider southeast and that the role of the Inter-Regional Planning Forum should be strengthened. In the latter report (London Assembly 2007a), the committee shared the concerns of the Outer London sub-regional partnerships that there was a risk of the suburbs becoming residential dormitories with employment growth being focused on Central London. The report argued that the Mayor and boroughs should do more to boost the suburban town centres, by developing public transport and amenities and by managing the balance between housing growth and the protection of the high-quality suburban environment which made the suburbs attractive to live in.

The Assembly also turned its attention increasingly to housing issues. As mentioned above, the Assembly had published its own study on key worker housing in 2001. After focusing on other issues for the following five years, in 2006 the committee published an investigation into the fact that the proportion of housing output in London which was family homes was falling (London Assembly 2006e). This research was not new but picked up some of the debates over housing quality and density discussed in some detail in Chapters 6 and 7, based on information published in the Mayor's annual London Plan monitoring reports, the density and space standards review, and data also used in the similar *Think Big* report published jointly by the ALG and the London Housing Federation in November 2006 (London Housing Federation and London Councils 2006). Recognizing that the Mayor was likely to be granted housing strategy powers, the committee then published three further reports relating to housing: a study of the role of Housing Corporation grant in providing affordable housing, a response to the consultation on the draft Mayor's Housing Strategy and then a study on the operation of planning obligations (London Assembly 2007b, 2008b,c). None of these reports identified new issues or came forward with radical proposals, though the reports did contribute to the wider debate on the issues and pointed to the need for more consistency in the application of policy across London. The reports, however, focused on the activities of agencies other than the Mayor. In May 2008 the committee changed its name to the Planning and Housing Committee. It was now chaired by the former Deputy Mayor, Nicky Gavron.

There is little if any evidence that the Assembly's work on planning and housing had any direct impact on Ken Livingstone's overall policy approach or his planning interventions in specific cases. Livingstone generally ignored the Assembly and at times could be robust with individual Assembly members, even those who were members of his own political party. The Assembly soon realized it could not influence the Mayor and after 2002 lost interest in individual planning decisions made by the Mayor, instead trying to add to more general debates on what they saw as key issues, or the more personal interests of individual Assembly members; for example, the affordable housing study was an initiative by John Biggs, with other committee members showing little interest. After the May 2008 election, the committee was to focus its attention mainly on the Mayor's Housing Strategy and whether, in the context of the market downturn, the new Mayor's 50,000 affordable homes target could be achieved over three years. Following a series of sessions with expert witnesses, including Sir Bob Kerslake, the chief executive designate of the new Homes and Communities Agency, the committee concluded that the target would not be met, but that neither they nor the Mayor could do much about it (London Assembly 2008d).

The 2007 Greater London Act: increasing the Mayor's powers

In April 2008, the Mayor of London's powers were extended. He was given positive planning powers for strategic schemes: whereas before he had the power to veto major development schemes, he now has the power to take over a scheme from a local planning authority and grant consent himself, if he considers the proposal to be consistent with the London Plan, even if the borough objects to a scheme. This was a fundamental shift of power from local to regional government, and is in contrast with the position in the rest of England, where the government intends to abolish regional assemblies and transfer their regional plan-making powers to Regional Development Agencies, which are private sector-led inward investment agencies. In London, the strategic referral threshold was lowered from 500 homes to 150 homes, giving the Mayor a decision-making role in a wider range of projects, including schemes which are arguably not of regional significance. This shift of power derived from the fact that the government saw the Mayor as more in favour of growth and housing development than boroughs. The Mayor was also made the strategic housing authority in that he was given responsibility for the London Housing Strategy, previously the responsibility of the central government. The strategy sets the framework for the use of public housing investment resources. The Mayor was also invited by ministers to chair the London board of the new Homes and Communities Agency, which as from 1 December 2008 would combine the roles of the Housing Corporation and English Partnerships. This was to give the Mayor considerable influence over the investment budget, some 40 per cent of the national housing investment budget – a major transfer of power from central to regional government.

The new arrangements in London contrast with government proposals for the future of spatial planning in regions outside London. In 2006 the government introduced new structures by which the responsibility for Regional Housing Strategies was transferred from the government regional offices to regional assemblies so that Regional Spatial Strategies and Regional Housing Strategies could be developed on an integrated basis. However, the government was not impressed with the position of Regional Assemblies in the south of England, which were in its view not giving sufficient support to higher housing targets, and considered that Regional Development Agencies, with their focus on economic growth, were more constructive. Regional assemblies had never been very popular with county and district councils; following the government's decision not to proceed with directly elected regional bodies, after the negative referendum vote in the North East in November 2004, they had had a rather tenuous existence.

The government in March 2008 therefore proposed major changes to the regional planning structure (BERR 2008). This would involve the abolition of regional assemblies outside London. No further Regional Strategy Statements would be produced after the current round. As from 2010, Regional Development Agencies would be responsible for developing Integrated Regional Strategies incorporating regional economic, spatial planning and housing strategies. These strategies would be signed off by a conference of local government leaders as well as by the Regional Development Agency Board (the latter is led by the private sector and appointed by the central government) before being submitted for joint approval by the Secretary of State for Business Enterprise and Regulatory Reform (BERR – the renamed Department of Trade and Industry) and the Department for Communities and Local Government. These proposals will require a significant amendment to the 2004 Planning and Compulsory Purchase Act. The government also considered establishing a new structure of House of

Commons regional committees to scrutinize the work of both regional ministers and Regional Development Agencies in their enhanced role, though this was not progressed. These proposals will lead to a significant weakening of spatial planning outside London, with spatial planning becoming subservient to economic growth objectives, putting at risk environmental and equity/social justice objectives.

Chapter 14
London's experience of spatial planning

The practice of spatial planning in relation to theory

The theories of planning considered in the first chapter are not necessarily mutually exclusive. Moreover many of the theories are in effect derived from other social sciences rather than developed for specific application to planning practice. However, it can be argued that the practice of spatial planning by the Mayor and his strategic planners had some of the elements of positivism, derided by some theoretical commentators. For example, Davoudi and Strange (2009) considered that planning interventions by the Mayor could have a positive influence on the quality of life of people living in, working in or visiting London. Planning practice in London also contained an element of rationalism: plans should be based on evidence and analysis, an approach that is required both by government guidance and by the statutory planning framework, which sets out tests of soundness to be examined through a public inquiry. The strategic planners at City Hall, however, never fell into the trap of systems theory; modelling and scenario testing were undertaken in order to seek to anticipate future changes, demographic and economic, but were never seen as a determinant of the future or as a mechanism to control external factors.

The London Plan as published reflected the institutional relationships between different elements of government and with the Mayor. In effect the Mayor was the middle tier of a planning hierarchy, with the central government as the top tier and the London boroughs as the bottom tier. It is important to note that, whereas the Mayor saw himself as representing London interests to central government, he saw this not as a representative function on behalf of the boroughs, but as a function he was entitled to carry out as directly elected Mayor. He therefore did not see his role as mediating between the central government and the boroughs as local planning authorities. Where he agreed with the central government, he would collaborate with it to impose policies on the boroughs. Where he disagreed, he would use both the statutory planning system and his political status to challenge the central government, whether or not he had borough support.

The Mayor was also conscious of the institutional relationships between public, private and independent sectors. In practice he did not fully use his powers to seek to direct the market sector. Although the London Plan had within it components, for example the policy of planning obligations, which sought to utilize market-led development for wider public benefit, the analysis within this study has demonstrated the extent to which in practice this approach was reactive rather than proactive, and that his planning decisions tended to serve market interests rather than wider public sector interests. Missing from the Mayor's planning policies and practice – a somewhat surprising omission given the historic political position of the Mayor and his political advisers – was any critique of the market's domination of development and consequently of the planning system as it operated in London. The critical theory of Harvey and his disciples was largely absent from debates within the Greater London Authority, and on the rare occasions on which it was propounded in more public environments, such as the Examination in Public, such perspectives were easily marginalized (Edwards 2004).

As a regional strategic planning authority, it would have been difficult for the Mayor to adopt an advocacy approach to planning, through pursuing the interests of specific community groups. As presented by Davidoff (1965), an independent planner can be the advocate of community interests. As a decision-making authority, the Mayor is generally a recipient of advocacy – that is the target of a specific lobby, rather than the promoter. There were exceptions. For example the Mayor became the advocate for a number of developments related to the Olympics and because of a perceived conflict of interest had to delegate his executive powers to planning officers who would be seen as neutral. His advocacy of a proposed aquarium in the Royal Docks and the Thames Gateway Bridge raised similar issues. His opposition to the extension of Heathrow airport could also be seen as adopting a position which advocated the perspective of residents living near the airport, though the Mayor argued that his position was based on sound independent professional advice rather than on simply supporting a specific interest group. There is, however, a specific contrast with the former Greater London Council's planning role in the late 1970s and early 1980s when that strategic planning agency had adopted planning policies based on advocacy of the interests of a specific group of residents: those in residential areas in the city fringe threatened by city expansion (GLC 1984, Nicholson 1990,1992). By not taking this position in his 2000–8 term, the Mayor was in effect supporting by default, and at times publicly advocating, the interests of the market-led developers.

As the approaches to spatial planning categorized by Salet and Faludi (2000) are descriptors rather than mutually exclusive determinants of a policy process, it is possible to see all three streams represented within spatial planning practice in London in the 2000 to 2008 period. Elements of the London Plan are clearly aimed at legitimizing the Mayor's role as the strategic planning authority, though this is building on powers given to the post in statute rather than seeking to invent the role. However, the London Plan and related strategies were innovative in terms of using the concept of spatial planning to extend the role of planning policies beyond the historic land use basis. This led to a number of disputes with the central government as to whether certain policy proposals went beyond established planning powers and processes. The Mayor's strategy was largely successful and led to a significant extension of the Mayor's powers through the 2007 Greater London Authority Act.

Spatial planning policy and practice in London has also recognized the interactive nature of planning. However, it can be concluded that the approach is largely top-down and consequently does not achieve a balance between top-down planning and bottom-up planning as implied by Salet and Faludi. It is arguable that a strategic plan by its very nature has to be something more than an aggregation of bottom-up representations from different interest groups. Salet and Faludi's descriptors do not distinguish between different levels of spatial planning. A failure to recognize these important differentiations has been common in both government policy guidance and academic analysis. An approach involving extensive active engagement of local community groups which would be appropriate and achievable at a localized level is neither appropriate nor deliverable at regional or for that matter national level.

This brings us to a further interesting theoretical issue which relates to a point raised by Davoudi and Strange (2009) – the relationship between planning for specific places and the development and implementation of regional spatial planning. This issue has been raised explicitly by Boris Johnson as the new Mayor of London in his statement of possible changes to the London Plan (GLA 2008k). The new Mayor has expressed the view that the Livingstone plan gave insufficient attention to the importance of neighbourhood and place making by focusing on Londonwide strategy and a number of specific Londonwide objectives and targets. Johnson has implied that this approach fails to recognize the different characteristics of different locations and the interests of their residents. Johnson has also picked up on the increasing focus on place making within government guidance, and the increasing influence of concepts based on urban design and urbanism, promoted by former advisors to Ken Livingstone such as Richard Rogers and Ricky Burdett, within both planning policy and planning process.

The London Plan identified areas which had a potential for growth; although the density policy had regard to existing neighbourhood character, the plan was not aimed at protecting the character of specific areas from the pressures of change, nor did it seek to define what the form or components of any new community should be. This was because, as a strategic plan, the London Plan had to focus on using London's resources in terms of space, existing built form and future development capacity, to meet the needs of London's existing and future population for housing, employment, leisure and cultural space, transport, utility and social infrastructure.

Moreover, in terms of English planning law, a strategic spatial plan cannot make specific land use allocations or determine the application of specific policies to specific sites.

A spatial plan at regional level has to recognize the differentiation between places but has to be very cautious about promoting different policies for different places. A strategic spatial plan cannot be just a crude aggregation of locally determined place-based policies derived from the interests of existing residents. Urban design-based place making is an inadequate basis for spatial planning as it cannot consider strategic issues of resource allocation and access to space and place. Place making is an important component of spatial planning; despite the advocacy of urban design practitioners and academics such as Davoudi, it is not a substitute for a strategic spatial planning which fully considers economic, environment and equity objectives and the inter-relationships and conflicts between them.

London planning in 1988 and 2008

It is helpful to return to the analysis of London planning in the late 1970s and early 1980s in Savitch's *Post-Industrial Cities*: his study of politics and planning in New York, Paris and London (Savitch 1988).

Savitch defined the London planning regime as *liberal corporatism* (Savitch 1988 p. 197). This is contrasted with a *pluralist–corporatist hybrid* in New York, and a *mobilizing corporatist* regime in Paris. Savitch saw the three-tier system of planning in London – central, regional and local – as representing a rationalization of the planning system. He considered the establishment of the Green Belt as being critical to London's having a distinct identity, but he also considered that measures taken by both the central government and the GLC had slowed down London's growth. He then traced the policy reversals in the 1970s, which abandoned the policies of both residential and commercial dispersal and supported the development of the Central Activities Zone. This was, however, itself geographically constrained by the 1984 community areas policy, which sought to protect residential areas of Inner London from commercial expansion. Savitch, however, also draws attention to the GLC's polycentric approach with its focus on twenty-eight strategic centres outside the CAZ area. Savitch commented that the GLC approach to planning 'stemmed from a socialist orientation that wanted to control growth, preserve existing communities, and restore London's lost manufacture' (p. 202). The Tories were seen to 'favor aggressive expansion, see neighbourhood change as inevitable, and are convinced that old industry is forever gone' pointing to the irony that socialist Labour was 'conservative' whereas the Conservatives supported radical physical change (ibid.).

Pluralism and interest groups

Savitch also drew attention to the differing relationships between government and pressure groups in the three cities. In New York, pressure groups are seen as 'hit and run guerrillas' operating outside the decision-making process. In Paris, with power centralized, interest groups were activated by factions within the power structure only when support is needed – he refers to them as a 'reserve army'. Savitch, however, considered that, in London, interest groups were integral to the planning process, with a great deal of continuity, often funded by central, regional or local government, and influential. Alliances could be formed between different components of the decision-making structure and different interest groups. Savitch referred to London interest groups as a 'standing army'.

Savitch also focused on the party political nature of London's planning processes, with divisions uncommon within a political party and with tight discipline applied, and clear divisions between Labour and Conservative policies. He also pointed to the extent to which governing bodies are able to coopt, diffuse and in effect subvert opposition, giving interesting examples from Covent Garden and London Docklands. Personalities were seen as having less significance than in Paris or New York.

It is interesting to note how much has changed in twenty years. While interest groups in London can still be seen as a standing army, with some of its members from the 1970s and early 1980s still serving, its influence is perhaps less. Of the Londonwide representative groups, the London Forum of Civic and Amenity Societies, which represents civic and amenity societies across the capital and has been advised by some experienced professional planners, has made a well-informed and constructive contribution to the London Plan process, though not a contribution always welcomed by the Mayor and his political advisers. The proposition Savitch makes that government planning bodies rarely overcome local opposition is less true today, and in many ways government at all levels has become more arrogant and dismissive of opposition. This, however, could also reflect a greater recognition that to achieve strategic objectives local objections need to be overridden, and a greater determination by agencies of central and regional government to do so. Whereas a few individuals within interest groups have some influence in central and regional government circles, it is more because they are recognized as experienced professional experts, rather than that government has granted any concessions to interest groups. Although the consultation processes undertaken in developing the London Plan were extensive, there is little evidence of concessions being given to any interest group, and many interest groups found the process unproductive. From the Mayor's perspective, consultation was little more than a process and there was never any intention to make more than minor changes in response to interest group representations.

It is also interesting that the preparation of the 2004 London Plan and the revisions in 2006 and 2008 were largely uncontroversial. The Mayor and the GLA met with some opposition from environmentalist groups, but all but a few more 'purist' environmentalists who argued for a no-growth option were satisfied with the Mayor's strong support, at least on paper, for a range of strong environmentalist policies including the congestion charge, policies on energy and waste and his advanced position on climate change and carbon emission reduction targets. The most vociferous individuals at the Examinations in Public focused on protection of the banks of the River Thames and affordable houseboats.

Governance and the three-tier planning system

Savitch focused on the three-tier planning system, a system which was abandoned with the abolition of the Greater London Council in 1986. This created a vacuum in regional governance, which the establishment of the Government Office for London in 1994 as a regional outpost of central government did not fill. Although the first director of the Government Office for London, Robin Young, was initially referred to in the press as a 'tsar', he and his successors had low profiles and there is little evidence of GOL either effectively representing London's interests to the central government, or developing a regional strategic approach. GOL in fact was mainly to focus on monitoring borough performance and implementing the government's increasing obsession, inherited from the Conservative Prime Minister John Major by Tony Blair, with indicators, inspections, awarding stars and 'beacon awards' for good performance. As has been discussed in Chapter 3, as far as regional planning was concerned, the vacuum was at least partly filled by the London Planning Advisory Committee. Though this organization had only an advisory role, it was indirectly accountable to the electorate as it comprised representatives of the thirty-three local planning authorities and produced a comprehensive range of strategic planning advice which established a framework for boroughs to produce their Unitary Development Plans. This was an essential role given that GOL did not produce its Regional Planning Advice until 1996, a document that was thin and demonstrated that the central government, still then under Conservative control in the last year of the Major government, did not see the strategic planning of the capital city as a significant policy priority.

So, although the Mayor in 2000 had to re-establish the regional tier in the three-tier system of planning, he had a sound cross-party base in the guidance inherited from LPAC as well as a strong legal basis in terms of the 1999 Greater London Authority Act and circular 1/2000. Consequently his new power was challenged less by either the central government or the boroughs than might have been expected. Boroughs generally accepted that there was a case for a strategic planning body and supported the London Plan process. Moreover there was surprisingly little objection to the Mayor's development control intervention, a power which the Greater London Council had not possessed. It is not insignificant that it was not till eighteen months after LPAC staff were incorporated into the GLA that the Association of London Government, representing the London boroughs, recognized that they needed their own independent planning advice and professional staff as they might have a different position from the new strategic planning body. The consensus in London contrasted with the position outside London, where the three-tier system was in disrepute, with the government abolishing the county councils' structure-planning functions in 2004, transferring strategic planning powers to unelected regional assemblies and then in 2008 proposing to abolish them as well.

Personalities and parties in politics

More significant perhaps is the change in the relationships between politicians and political parties. In 1988, Savitch focused on the discipline within political parties and the extent to which decisions were made within political groupings, with distinct differences between party positions and policies changing only when political control of a public body changed after a popular election. Twenty years later the position is fundamentally different. First, with the 'New Labour' governments of Blair and Brown following many of the approaches of Thatcher and Major, not just the neo-liberal approach to economic policy but also a mixed provision approach to public services, with local government being transformed from delivery agencies to enabling bodies, the whole nature of the 'public sector' and the role of planning within governance fundamentally changes. This change has been studied by David Marquand (2004) in his works on the changing nature of governance, and in relation to planning has been traced by Philip Allmendinger among others (Allmendinger and Thomas 1998).

Second, discipline within political parties has broken down, and this is especially the case in London. In seeking to stand initially as the Labour party candidate in 2000, being rejected by the party after interference by Tony Blair and Gordon Brown as leaders of both the national Labour party and the central government, and then standing as an independent candidate and winning by defeating the official Labour candidate, Frank Dobson, who had resigned from the government to contest the election, Livingstone split the London Labour party, a party which had already seen a significant fall in membership and decreasing activism by its remaining members. The election was the triumph of personality over party politics and saw the emergence of a new celebrity style of politics in British political life. It could be argued that this was an inevitable consequence of the creation of the post of Mayor of a city of over 7 million people with direct election from an electorate of over 4 million, fifty times the electorate of the average British parliamentary constituency. In such a context the media are certain to have a greater impact than political meetings and canvassing. The main opposition parties recognized that they needed a candidate who could generate media coverage and to do so needed to be somewhat idiosyncratic; so the Conservatives chose first Jeffrey Archer until he was forced to resign after scandals over share deals and prostitution, and then Steve Norris, a rogue MP with a personal life covered in the tabloids, while the Liberal Democrats made the mistake of not selecting the popular south London radical MP, Simon Hughes, who also had a high profile but was caught up in a murder trial and needed a guard to protect him from a local gang, but instead selecting Susan Kramer, a local Liberal activist who was without political experience other than as President of the Oxford University Union Society but put up a strong performance, being referred to by two commentators as radiating 'the super-confidence of a *Cosmo* woman on steroids' (D'Arcy and Maclean 2000).

The mayoral election therefore focused more on personalities than on the policies of the opposing candidates, with the dogged and browbeaten former cabinet minister Frank Dobson soon becoming the underdog against the resurgent former GLC leader, who was perceived as the one man to have London's interests at heart and take on Blair and anybody else who stood in his way. It is arguable that the London Labour party never really recovered from the split, even when Livingstone was allowed back in to the party in 2004, quickly replacing his loyal deputy Nicky Gavron as Labour's official candidate. The Conservatives, especially after their second defeat in 2004, also realized they needed a new celebrity candidate. After considering a number of media-friendly individuals, including a radio disc jockey and a former New Labour associate and sacked BBC director, Greg Dyke, they opted for one of their most maverick members. Journalist, star of TV comedy shows and, like Archer and Norris, a man with a tabloid-friendly private life, the MP for Henley in leafy Oxfordshire, well beyond the London boundary, Boris Johnson was selected partly because he was the only British politician other than Ken who was generally known by his first name. Both Ken and Boris were to reach beyond traditional political alliances, completely ignoring political affiliations, happily working with individuals from competing political parties or none – and in some cases in reaching out too far, making bizarre appointments which were to backfire. In Livingstone's case, his reach eventually extended to Labour loyalists, with not just Nicky Gavron being appointed Deputy Mayor but also the former Labour council leaders Val Shawcross, Toby Harris, Len Duvall and John Biggs all being given salaried posts in the mayoral family: the functional bodies, the Development Agency, the Police Authority, and the Fire Authority.

The new neo-liberal paradigm

The most fundamental change since Savitch's study of 1988 is the radical shift in the framework in which governance in both London and the United Kingdom as a whole operates. In 1988 Margaret Thatcher had still two years to serve as Prime Minister. At that time, Savitch could not know that Thatcher's neo-liberal approach would not only be continued by a Conservative successor but later be maintained and in fact expanded in new areas of the traditional public sector under a decade of New Labour government. By May 2000, when the Mayor came into office, as a socialist MP with a keen interest in economics, and his own personal think tank of left-wing economists active in a Trotskyite group called Socialist Action (Hosken 2008 Chapters 18 and 22), the new paradigm was fixed and unchallengeable. Livingstone and his advisers were quick to recognize the position. He realized that he had no delivery powers and no ability to raise finance for investment. His levy powers were limited to funding the revenue costs of his staff including those of the functional bodies such as the Police Authority. He depended on fares and government support to run the buses and the Underground. He needed government grant for the London Development Agency's regeneration programme.

If Livingstone was going to deliver any of his policy objectives he needed friends in the City. It did not take long to follow Gordon Brown's route to the City of London Corporation's headquarters at Guildhall. In his first week in power he appointed the City Corporation leader, Dame Judith Mayhew, as his City advisor and he was setting up formal liaison arrangements with the business lobby group London First. As discussed earlier, it was largely their lobbying that London needed its own mayoralty to be a real world city that had led to the post being created, so Livingstone had a lot to thank them for. A deal was done. The Mayor would support the continuing role of the City Corporation, despite the fact that it was a feudal anachronism, while the City would support the Mayor's ambitions and even help fund them. Livingstone abandoned not just any idea of fighting the City, but even any idea of reforming them, and hitched both his own vision, and with it the London Plan, to the City's vision of unconstrained economic growth and wealth appreciation based on unregulated and unconstrained operation of capitalism and all its derivatives.

It could be argued that this pact was predicated on an agenda for using the benefits of unconstrained capitalism for the wider benefit of Londoners. Rather oddly, that argument tends to be absent from both the Mayor's polemics and the technical reports of his economists and planners. If economic growth based on unconstrained capitalism was good for London, it was therefore good for all Londoners, so by definition any constraint or attempt to divert its profits would be bad for London's economy and bad for Londoners. The neo-liberal paradigm was to reign supreme and condition every decision the Mayor took. By the time the paradigm collapsed in the autumn of 2008, Livingstone was no longer in office, and in happy media-friendly exile could of course argue that, now the neo-liberal paradigm was dead and gone, socialism was a good thing after all.

The role of academics and the professional bodies

There has been a further shift in the framework of planning policy making over the last twenty years. There would appear to be less engagement by the academic community and the chartered institutes in the London strategic planning process than twenty years ago. Although the LSE London studies group originally established by William Robson is still operating under the leadership of Tony Travers, the group has focused on governance and funding issues rather than strategic planning, and there is no parallel group of planning academics contributing to the development of London planning policy. This appears to be in contrast with the position in New York and Paris, where there seems to be greater engagement by the academic community in governance and regional planning, assisted in the former case by the Regional Plan Association of New York set up in 1929 (Hays 1965), and in the latter by the Institute d'Urbanisme de Paris at Université Paris XII Creteuil.

Robin Thompson and Drew Stevenson, both former planning practitioners as well as academics, acted as planning advisers to the Mayor between 2000 and 2008, but the engagement of the wider academic planning community has been more limited. As referred to earlier, there have been a number of academic studies of elements of the London strategic planning process. As is, however, demonstrated in the bibliography, relatively little has been written since the Plan's publication in 2004.

Sir Peter Hall, the author of two books on planning in London as well as a more recent sociological study (Hall 1969, 1989, 2007), was invited by the Mayor to chair an external advisory group on the Plan, which was dissolved before the draft London Plan was published, having been sidelined as the Plan's focus was shifted onto an economic growth/compact city basis, discounting London's relationship with the wider metropolitan region. At the first Examination in Public in 2003, Hall appeared in his role as President of the Town and Country Planning Association. It is significant that the GLA generally chose not to seek external academic advice, but that also very few academic planners, even those based in London, chose to engage in the strategic plan-making process. The notable exception is Michael Edwards, senior lecturer in planning at the Bartlett School of Planning, who represented the Kings Cross Lands Group and the London Social Forum at the EiP and has published on the London Plan as well as making formal submissions to the Mayor (Edwards 2004, 2008, 2009)

The position of the Charted Institutes is also less significant than in the past. In the early postwar period, both the Architects and Planners Institutes were more engaged in the plan-making process. For example, in 1943, the RIBA published its own report on the reconstruction of London (RIBA Greater London 1943). Yet neither the London Royal Town Planning Institute (RTPI) nor the London RIBA has had significant engagement in the London spatial plan-making process. London RIBA has recently established a London urbanism and planning group, but the group focuses on urban design issues and has limited planning input, and has not engaged in the London Plan process since responding to the draft London Plan in 2003. The London branch of the RTPI is even less well resourced and has been unable to engage with the London Plan process. This to a large extent reflects the pressure on planning practitioner workloads, with the RTPI having to focus on providing support and training for practising planners rather than on policy development. This is a reflection of the extent to which planning as a profession is on the defensive. The London Planning and Development Forum, which is an informal forum of public and private sector planners and architects, has been more engaged in the London Plan process in that it both runs bimonthly meetings with invited speakers on both regional and national planning and development issues, and has held special meetings with mayoral planning advisors at key stages of the London Plan and London Plan review processes. It also publishes the quarterly journal *Planning in London*, which includes articles and commentary from both practising and academic planners and architects.

The role of consultants, professional staff and mayoral policy advisers

Another contrast with 1988 is the increasing role of private consultants in undertaking research and consultancy work which has contributed to the strategic planning process. The Mayor's strategic planning team has been very compact, comprising only ten to fifteen professional planners. In fact it is smaller than the LPAC team, which had no statutory functions, and not much larger than the GOL planning team, which now has a much more limited role. The team was first led by a consultant from the GLA set-up team, then by Greg Lomax, previously assistant chief executive of the Housing Corporation, and then from 2003 to 2008 by Debbie McMullen, a professional planner who had worked for LPAC, with John Lett, also from LPAC, as strategic planning manager. The Mayor's planning decisions team, which advised the Mayor on the referral of strategic planning applications, had fewer than twenty staff and was led throughout Livingstone's term of office by Giles Dolphin, who had also previously worked for LPAC. The Mayor's total planning capacity to carry out his primary statutory function was therefore only thirty-five staff, out of a total direct staffing resource of over 600. The GLA therefore has depended on external consultants for much of the technical support work on which the plan is based.

As shown in the chapters above and the bibliography, the planning policy and research output published by the Mayor between 2000 and 2008 has nevertheless been extensive, with a total of 114 separate planning documents published during Ken Livingstone's eight-year term. The majority of the research documents and some of the more specialist Supplementary Planning Guidance and Best Practice Guidance documents were drafted by private consultants. It is important to note that these projects were all working to briefs prepared by GLA professional planning officers, with projects managed by and publications vetted by both GLA planners and the Mayor's policy and political advisers, known as policy directors: Neale Coleman, Eleanor Young, Alex Bax and Dan Hawthorn. In relation to economic and equalities policies they were vetted by John Ross and Lee Jasper respectively. A few consultants' reports which did not support the Mayor's overall policy direction were not published, though it is fair to say that the GLA's commissioning to publication record and commissioned to published ratio was probably considerably better than that of the relevant central government departments.

The role of private consultants was therefore central to the development of strategic planning policy in London and generally a constructive contribution.

However, the role of the Mayor's policy advisers, some of which were personal political appointments, cannot be overstated. They operated a power of veto on behalf of Livingstone. They could and often did override both external consultancy and internal professional advice, and cleared every report which went to the Mayor, whether in relation to a research report, proposed planning guidance, comments on a borough plan or a recommendation on a specific application. Although Livingstone personally read all reports and had a phenomenal capacity to absorb information and pick out the most essential components, he did rely on his policy advisers to act on his behalf. The policy advisers therefore had a key role in ensuring the Mayor was told only what they thought he should know. This role of political gatekeepers was more central than in 1988, when the concept of political advisers to ministers and local government leaders in the UK was in its infancy.

It is now necessary to move on from considering contextual and process issues to assessing the achievements and impacts of the Mayor's two four-year terms and to assess the product of the new governance structures in relation to strategic planning and housing.

Quantity and quality

The Mayor of London's main focus has been on increasing housing output in numerical terms. This is partly by demonstrating that not only could the original London plan target of 23,000 homes a year be achieved, but also the new target of 30,500 could be achieved and in fact exceeded. This objective was strongly supported by the central government, which, following Kate Barker's review of housing supply, considered increased housing output as the best means of stabilizing the rate of house price inflation, which was both a key government objective in its own right and a key factor within the move towards harmonization of economies within the European Union, at a time the United Kingdom was still actively considering joining the European Monetary Union (EMU). Even after the pursuit of EMU membership lapsed, the government continued to put pressure on all regional planning authorities to increase housing output, based on a macroeconomic formulaic modelling of the relationship between new housing construction and house prices. Even in late 2008 with a fall in house prices, the government was encouraging the Mayor to undertake a further housing capacity study to meet projected future housing demand, though government arguments have moved away from macroeconomic formulae to demographic projections, having discovered that the rate of population growth is likely to be somewhat higher than previously expected.

The consequence has been that both the central government and its agents in the form of government regional offices have intervened in strategic and local planning matters on the issue of total housing targets and their delivery, without adequate consideration of more complex issues in relation to tenure mix, affordability (other than in relation to the affordability of market housing to first-time buyers) or housing type in terms of built form or bedroom size mix. The government has no targets in relation to these key elements of housing output and the attitude of the government to the Mayor's representations on the low affordable housing policy targets of some boroughs has not always been supportive. However, there have been occasions on which ministers have expressed both concern and surprise at the limited number of family-size homes being built; on one occasion Yvette Cooper, then Housing and Planning Minister, expressed surprise that plans for the Lower Lea Valley did not envisage significant numbers of family homes with gardens. The Mayor's reluctance to enshrine the housing mix targets in the Housing Supplementary Planning Guidance in formal London Plan policy also reflected a concern that such prescription would reduce housing output in quantitative terms. The reluctance of the Mayor's advisers to adopt internal housing space standards within the London Plan review reflected similar concerns.

Density, bedroom size mix and built form

The analysis in Chapter 6 has clearly demonstrated a correlation between density and bedroom size mix. The push to increase housing output, which has led to over half of planning consents granted over the three years to 2006/7 being above the Mayor's own sustainable residential quality guidelines, has contributed to the bedroom size mix of new development output falling far short of the balance of needs demonstrated by the 2004 housing requirements study as encapsulated in the Housing SPG. Built form clearly has an impact on bedroom size mix. Most of the developments over ten stories are at densities over 435 dwellings per hectare, with some schemes at densities of over 1,000 dwellings per hectare. It is generally regarded as inappropriate to provide family homes in higher floors of blocks. Until fairly recently, children in social housing above the fifth floor were one of the factors that contributed to the index of deprivation that was the basis of allocating government funding to disadvantaged areas, with many councils having formal policies to transfer such households to lower-rise accommodation. Moreover it is difficult to meet standards on access to children's playspace, including the Mayor's new 10 sq m per child standard, through including significant family provision in high-rise schemes. Options of providing playspace at roof level may not always be appropriate.

An analysis of housing mix in a sample of high-rise schemes confirms that the proportion of three-bedroom and larger homes in high-rise schemes is low, whereas developers generally assume that larger market homes in high-rise schemes, including penthouse flats, will generally not be sold to households which include children where the accommodation is the household's sole home. This is confirmed by the child occupation model used for calculating demand for school places, which is based on surveys of the occupation levels of recently completed developments, which assumes a very low child occupation for flatted three-bedroom or larger market homes. It is therefore not surprising that the drive to high-rise development has led to a lower output of family-sized housing.

The viability of affordable housing without subsidy

Although the London Plan set a Londonwide 50 per cent affordable housing target, the application of the target to an individual site depends on the ability of a private development to deliver this affordable housing output. As described above, the Mayor's practice has been that any strategic development referred to him under his planning powers is subject to a financial appraisal to test the viability of a scheme at different levels or mixes of output if it includes housing but does not meet his targets on bedroom size mix and proportions of affordable housing, social rent and intermediate housing. Part of this assessment is to test assumptions about the availability of public subsidy, normally in the form of grant from the Housing Corporation, the government's social housing investment agency, and whether targets could be achieved if more grant is made available. A number of London boroughs also undertake financial appraisals of proposals for housing development which are locally determined and not referable to the Mayor.

Very few schemes could achieve 50 per cent affordable housing without some form of public subsidy. Over the last few years 98 per cent of London housing development has been on previously developed land, which already has an existing use value, which can be as high as £30m–£50m a hectare. On premium sites high sales values will be reflected by high land acquisition costs. In Central London, the value can be over £100m a hectare. Brownfield sites generally have high development costs; where sales values are relatively low, developments may only be marginally profitable for developers even without a contribution to affordable housing. Private residential developments in aggregate in London contribute less than 10 per cent of the overall investment requirement of the social housing programme, so the availability of grant is essential. Even relatively high-value low-cost developments will rarely deliver more than 30 per cent affordable housing without grant.

The government has had an expectation that private developers can provide a greater subsidy to affordable housing, and this belief, not supported by any sound evidence, has been at the centre of the government's successive proposals to reform the planning obligations regime: the tariff proposal, the Optional Planning Charge (OPC), the Planning Gain Supplement (PGS) and now the Community Infrastructure Levy (CIL). At the same time the Housing Corporation was reducing the amount of social grant it provides per social housing unit, with a target set by the Treasury for a 7 per cent saving per annum – this at a time of rising construction and land costs. Consequently the economics of development has meant that, at least in London, affordable housing output has been squeezed. The programme has been maintained to a large extent by housing associations using reserves or receipts from property disposals to support new development, often at the level of £25,000 a home, but such an approach is not sustainable in the long term. With sales values now falling, and increases of Housing Corporation grant being short-term, the affordable housing programme is set to be squeezed further. It is the economics of development rather than the Mayor's planning policy requirements that is the main reason for the fall-off in proportionate affordable housing output over the last few years, though it is also significant that the move to more complex developments and built forms such as high-rise schemes which have high unit construction costs, and are not very profitable unless on premium sites, has added to the problem.

Competing policy priorities

Maximising or optimizing affordable housing output is not the only priority of planning policy. The London Plan gives two key priorities for planning obligations – affordable housing and public transport – but also recognizes that planning obligations will also be used to support health, childcare and training objectives. In the 2008 revision to the London Plan, climate change mitigation was also added as a strategic priority. In practice, planning obligations are used by boroughs to support a range of social infrastructure provision including education and public realm, and often to support employment generation in the context of mixed-use objectives. The costs of meeting energy renewables and climate change mitigation objectives have also contributed to the reduced ability of schemes to meet affordable housing targets. The consequence has been a lower priority being given by the Mayor, and often by boroughs as local planning authorities, to meeting affordable housing targets. This is especially the case in mixed-use schemes which include non-profit-making non-residential activities. There have been a number of recent major projects with limited or no affordable housing content; for example the Silvertown Quays scheme in the Royal Docks, which includes an aquarium but only 27.5 per cent affordable housing, and the Doon Street development on the South Bank, which has a swimming pool but no affordable housing. With the Mayor giving increasing priority to improving public transport, major residential development schemes at stations, for example at Victoria and Dalston Junction in Hackney, have been used to support station improvement, with affordable housing requirements being waived. It is significant that, in the case of strategic schemes considered by the Mayor, the affordable housing output fell significantly in the last two years of Ken Livingstone's eight-year term of office.

The limitations of planning in controlling the market and ensuring housing delivery

Planning can only create a framework for development. Granting planning permission does not in itself make development happen. Moreover very little development is undertaken directly by public sector agencies. Even where boroughs, the London Development Agency or English Partnerships controlled land, development was undertaken in partnership with private developers and was often supported by private investors. The fact that planning consents in London have increased to over 60,000 homes a year, with completions running at half this level, demonstrates that the main obstacle to increased housing output is not a lack of planning consents, but the fact that major schemes, such as Greenwich Millennium Village, Barking Riverside, Stratford City, Kings Cross and Silvertown Quays, have extensive build-out periods, extending to fifteen years or more, with social and transport infrastructure required as well as housing. These issues were considered fully in the GLA's report on *Delivering Increased Housing Output* (GLA 2006b). The recent slowing down in the London property market will lead to reduction in both overall housing output and affordable housing output unless the government provides additional investment to secure returns to landowners and developers. The Barker report, which saw planning and land supply as the main constraint, should have paid more attention to external economic factors. Whereas increased housing output in London has not significantly reduced house prices as Barker assumed, falls in house prices significantly reduce housing output.

The policy changes necessary for the London Plan objectives to be achieved

The analysis in earlier chapters has demonstrated that the density policies set out in the 2004 London Plan, based on the principle of sustainable residential quality, were not properly applied either by the Mayor himself or by many London boroughs. This was partly attributable to the fact that the density matrix allowed for significantly higher densities where a proposed development was predominantly flats, but also because the matrix implied that developments in central and accessible locations should primarily be small units. It is not surprising that when combined with development economics this led to a focus on small units at higher densities. This neither increased affordable housing on site nor generated additional value to support contribution through planning obligations to affordable housing on other sites. The Mayor therefore modified the density matrix so that neither the built form of the proposed development nor car-parking provision was an element in the density calculation, with habitable room density, the new primary measure, being driven solely by public transport access and neighbourhood characteristics including town centre location. By allowing for a range of different unit sizes in all locations, with different unit ranges within each density habitable room range, the matrix now allows for family-sized units in central locations, as well as for smaller units in suburban locations. The critical issue is that the form of development should be driven by an assessment of housing requirements and the assessment of the suitability of a site to meet these requirements, based on a planning brief prepared by the local planning authority, rather than by developers' profit margins or architects' design concepts. This process should be aided by changes in market demand, which should lead developers to redesign some projects to focus on homes for occupation rather than investment, which should include more family homes at lower unit densities.

As also demonstrated in this analysis, there is increasing evidence from the GLA's report on housing space standards of low and falling internal space standards in new development in London (GLA 2006d). Though the Mayor of London recently adopted an external playspace standard of 10 sq m per child, and the London Plan encourages higher internal space standards, no minimum standard was set. The adoption of a minimum standard would be helpful in ensuring quality across all sectors and would help to ensure that homes built for the market sector are also useable for social housing when the private market slows down, as at present. It is regrettable that the combination of density policies and market pressures has led to a significant element of recently completed market development failing to meet the Housing Corporation's Housing Quality Indicator (HQI) standards for social housing, forcing the dilemma of whether to lower these standards or to leave the housing empty. This dilemma could and should have been avoided.

The fundamental challenge, however, remains the economics of development – a challenge that the Mayor's use of development appraisal as part of his planning decision process has exposed rather than resolved. The government's assumption that costs will be reduced by public sector bodies giving away land for housing development is predicated on the false assumption that government departments and local authorities are not themselves seeking to maximize receipts. Moreover housing development value is always competing with alternative use value, and for brownfield sites this will only fall, unless the office, retail, logistics and hotel markets also slow down. For housing output to be maintained in the current market, let alone increased to meet outstanding requirements, government subsidy to affordable housing output has to be increased significantly and the government has to directly fund health, education, transport and leisure facilities rather than assume that costs can be covered from developer profit and rising sales values.

Both the Mayor and boroughs as local planning authorities need to focus on lower-level intensification in suburban centres with good facilities and good public transport access, raising development densities from the current 40–60 dwellings per hectare to 70–125, which will still allow for significant proportions of family-size homes including some houses and maisonettes as well as flats. This is far more sustainable and, in the current market, more profitable for developers than focusing on hyperdense high-rise schemes, often in unattractive and now unmarketable locations. Both in the medium term and for future generations, the focus has to shift to the needs, not just of the immediate investment market, but of the long-term occupier. This includes a much greater focus on both quality and affordability.

London's housing capacity needs to be reviewed. If we are to build better-quality housing, with more internal space and more amenity space, and leave room for schools, health services, leisure facilities and other social infrastructure essential to sustainable communities, we need more space. Recent experience has demonstrated that city cramming is not the answer. This means that, to meet projected population growth, we need to reconsider the potential for significant new development on the periphery of London, and this may need to include some development on accessible sites within the Green Belt. The positive role of the Green Belt can be protected while allowing for some 'finger' development, following the example of Stockholm and Copenhagen, where new communities would still have access to protected open space. It is no longer sound policy to have a Green Girdle that strangles London and forces overdevelopment and overcrowding within the London boundary.

Combining strategic plan making and strategic intervention in development control

The Mayor of London had a novel combination of powers in that, as well as being the regional planning authority responsible for publishing the regional spatial plan, he also had development control powers. As far as the UK was concerned, the 1999 GLA Act created a new planning process: strategic development control, an innovation that has not to my knowledge previously been assessed by academic planners. The Mayor's powers therefore do not just relate to setting the framework for the thirty-three borough plans, which must be in general conformity with the regional strategy; the Mayor has had the power to intervene to ensure major developments also conform with the plan. Up to April 2008, this was the power to veto non-conforming developments, but the 2007 GLA Act gave the Mayor the power to take over such applications and grant consent directly. The power only came into effect just as Livingstone's second term came to an end and has not at the time of writing been used by his successor. What was curious about the government's decision to extend the Mayor's powers was that, although the parliamentary debate raised questions as to the Mayor's actions in specific cases, no systematic analysis of the Mayor's practice in terms of using his pre-existing powers was undertaken by the government, the Mayor, the boroughs or any other interested party.

The Mayor in his proposals for a positive development control power gave some examples of cases which in his view would have proceeded more quickly to planning consent had he had a positive power (GLA 2006m). Curiously this list of thirty cases included several major schemes which breached the Mayor's policy guidance on density and affordable housing, for example the schemes at Lovell's Wharf, Vauxhall Tower, Commerce Road and Lots Road. The Mayor gave a number of examples where he considered boroughs were wrong to object to schemes on the ground of height, irrespective of whether the components of the application were consistent with other London Plan policies. As referred to earlier, the Assembly's second report on the Mayor's planning decisions (London Assembly 2006a), by looking at only a few cases rather than undertaking a systematic analysis of interventions in relation to published policy, was also insufficiently critical of the Mayor's actual planning decisions.

The Mayor and his planning decisions officers were selective in relation to which policies in the published plan they chose to apply and which they chose to disregard. Density guidance was generally disregarded on the grounds that the tops of density ranges were not intended to be caps. The requirement for justification for development outside the density range was largely ignored. Moreover, within the GLA, the London Plan team and the planning decisions unit operated as separate entities. Leaving aside the specialist technical support to the planning decisions unit by the London Plan team specialist housing planner, the London Plan team was generally not consulted on individual strategic referrals, unless a planning decisions officer chose to seek advice. London Plan team members were therefore not expected to intervene in planning applications. Given that such interventions were discouraged, the plan-making and development control functions became increasingly separate, not an uncommon experience within a local planning authority. So plan making had little or no regard to whether a policy could actually be implemented or monitored, and development control staff chose which if any policies were considered to be relevant to a specific scheme. Development control staff did not engage in policy development and the plan-making team did not engage in its implementation.

The analysis in Chapter 6 above, which is the first systematic analysis of overall housing output in London and of cases referred to the Mayor, is clear evidence of the extent to which development control decisions by both the Mayor and individual boroughs were not consistent with the London Plan. Objectors at public inquiries, for example at the Commerce Road and Lots Road inquiries, found themselves quoting London Plan policies to support their objections, only to find themselves opposed by the Mayor's representatives. It can be argued that this is all a matter of degree, but an output so seriously divergent from mayoral guidance on density, tenure mix and bedroom size mix represents a systematic failure of policy implementation. Moreover, by encouraging developers to deviate to such an extent from published policy, it is arguable that the Mayor's interventions did more damage to his own declared policy objectives than any actions of dissenting boroughs or of the central government.

The Mayor's focus on enabling development was absolute, and both he and his advisors ensured that what developers wanted they got, and developers soon learnt that, if they offered the Mayor some of his favourite outputs in relation to more energy efficiency or a change to London's skyline, more substantive policy requirements could be forgotten about. For such a scheme, any planning officer or legal adviser who might wish to draw attention to negative aspects was soon made aware of the Mayor's direction, and increasingly reports were written to give the Mayor the answer he wanted, or that his political advisers wanted. Developers who thought the planning officer was being awkward could easily bring pressure to make sure their scheme was consented, and unless they did something to upset the Mayor personally, they were guaranteed success, which is why developers were so enthusiastic about the Mayor's powers being extended and decision making for strategic schemes being taken away from the boroughs. As an experiment, the unique combination of plan making and development control powers, which could have had a positive impact, was a failure because the powers were used inappropriately and inconsistently. From the perspective of developers and to a certain extent the government, which had its eyes on housing numbers and nothing else, it was a roaring success.

Combining strategic planning and strategic housing policy

Ken Livingstone was granted a statutory housing function only as he was nearing the end of his second term, when he took over responsibility of the Regional Housing Strategy from the Government Office for London and the Secretary of State. The original 1999 GLA Act had debarred the Mayor from undertaking expenditure to provide housing. Housing provision and homelessness had remained the statutory responsibility of the thirty-two London boroughs and the City of London Corporation, although most had chosen to transfer the ownership and/or management of all or part of their housing stock to housing associations or other providers. Livingstone was always interested in housing; in his youth he had been vice-chair of the housing committee of the London borough of Lambeth. He therefore would not let the restrictions of the 1999 Act stop him from pursuing his interest – thus the appointment in early 2000 of the Mayor's Housing Commission and his later takeover of the joint forum with the boroughs, which was transformed into the Mayor's Housing Forum, though he personally attended only one meeting and delegated his responsibility for chairing it first to Neale Coleman and then to David Lunts, his policy director.

It is also arguable that, the more housing responsibilities the Mayor took on, the less the Mayor's housing team actually did. In the early years, carrying on the tradition of its predecessor body the London Research Centre, from which Julia Atkins and many of her team came, the housing group produced a plethora of research reports and comprehensive statistical analyses, including the London Household Survey, the 2004 housing requirements study, an annual housing statistics report and a series of bulletins on homelessness, private sector rents and empty properties. The team also did most of the drafting work for the annual regional housing strategies published by GOL. However, by 2003, with Julia

Atkins replaced by Mark Kleinman, and then a year later by Alan Benson, while the housing statistics evidence base was maintained, research output was reduced, with resources devoted to servicing the structure of the Mayor's Housing Forum and its subgroups. The team also held liaison meetings with the Housing Corporation in an attempt to influence their housing investment decisions, an attempt that was of little impact as the Mayor and his advisors had little view on how investment should be distributed between either geographical areas or types of affordable housing product, other than a general line that investment was needed in the Thames Gateway, and later to support the Olympics housing project.

When it came to drafting the Mayor's Housing Strategy, which Livingstone and his advisors rather presumptuously wanted to publish in advance of the new power coming into effect, they passed out both the research and the drafting to consultants, so Steve Wilcox of York University and Peter Williams, who had been deputy director at the Council of Mortgage Lenders, wrote a report on intermediate housing (GLA 2008l). This was completed in April 2007 but not published until sixteen months later. The consultant Steve Hilditch, previously a partner in Paddington Consultancy Partnership with Neale Coleman, drafted the strategy, with fairly limited input from members of the housing team or from members of the specialist sub-groups. The sub-groups, like the Forum itself, became talking shops, rather than working up and refining policy options. Consequently, when the *Draft Mayor's Housing Strategy* appeared in September 2007 (GLA 2007b), although including a fairly comprehensive policy analysis, it was relatively short on policy proposals and did not really go beyond the housing policies in the London Plan published four years earlier. The two main initiatives were to increase the proportion of family rented homes, but with a target still far below that in the Housing SPG, and to pool lettings to council and housing association stock across London, a proposal objected to by the boroughs.

The Housing Corporation continued to allocate the investment programme and in April 2008 issued allocations which committed most of the resources available for the 2008–11 three-year programme (Housing Corporation 2008). The draft Housing Strategy agreed with GOL and the Housing Corporation had proposed a set of new initiatives for direct funding to local authorities outside the main National Affordable Housing Programme managed by the Housing Corporation. Responsibility for coordinating these innovation programmes was transferred from GOL to the Mayor. The Mayor issued in March 2008 a bidding prospectus for this targeted funding stream – the first time the Mayor had had an explicit role in determining allocation of housing investment resources. However, by the time the bids were in, Livingstone was no longer in office, so had lost the opportunity he had sought for so long to allocate a housing capital programme. The new Mayor did not allocate the resources until December 2008. This process apparently required the consent of the Housing Corporation Board and the board of the new Homes and Communities Agency, which was appointed only in late October. A new draft of the Mayor's Housing Strategy approved by the new Mayor was published in May 2009.

Interestingly, with the new powers transferred to the Mayor, the GLA found it had no experience of a housing investment decision-making process. Having been granted housing powers under the 2007 GLA Act, it chose to delegate the management of the process to the London Development Agency, which, although having some experience of project-managing development, did not have any investment allocation experience either and had no housing powers of its own. The allocation process included officers from LDA, GLA, the Housing Corporation and the central government as well as specialist external consultants on each programme area and was a rather confused as well as time-consuming process as, despite the publication of the bidding guidance, there was little agreement between the parties on allocation criteria. The first announcement of mayoral housing investment decisions led to a public dispute with the Housing Minister.

Although the regional housing and planning strategies were to a large extent consistent, this was not necessarily a consequence of the bringing together of strategic planning and housing functions under the Mayor. The previous London Housing Strategy, published by GOL, had also been consistent with the London Plan (GOL 2005). The difficulty was therefore not inconsistency of strategies but the implementation; ensuring investment decisions were consistent with strategy was not within the Mayor's power, and any public sector agency, whether the central government, the Housing Corporation or the Mayor, can only set a policy framework for investment. It is for developers and housing associations to bring development proposals forward. As demonstrated above, coordination between planning and investment decisions, whether at regional, sub-regional or borough level, has been poor, with planning decisions more often than not having to be made on the basis of inadequate information on the availability or lack of public subsidy. Without this case-by-case collaboration, including joint appraisals and joint decision making, consensus over strategy is of limited use. It is ironic that, when the opportunity to improve collaboration is available, the policy consensus may collapse, as the new Mayor seeks to use the new housing strategy to override existing strategic planning policy by abandoning the 50 per cent affordable homes target and trying to sift the balance of the programme away from social rented housing towards intermediate housing. Moreover, by abandoning a regional strategic approach, not only the strategic plan will be put at risk but the delivery of the investment programme as well. So, arguably, the novel approach to combining planning and housing strategy and delivery at regional level has broken down before it has had a chance to bed down.

Lessons for other world cities?

It is always somewhat presumptuous to assert that other world cities can learn from London. As Savitch demonstrated in his book twenty years ago, the governance arrangements in New York and Paris, for example, are very different from London. Although the institution of a mayoral system in London in 2000 introduces elements of the American system into London politics, it should be recognized that the Mayor of New York has greater powers and functional responsibilities than the Mayor of London. The Mayor of Paris has greater powers to intervene in local government matters – in the *arrondissements* – than the Mayor of London has in relation to the London boroughs, though the 2007 GLA Act in giving the Mayor positive planning powers brings his position somewhat closer to his Parisian equivalent.

Savitch also drew attention to the differences in relationships between governing bodies and interest groups in the three cities. mayoral government in London has perhaps over time become as autocratic and dismissive of external pressures as that of New York. Livingstone did manage to rally external parties in the manner suggested by Savitch in his analysis of Paris, though interest groups in London cannot as yet be manipulated by politicians in the way that Savitch implied was the case in Paris. It could be argued that in London the media performs that role, especially the *Evening Standard* in the 2008 mayoral election. The trajectory of Livingstone's political career depended as much on his presentation in the media as it did on his relationship with the central government or his performance on his manifesto objectives. The media gave far more attention to personal incidents than to the facts of London governance, but this is an inevitable consequence of the growth of celebrity culture and its invasion of political life – perhaps the most significant change in the external context since 1988.

In this sense London politics has grown closer to that of New York and the political scandals of the 1980s Koch era studied by Savitch than to the less scandal-ridden politics of Paris, but we should remember that the French are perhaps more relaxed about personal or even financial scandals than the British electorate. This may reflect media as well as culture. Perhaps the Parisian electorate have better ways of spending their time than immersing themselves in the tabloids; perhaps they are still a bit more sophisticated than Londoners. It may be that this contrast also reflects the different social mix in Paris, where the majority of working-class households are resident outside the Paris boundary. The Paris Mayor can have a Zone 1 plan, as he is not responsible for governing the outer zone, and this is a fundamental difference between the two cities. Livingstone lost the 2008 election partly because of the revolt of the Tory suburbs. Had his remit been limited to Inner London, the old London County Council boundary before 1964, which in many ways parallels the Paris boundary, the 2008 election result would perhaps have been very different.

As pointed out by Savitch, the public sector/private sector balance was different in the three cities. Savitch considered that the tradition of public sector-led municipal governance was stronger in London but he rightly pointed out how the Conservative government of Margaret Thatcher was in the process of changing the public/private sector balance. Twenty years later the position is unrecognizable. The 150-year-old British tradition of strong democratically accountable municipal government is largely destroyed. The majority of London boroughs have either sold off or transferred the management of their housing stock to independent or semi-independent agencies. NHS trusts operate on a commercial basis and have little relationship with local authorities. Schools operate largely independently of the boroughs as education authorities and central government support for individual schools is driven primarily by the degree of their independence from councils. Increasingly, basic council services are contracted out, with senior council officers being more contract managers than the deliverers of services. Councils are now enablers of the private sector. Their role is to establish a framework in which the private sector can make sufficient profit from providing services to ensure continued investment from their shareholders. The public/private sector balance appears to have shifted in favour of the private sector far beyond the position in Paris and New York. Paris and New York still have strong publicly accountable forms of regional and local government. London does not. This state of affairs is often a surprise to international visitors who have been interested in learning from London. A recent group of Nigerian regional and local government officials cannot have been the first to question why British governments had handed over local government to the private sector.

So the main lesson from London's experience for Paris and New York and other major cities is that regional and local governments needs to retain control over both investment and service provision if it is to succeed. The public sector can make use of the private sector, but it must set the terms on which the private sector operates. Similarly a regional strategic authority cannot rely entirely on the private sector for implementation of its policies. Planning does not go beyond plan making if the planning authority has no power to implement. It is of limited use for the Mayor to direct a borough to implement a strategic policy if the borough has no resources or power of implementation. A strategic plan, even one containing detailed targets and policies, such as the London Plan, still relies on the private sector to implement it and, as the analysis in this book has shown, the implementation will be on the private sector's own terms.

London's experience is that, without resources and direction, you do not get the quality of outputs you require. The Mayor of London, by pushing the compact city case and creating a framework for intensification of development, and by not stopping developments which did not conform with his sustainable development criteria, has enabled house builders to benefit at the expensive of his qualitative objectives. This must be a lesson for cities such as Paris which are considering more intensive development. The lesson from London is clear: hyperdense developments and high-rise housing do not increase the quantum of housing output affordable by and appropriate for lower-income family households. This type of housing is suitable for some households but to impose it on all households is a serious error which can only have serious negative social policy repercussions.

Another lesson from London's experience is the importance of providing transport and social infrastructure to meet the needs of a growing population. London's record of investment in the basic physical and social infrastructure over the last twenty years is poor. Services have not kept up with population growth and London's transport infrastructure is seriously overstretched. Although the Mayor and Transport for London have made significant improvements to the bus system, partly funded by the successful congestion charge, the underground system and the commuter overground network system are in a poor state of repair, with maintenance and provision of new networks overdependent on private finance. This is not helped by the privatization of basic physical and social infrastructure services, from the railway franchise and the underground maintenance contracts to the energy providers and the water and sewerage companies. It is self-evident that the government has not adequately planned for physical and social infrastructure in the Thames Gateway and other growth areas, where development will be mainly on isolated brownfield sites where no such infrastructure exists. Even less provision has been made for the rest of London, where 50 per cent of residential growth is to take place. Similarly the Mayor has no power even to bring infrastructure providers together, let alone to make them do anything. It is an absurd situation, in which government agencies such as the Environment Agency or regulated utilities such as Thames Water can object to development proposals which are necessary to meet government housing targets on the grounds that there is insufficient water supply or sewerage. This would not have happened 150 years ago when, even before the founding of the London County Council, the Metropolitan Board of Works, a publicly accountable body, provided water, sewerage, bridges and roads.

So the lesson for other cities is not to follow London's example. As the recent report *Beyond Eco-Towns* (PRP 2008) so clearly demonstrates, many European countries such as Germany, Sweden, the Netherlands and Ireland, on which the report focuses, are far better at delivering sustainable communities than we are in the UK.

This also raises the issue of the relationship with the wider metropolitan region, a point focused on by Sir Peter Hall in his works and his representations at the original

London Plan Examination in Public. The British planning and governance system has never dealt adequately with this issue. It is interesting to contrast the position in New York, where regional planning since 1929 has operated on a tri-state basis (Johnson 1996, Yaro and Hiss 1996). The Paris governance framework is even more problematic than the London system: the Mayor has no control beyond the ancient City of Paris boundary; the Isle de France region, which surrounds Paris, is a separate planning authority. This is quite rightly being reviewed (Thibault 2000, Paris 2007). As commented above, there has been a lack of reality in the Mayor's compact city objective set out in the 2004 London Plan, which in effect ignored the relationship of London to the wider metropolitan region and the fact that a third of London's workforce commuted in from outside the London boundary. It was not surprising, however, that the Home County councils were suspicious of the Mayor taking over the commuter rail franchises on which so many of their residents depended. The fact that there is no statutory strategic planning body for the wider London metropolitan area is a significant deficiency. As recognized by the new Mayor, Boris Johnson, the fact that the Inter-Regional Forum as an informal body meets so irregularly and does so little when it does meet is also a matter of serious concern, and it is equally worrying that the central government does not itself recognize this deficiency. Symptomatic of this failing is that the last meeting of the Forum deferred consideration of physical and social infrastructure planning requirements, to focus on considering solely 'green infrastructure' – this in an area which is largely undeveloped countryside.

There is a final point which needs to be made. The globalization of the economy and the role London and other world cities play within it have implications for regional planning in a metropolitan region. Much has been written on economic and environmental impacts of globalization. These are not unimportant, though there is little that planning can actually do other than prepare for economic or environmental calamity. A more immediate impact is the extent of population churn that results from labour and other migration. This relates not just to long-term international immigration and out-migration, but to movement between London and other UK regions and the increasing mobility of individuals and households both within the working and non-working week and over longer periods. This includes commuting between regions but also people having more than one job at the same time, one within London and one elsewhere, and people with more than one residence at the same time, one within London and another elsewhere. The second section in Chapter 9 gave some information on the significance of what I called transience, as important for planning service provision and social and transport infrastructure and housing as the issue of international in-migration on which so much political and media attention is focused. This presents a challenge to planners in terms of the validity of survey and administrative data they use as evidence for policy; but it presents a much greater challenge for both governance and community engagement. How can governance be accountable to a population which is continuously on the move and generates demands and can contribute both spending and investment in a number of locations simultaneously, while having no single residential base or community identity? A large proportion of London's population are only transient residents with no real desire to be in a stable community. Ours is not the only government which is focusing planning on an ideal which may be derived from Ebenezer Howard or Robert Owen but does not relate to the lifestyles and aspirations of many if not most twenty-first-century Londoners. Planning in Britain is at risk of following the wrong agenda and chasing a mirage.

Spatial planning in boom and recession

This work has focused on the period 2000 to 2008, which coincided with a high level of economic growth in which London strengthened its role as one of the economic hubs of the world economy, becoming the pre-eminent centre of international finance. This period was one of sustained economic growth, enabled by an unregulated finance and property market. Livingstone's vision of London as a 'world city', which was the ideological basis of his strategic planning policy, was predicated on an assumption that London's population as a whole both now and in the future derived benefits from this boom period. The arrival of the market downturn in August 2008, deepening by April 2009 into the worst recession since 1929, has generated a debate over what went wrong and whose fault it was, but much more importantly has presented the necessity of reviewing the whole approach to markets, the private sector and governance, both to plan the way out of the recession and also to plan a way of ensuring that, if another recession arrives at some time in the future, both governments and the private sector are better equipped, in terms of both theoretical understanding and mechanisms for appropriate policy interventions (Bowie 2008c).

The government is seeking, through new legislation in the Local Democracy, Economic Development and Construction Bill, to integrate planning and economic strategies into new regional strategies. However, regional economic strategies for the English regions have to a certain extent been aspirational rather than deliverable and to hitch our spatial strategies to them would appear misguided as it is a further step in the process of making spatial planning dependent on the market. Moreover there is a risk that, with regional strategies being led by economic targets, there will be insufficient focus on the environmental and social justice objectives which were the other two components of the trinity of principles set out in the European Spatial Planning Perspective, which were incorporated into the 2004 Planning and

Compulsory Purchase Act as well as into the London Plan vision.

In this context it should be noted that the proposed new arrangements will not apply to London, where the Spatial Development Strategy will continue to be the overarching statutory plan. Not only will London be the first region to test the concept of regional spatial planning, it will be the only region in England in which the principle of spatial planning is continued beyond 2010.

However, with the change in the external economic context, London, like other regions, does need a Plan B. Plan B is not about constraining population and employment growth. London is facing a combination of economic decline and continued population growth, although potentially somewhat less rapid than previously projected. There is little evidence that unemployed people have fewer children or die earlier in a recession, and economic slowdown will not necessarily significantly reduce in-migration or increase out-migration as this downturn is a worldwide phenomenon. Many people will still want to come to Britain because they would still have more opportunities in Britain than in their country of origin. Climate change will generate its own refugees, and it is not Britain which is going to be subject to desertification.

If we could not rely on the market to deliver what London needed in the boom period, we certainly cannot depend on the market to achieve public policy objectives in the recession. It is not surprising that John Maynard Keynes, confined to the historical dustbin by twenty years of neo-liberalism, is now back on the reading lists of politicians and civil servants. This is relevant to planning, as planning and planners can no longer achieve affordable housing, health, schools and transport by piggybacking these requirements onto private development. There is increasing evidence that the private sector now needs public subsidy just to maintain activity and avoid bankruptcy. Planners need to understand development economics and the preconditions of effective plan implementation.

It is essential that the public sector take the lead because, if it does not, there will be little or no new development of any kind until the market revives, and when it does there is a risk that market-led development will repeat the mistakes of the last ten years unless the parameters under which planning operates are radically changed. With the private sector dependent on public sector support, now is the time for the public sector to impose the terms which benefit the public as a whole. This is the public sector's duty to the electorate to whom we are accountable, whether professionals or politicians. No politician, irrespective of political affiliation, or public sector official is elected or appointed to promote private profit, if this is at the expense of the interests of the electorate as a whole.

This is relevant to planning and governance. Regional and local government needs to be empowered and resourced to take the lead as in the northern European model. Planning powers now need to be conjoined with public investment and public sector control. Public investment without public sector equity is an inefficient use of public resources. Government agencies should use the opportunity to take the lead on joint ventures: to buy land and agree that a developer or developers build homes and other social infrastructure as contractors. Where land is not publicly owned, planning consent for development would be conditional on the planning authority taking equity, with any value appreciation in the short, medium or longer term paid back to the public sector.

Planning authorities should grant consent only for projects which are of public benefit. If a developer in the current market applies for consent for a high-rise development of small flats in the hope that the market will revive and he will still make a profit, the planning authority should turn the application down on the basis that it does not meet planning policy guidance which is based on an assessment of long-term housing requirements. The developer will have no choice other than to sell on the land at a discount or come forward with a more appropriate development proposal. Moreover the public sector needs to provide up-front funding for those programmes the market sector can no longer support: affordable housing, transport and social infrastructure.

Planning and planners have a critical role both in maintaining a housing and regeneration programme during the recession and in setting new rules for the longer term. This is a challenge to both politicians and planners at all levels of government. The new Mayor of London has to recognize the necessity of taking a much tougher approach to the market and the protection of the long-term interests of Londoners than his predecessor ever did. There is experience from European cities where municipal leaders have been more interventionist. British regional and municipal leaders can also draw on the British tradition of intervention from the Victorian period and from the periods after both the First and Second World Wars, as well as the response to the 1930s recession. In terms of planning theory, this could be called a 'pragmatic' approach to planning – the use of planning tools which are appropriate to the context.

Appendix
Additional tables

Table A.1 Borough affordable housing targets 2002 and 2007

Borough	December 2002	December 2007
Camden	50%	50%
Islington	25%	50%
Kensington and Chelsea	33%	LP*
Lambeth	35–50%	40% (50% on sites with grant)
Southwark	25%	50%
Wandsworth	No policy	LP* 33% proposed
Westminster	30%	50% (30% within Central Activities Zone)
City of London	None	LP*
Barking and Dagenham	25%	LP*
Bexley	25%	35%
Greenwich	35%	35% (50% on large sites)
Hackney	25%	50%
Havering	None	50%
Lewisham	30%	35%
Newham	25%	LP*
Redbridge	25%	50%
Tower Hamlets	25–33%	LP*
Brent	30–50%	50%
Ealing	50%	50%

	65% proposed	Reduction to 50% proposed
Hammersmith and Fulham		
Harrow	30%	50%
Hillingdon	25%	LP*
Hounslow	50%	50%
Barnet	30%	50%
Enfield	25%	LP*
Haringey	30%	50%
Waltham Forest	40%	50%
Bromley	20%	25% (site-specific 35%)
Croydon	40%	50%
Kingston upon Thames	50%	50% starting point
Merton	30%	LP*
Richmond upon Thames	40%	40%
Sutton	25%	LP*
Boroughs consistent with London Plan target	5 of 33	27 of 33

Source: GLA London Plan Annual Monitoring Reports with adaptations.

LP*   Where Unitary Development Policy target not saved and consequently London Plan policy target of 50% applies by default. In the case of Redbridge and Havering, the Secretary of State directed that core strategies be amended to 50% target.

Table A.2 Borough completions 2003/4 to 2007/8 homes and percentage by tenure

Borough	Social rent	Intermediate	Affordable	Total	Social rent (%)	Intermediate (%)	Affordable (%)
Camden	535	215	750	2221	24	10	34
Islington	1417	1237	2654	6216	23	20	43
Kensington and Chelsea	301	35	336	1386	22	3	25
Lambeth	932	600	1532	5795	16	10	26
Southwark	1650	1435	3085	7195	23	20	43
Wandsworth	213	805	1018	6433	3	13	16
Westminster	1007	188	1195	5146	20	4	23
City of London	48	55	103	533	9	10	19
Barking and Dagenham	709	460	1169	2726	26	17	43
Bexley	266	154	420	1701	16	9	25
Greenwich	930	793	1723	7950	12	10	22
Hackney	1352	1187	2539	5460	25	22	47
Havering	365	189	554	2571	14	7	22
Lewisham	915	312	1227	3291	28	10	37
Newham	1245	862	2107	5077	25	17	42
Redbridge	426	478	904	3268	13	15	28

Tower Hamlets	2868	996	3864	12036	24	8	32
Brent	1400	392	1792	4003	35	10	45
Ealing	1041	809	1850	4366	24	19	42
Hammersmith and Fulham	877	602	1479	2141	41	28	69
Harrow	285	441	726	2631	11	17	28
Hillingdon	384	151	535	1600	24	9	33
Hounslow	897	1306	2203	5074	18	26	43
Barnet	620	224	844	4197	15	5	20
Enfield	917	335	1252	3114	29	11	40
Haringey	974	585	1559	3251	30	18	48
Waltham Forest	748	319	1067	2554	29	12	42
Bromley	650	300	950	3596	18	8	26
Croydon	1497	591	2088	4713	32	13	44
Kingston upon Thames	286	99	385	2004	14	5	19
Merton	414	203	617	2168	19	9	28
Richmond upon Thames	418	173	591	2373	18	7	25
Sutton	754	267	1021	2530	30	13	44

Source: GLA London Plan Annual Monitoring Reports 1–5.

Table A.3 Borough housing targets 2004 and 2007

Borough	2004 target	2007 target
Camden	850	595
Islington	900	1160
Kensington and Chelsea	540	350
Lambeth	1450	1100
Southwark	1480	1630
Wandsworth	820	745
Westminster	970	705
City of London	110	90
Barking and Dagenham	510	1190
Bexley	280	345
Greenwich	800	2010
Hackney	720	1085
Havering	350	535
Lewisham	870	975
Newham	890	3510
Redbridge	540	905
Tower Hamlets	2070	3150

	2004 target	2007 target
Brent	680	1120
Ealing	650	915
Hammersmith and Fulham	400	450
Harrow	330	400
Hillingdon	440	365
Hounslow	470	445
Barnet	890	2055
Enfield	660	395
Haringey	970	680
Waltham Forest	480	665
Bromley	570	485
Croydon	850	1100
Kingston upon Thames	340	385
Merton	430	370
Richmond upon Thames	270	270
Sutton	345	370

Sources: GLA (2004a, 2006g).

2004 targets refers to target set by 2004 London Plan. 2007 target refers to new target set by 2007 Alterations to London Plan, which applied from 2007/8.

Table A.4 Density of residential development by borough (dwellings per hectare)

Borough	Sub-region	Inner/Outer London	1999–2002 completions	2007/8 permissions	% change
Camden	Central	Inner	92	100	+9
Islington	Central	Inner	99	293	+195
Kensington and Chelsea	Central	Inner	93	164	+76
Lambeth	Central	Inner	82	216	+163
Southwark	Central	Inner	88	273	+210
Wandsworth	Central	Inner	65	151	+132
Westminster	Central	Inner	116	242	+108
City of London	East	Inner	245	1263	+415
Barking and Dagenham	East	Outer	43	146	+239
Bexley	East	Outer	30	50	+66
Greenwich	East	Inner	43	236	+448
Hackney	East	Inner	88	240	+173
Havering	East	Outer	39	42	+8
Lewisham	East	Inner	55	173	+214
Newham	East	Outer	64	349	+445

Borough	Region				
Redbridge	East	Outer	30	114	+280
Tower Hamlets	East	Inner	113	446	+294
Brent	West	Outer	47	150	+219
Ealing	West	Outer	68	113	+66
Hammersmith and Fulham	West	Inner	68	227	+233
Harrow	West	Outer	30	90	+200
Hillingdon	West	Outer	37	69	+86
Hounslow	West	Outer	53	95	+79
Barnet	North	Outer	43	60	+40
Enfield	North	Outer	41	82	+100
Haringey	North	Outer	72	137	+90
Waltham Forest	North	Outer	38	117	+208
Bromley	South	Outer	28	50	+79
Croydon	South	Outer	41	109	+166
Kingston upon Thames	South	Outer	39	60	+54
Merton	South	Outer	51	94	+84
Richmond upon Thames	South	Outer	48	60	+25
Sutton	South	Outer	43	104	+142

Source: GLA London Plan Annual Monitoring Reports (completions data from DCLG Live Tables: Housebuilding http://www.communities.gov.uk/housing/housingresearch/housing statistics/housingstatisticsby/housebuilding/livetables/). Boroughs are grouped by 2004 London Plan sub-regions.

Table A.5 Land cost per home and land cost per hectare

Borough	Sub-region	Inner/Outer London	£ per home	£m per hectare
Camden	Central	Inner	209,000	54.1
Islington	Central	Inner	69,000	30.3
Kensington and Chelsea	Central	Inner	204,000	82.2
Lambeth	Central	Inner	46,000	21.0
Southwark	Central	Inner	54,000	19.8
Wandsworth	Central	Inner	155,000	30.6
Westminster	Central	Inner	963,000	348.7
City of London	East	Inner	270,000	161.1
Barking and Dagenham	East	Outer	37,000	4.8
Bexley	East	Outer	29,000	2.8
Greenwich	East	Inner	25,000	3.5
Hackney	East	Inner	82,000	27.3
Havering	East	Outer	111,000	14.4
Lewisham	East	Inner	43,000	12.5
Newham	East	Outer	37,000	14.6
Redbridge	East	Outer	43,000	9.3
Tower Hamlets	East	Inner	54,000	24.6

Brent	West	Outer	53,000	15.8
Ealing	West	Outer	77,000	21.9
Hammersmith and Fulham	West	Inner	253,000	58.7
Harrow	West	Outer	60,000	10.0
Hillingdon	West	Outer	60,000	5.5
Hounslow	West	Outer	37,000	7.1
Barnet	North	Outer	52,000	11.5
Enfield	North	Outer	75,000	6.1
Haringey	North	Outer	37,000	7.5
Waltham Forest	North	Outer	49,000	9.5
Bromley	South	Outer	134,000	12.0
Croydon	South	Outer	53,000	10.8
Kingston upon Thames	South	Outer	51,000	14.5
Merton	South	Outer	84,000	12.1
Richmond upon Thames	South	Outer	91,000	22.2
Sutton	South	Outer	36,000	2.2

Source: London Development Research dataset.

It should be noted that this dataset includes conversions and mixed-use schemes. Consequently the land cost will include the cost of acquiring any existing buildings on a site.

Table A.6 Borough housing stock 2001 and 2008

Borough	SR 2001	SR 2008	Private 2001	Private 2008	Total 2001	Total 2008	SR 2001 (%)	SR 2008 (%)
Camden	35,588	35,107	55,180	63,900	90,768	99,007	39.2	35.5
Islington	42,647	38,647	42,219	54,790	84,866	93,437	50.3	41.4
Kensington and Chelsea	18,927	19,084	68,630	67,032	87,557	86,116	21.6	22.2
Lambeth	52,587	47,702	67,960	80,967	120,547	128,669	43.6	37.1
Southwark	62,094	55,856	51,870	66,611	113,964	122,467	54.5	45.6
Wandsworth	28,069	27,252	94,482	103,281	122,551	130,533	22.9	20.9
Westminster	26,778	15,435	81,463	92,962	108,241	118,716	24.7	21.7
Barking and Dagenham	25,024	22,537	42,132	47,491	67,156	70,028	37.3	32.2
Bexley	13,642	12,633	78,812	81,645	92,454	94,278	14.8	13.4
City	927	796	3,932	5,043	4,859	5,839	19.1	13.6
Greenwich	38,135	35,453	54,684	65,583	92,819	101,036	41.4	35.1
Hackney	46,992	46,053	39,000	50,543	85,992	96,596	54.6	47.7
Havering	14,016	13,593	80,658	85,139	94,674	98,732	14.8	13.8
Lewisham	39,927	36,150	74,778	78,789	114,705	114,939	34.8	31.5
Newham	33,701	33,622	59,120	66.724	92,821	100,346	36.3	33.5
Redbridge	8,377	10,142	85,522	88,293	93,899	98,432	8.9	10.3
Tower Hamlets	44,023	40,640	38,828	58,159	82,851	98,799	53.1	41.1
Brent	25,559	25,739	78,493	81,763	104,052	107,502	24.6	23.9

Ealing	22,637	25,395	96,770	100,050	119,407	125,445	19.0	20.2
Hammersmith and Fulham	25,638	28,963	51,363	53,480	77,001	80,326	33.3	33.4
Harrow	8,538	8,976	72,846	75,638	81,384	84,614	10.5	10.6
Hillingdon	18,792	18,364	80,830	84,136	99,622	102,500	18.9	17.9
Hounslow	21,156	20,624	65,694	72,384	86,850	92,988	24.4	22.2
Barnet	19,047	18,277	116,318	117,341	135,365	135,618	14.1	13.5
Enfield	19,482	19,027	94,619	100,352	114,101	119,379	17.1	15.9
Haringey	27,427	28,062	66,711	72,382	94,138	100,444	29.1	27.9
Waltham Forest	22,041	21,189	71,089	75,393	93,130	96,582	23.7	21.9
Bromley	17,507	18,435	113,117	115,013	130,624	133,448	13.4	13.8
Croydon	23,543	24,071	113,314	117,797	136,857	141,868	17.2	17.0
Kingston upon Thames	7,541	7,264	53,697	56,417	61,238	63,681	12.3	11.4
Merton	11,811	10,969	64,812	68,326	76,623	79,295	15.4	13.8
Richmond upon Thames	9,017	9,635	68,415	70,959	77,432	80,594	11.6	12.0
Sutton	12,706	12,469	63,344	66,311	76,050	78,780	16.7	15.8
London	823,896	796,340	2,290,702	2,484,694	3,114,598	3,281,034	26.5	24.3

Source: DCLG Housing Strategy Statistical Annex.

SR: Social rent = local authority + housing association homes.

Bibliography

Note: All publications by the Mayor of London are listed under 'GLA'. Publications by the London Assembly are listed separately as 'London Assembly'. UK government publications are listed under the relevant department, some of which went through a number of name changes: Ministry of Housing and Local Government (MHLG); Department of Environment (DoE); Department of Environment, Transport and Regions (DETR); Department of Transport, Local Government and Regions (DTLR); Office of Deputy Prime Minister (ODPM); and Department of Communities and Local Government (DCLG). Other reports were published by the Treasury (HMT), the Government Office for London (GOL), the Planning Inspectorate and the National Planning and Housing Advisory Unit (NHPAU).

Abercrombie, P. (1944) *Greater London Plan*, London: HMSO.
Adams, T. (1927) *Planning the New York Region New York*. Reprinted by University of Michigan (no date).
Allmendinger, P. (2001) *Planning in Postmodern Times*, London: Routledge.
Allmendinger, P. (2002) *Planning Theory*, Basingstoke: Palgrave.
Allmendinger, P. and Thomas, H. (1998) *Urban Planning and the British New Right*, London: Routledge.
Andrusz, G., Harloe, M. and Szelenyi, I. (eds) (1996) *Cities after Socialism*, Oxford: Blackwell.
ALG (1999) *London Housing Partnership: Homelessness in London – A Way Out*, London: Association of London Government/London Housing Unit.
ALG (2001a) *A Housing Strategy for London*, London: Association of London Government.
ALG (2001b) *London Homelessness Strategy*, London: Association of London Government.
ALG (2006) *Note on Planning Obligations Circulated to Planning and Housing Working Group*. London: Association of London Government, August.
ATLAS (2007) *Cascades: Improving Certainty in the Delivery of Affordable Housing for Large Site Development*, London: Advisory Team for Large Applications, English Partnerships and the Housing Corporation. http://www.atlasplanning.com/lib/liDownload/323/S106_Cascades_Report.pdf?CFID=681994&CFTOKEN=72195356.
Baker, T. M. M. (2000) *London: Rebuilding the City after the Great Fire*, London: Phillimore.

Balchin, N., Sykora, L. and Bull, G. (1999) *Regional Policy and Planning in Europe*, London: Routledge.

Barber, S. (2007) *The Geo-Politics of the City*, London: Forum Press.

Barker, K. (2003) *Securing Our Future Housing Needs*. Review of Housing Supply. Interim Report. London: HM Treasury, December.

Barker, K. (2004) *Delivering Stability: Securing Our Future Housing Needs*. Review of Housing Supply. Final Report. London: HM Treasury, March.

Barker, K. (2006a) *Barker Review of Land Use Planning: Final Report*, London: HM Treasury, December.

Barker, K. (2006b) *Barker Review of Land Use Planning: Interim Report*, London: HM Treasury, July.

BBC (2005) News report. http://news.bbc.co.uk/1/hi/in_depth/uk/2005/london_explosions/default.stm.

Bell, C. and Bell, R. (1972) *City Fathers: The Early History of Town Planning in Britain*, London: Pelican.

BERR (2008) *Sub National Review*, London: Department for Business Enterprise and Regulatory Reform, March.

Booth, C. (1886–1903) *Life and Labour of the People in London*, London: Macmillan.

Bowie, D. (2008a) 'Density, Housing Mix and Space Standards of New Housing Development in London'. Paper presented to RIBA Research Symposium. http://www.architecture.com/Files/RIBAProfessionalServices/ResearchAndDevelopment/Symposium/2008/DuncanBowie.pdf.

Bowie, D. (2008b) *Housing and the Credit Crunch: Government and Property Market Failure*, London: Compass, August. http://clients.squareeye.com/uploads/compass/documents/CTP35CreditCruch.pdf.

Bowie, D. (2008c) 'Quantity and Quality: Who Are We Building for?', *Planning in London* 65: 20–3.

Bowie, D. (2008d) 'Housing Delivery and Sustainable Communities', *Planning in London* 66: 20–1.

Bowie, D. (2008e) 'Failure of Promise? Planning for Housing under the Mayor of London 2000–2008'. Paper presented to European Network for Housing Research conference, Dublin, July.

Bowie, D. (2008f) 'Bo-Jo: A New Dawn for Planning in London', in *London Calling*, London: RTPI London, August.

Bowie, D. (2009a) 'Housing and the Credit Crunch in London'. Paper for Highbury Group on Housing and the Credit Crunch.

Bowie, D. (2009b) 'The New Mayor's Housing Strategy', *Planning in London*, 68: 7.

Broudeheux, A. (2008) *The Making and Selling of Post-Mao Beijing*, London: Routledge.

Brownhill, S. (1990) *Developing London's Docklands: Another Great Planning Disaster?*, London: Paul Chapman.

Buck, N., Hall, P., Gordon, I. Harloe, M. and Kleinman, M. (2002) *Working Capital: Life and Labour in Contemporary London*, London: Routledge.

Buck, N., Turok, I. and Gordon, I. (eds). (2005) *Changing Cities: Rethinking Competitiveess, Cohesion and Governance*, Basingstoke: Palgrave.

Building for Life (2007) *Building for Life Standards*, revised February. http://www. buildingforlife.org/.

Burdett, R. with Sudjic, D. (2008) *The Endless City*, London: Phaidon.

Burke, G. (1996) *Greenheart Metropolis: Planning the Western Netherlands*, London: Macmillan.

Butler, T. (2003) *London Calling: The Middle Classes and the Remaking of Inner London*, London: Berg.

Butler, T. and Rustin, M. (1996) *Rising in the East: The Regeneration of East London*, London: Lawrence and Wishart.

van der Cammen, H. (1988) *Four Metropolises in Western Europe*, Assen: Van Gorcom.

Carter, E. (1972) *The Future of London*, London: Penguin.

Carter, E. J. and Goldfinger, E. (1945) *The County of London Plan Explained*, London: Penguin.

Carvel, J. (1984) *Citizen Ken*, London: Chatto & Windus.

CEC (1999) *European Spatial Development Perspective*, Luxembourg: Commission of the European Communities.

Cherry, G. (1980) 'The Place of Neville Chamberlain in British Town Planning', in Cherry, G. (ed.), *Shaping an Urban World*, London: Mansell.

City of London Corporation (1944) *Report of Preliminary Draft Proposals for Post War Reconstruction in the City of London*, London: City of London Corporation.

Clark, P. (ed.) (2006) *The European City and Green Space*, London: Ashgate.

Cohen, P. and Rustin, M. (eds) (2008) *London's Turning: The Making of the Thames Gateway*, London: Ashgate.

Collins, M. (1994) 'Land Use Planning since 1947', in Simmie, J. (ed.), *Planning in London*, London: UCL Press.

Colton, T. (1995) *Moscow: Governing the Socialist Metropolis*, Cambridge, MA: The Belknap Press of Harvard University Press.

Cooper, M. (2003) '*A More Beautiful City': Robert Hooke and the Rebuilding of London after the Great Fire*, London: Sutton.

Coopers and Lybrand (1994) *London: World City*, London: LPAC.

Coppock, J. T. and Prince, H. C. (1964) *Greater London*, London: Faber.

CPRE (2007) *Untapped Potential*, London: CPRE.

CPRE London (2006) *Compact Sustainable Communities*, London: CPRE.

CPRE London (2008) *Family Housing: The Power of Concentration*, London: CPRE.

D'Arcy, M. and Maclean, R. (2000) *Nightmare: The Race to Become London's Mayor*, London: Politicos.

Danielson, M. and Doig, G. (1982) *New York: The Politics of Urban Regional Development*, Berkeley: University of California Press.

Davidoff, P. (1965) 'Advocacy and Pluralism in Planning', *AIP Journal*, 31: 331–8.

Davis, J. (1988) *Reforming London: The London Government Problem 1855–1900*, Oxford: Clarendon Press.

Davoudi, S. and Strange, I. (2009) *Conceptions of Space and Place in Strategic Planning*, London: Routledge.

DCLG (2006a) *Planning Policy Statement 3: Housing*, London: DCLG, November.

DCLG (2006b) *Housing and Planning Delivery Grant: Consultation Paper*, London: DCLG, July.

DCLG (2006c) *Thames Gateway Interim Plan*, London: DCLG, November.

DCLG (2006d) *Changes to Planning Obligations: A Planning Gain Supplement Consultation*, London: DCLG, December.

DCLG (2006e) *Code for Sustainable Homes*, London: DCLG, December.

DCLG (2007a) *Thames Gateway Delivery Plan*, London: DCLG, November.

DCLG (2007b) *Strategic Housing Land Availability Assessment: Practice Guidance*, London: DCLG, July.

DCLG (2007c) *Strategic Housing Market Assessment: Practice Guidance*, London: DCLG, August.

DCLG (2008a) *Local Spatial Planning: Planning Policy Statement 12*, London: DCLG, June.

DCLG (2008b) *The Killian Pretty Review: Planning Applications: A Fairer and More Responsive System*, London: DCLG, November.

DCLG (2008c) *The Community Infrastructure Levy*, London: DCLG, August.

DETR (1999) *Draft Regional Planning Guidance for the South East RPG9*, London: DETR.

DETR (2000) *Planning Policy Guidance 3: Housing*, London: DETR.

DETR (2001) *Planning Guidance for the South East: Regional Planning Guidance 9 March 2001*, London: DETR.

DfES (2005) *London Challenge: Secondary Schools Places Planning in London*, London: Department for Education and Schools, March.

DoE (1989) *Strategic Guidance for London: Regional Planning Guidance 3*, London: DoE.

DoE (1995) *Thames Gateway Planning Framework: Regional Planning Guidance 9A*, London: DoE.

DTLR (2001) *Planning: Delivering a Fundamental Change*, London: DTLR, December.

Dijst, M. (2002) *Governing Cities on the Move*, London: Ashgate.

Edwards, G. and Isaby, J. (2008) *Boris v. Ken: How Boris Johnson Won London*, London: Politicos.

Edwards, M. (2004) 'London', in INURA (ed.), *INURA: The Contested Metropolis: Six Cities at the Beginning of the 21st Century: Berlin, Brussel, Firenze, London, Toronto, Zurich*, Basel: Birkhauser.

Edwards, M. (2008) 'Blue Sky over Bluewater', in Cohen, P. and Rustin, M. (eds), *London's Turning: The Making of the Thames Gateway*, London: Ashgate.

Edwards, M. (2009) 'King's Cross: Renaissance for Whom?', in Punter, J. (ed.), *Urban Design and the British Urban Renaissance*, London: Routledge.

Elkin, S. (1974) *Politics and Land Use Planning: The London Experience*, Cambridge: Cambridge University Press.

Evenson, N. (1979) *Paris: A Century of Change 1878–1978*, New Haven: Yale University Press.

Eversley, D. (1973) *The Planner in Society*, London: Faber.

Fainstein, S., Gordon, I. and Harloe, M. (1992) *Divided Cities: New York and London in the Contemporary World*, Oxford: Blackwell.

Faludi, A. (1973) *Planning Theory*, Oxford: Blackwell.

Festenstein, M. (1997) *Pragmatism and Political Theory*, Cambridge: Polity Press.

Foley, D. (1963) *Controlling London's Growth: Planning the Great Wen 1940–1946*, Berkeley: University of California.

Foley, D. (1972) *Governing the London Region: Reorganization and Planning in the 1960's*, Berkeley: University of California.

Forrester, A., Lansley, S., Pauley, R. (1985) *Beyond Our Ken: A Guide to the Battle for London*, London: Fourth Estate.

Gilbert, A. (2002) *The New Jerusalem: Rebuilding London: The Great Fire, Christopher Wren and the Royal Society*, London: Bantam.

GLA (2000a) *London's Housing Capacity*, London: GLA, September.

GLA (2000b) *Homes for a World City*. Report of the Mayor's Housing Commission, London: GLA, November.

GLA (2001a) *Towards the London Plan*, London: GLA, May.

GLA (2001b) *Affordable Housing in London*. Spatial Development Strategy technical report 1, London: GLA.

GLA (2002a) *Affordable Housing in London: Commercial Impact Assessment of Three Dragons/Nottingham Trent University Report*, London: GLA, August

GLA (2002b) *Affordable Housing Update: Response by Three Dragons and Nottingham Trent University*. SDS technical report, 22 September.

GLA (2002c) *Future Housing Provision: Speeding Up Delivery*, London: GLA, February.

GLA (2002d) *Planning Obligations in London*, London: GLA, June.

GLA (2002e) *Draft London Plan*, London: GLA, June.

GLA (2002f) *City of Villages: Promoting a Sustainable Future for London's Suburbs*. URBED SDS technical report, 11 August.

GLA (2002g) *Investigating the Potential of Large Mixed Use Housing Developments*. Urban Initiatives SDS technical report, 18 August.

GLA (2002i) *Analysis of Responses to Consultation on Draft London Plan*, London: GLA.

GLA (2002j) *GLA Population and Household Forecasts 2001 to 2016*. SDS technical report, 5 May.

GLA (2003a) *GLA Population and Household Forecasts 2001–2016 based on first results from 2001 census*. SDS report, 23 January.

GLA (2003b) *Planning Obligations in London*. SDS technical report 7, June.

GLA (2003c) *Housing for a Compact City*. Mayor's Architecture and Urbanism Unit, June.

GLA (2003d) Published for independent Examination in Public panel *Report of Examination in Public panel*. July. http://www.london.gov.uk/mayor/strategies/sds/eip_report/panel_report_all.pdf.

GLA (2003e) *London Housing Capacity Methodology Study*. ERM, August.

GLA (2003f) *Thresholds for the Application of Affordable Housing Requirements*. Three Dragons and Roger Tym, March.

GLA (2003g) *Housing for a Compact City.* Mayor's Architecture and Urbanism Unit, June.

GLA (2003h) *Schedule of Matters and Sub-Matters for the Examination in Public.* Published for independent Examination in Public Panel.

GLA (2003i) *Industrial Provision: Draft Supplementary Planning Guidance,* London: GLA, September.

GLA (2004a) *London Plan,* London: GLA, February.

GLA (2004b) *Greater London Housing Requirements Study,* London: GLA, December.

GLA (2004c) *Mixed Use Development and Affordable Housing,* London: GLA, March.

GLA (2004d) *Green Light to Clean Power: The Mayor's Energy Strategy,* London: GLA, February.

GLA (2004e) *London Stansted Cambridge Corridor: Initial Assessment of Growth Potential in London,* London: GLA, October.

GLA (2004f) *London's Housing Submarkets.* GLA Economics, April.

GLA (2004g) *Office Policy Review,* London: GLA, August.

GLA (2004h) *'Sounder City' Ambient Noise Strategy,* London: GLA, March.

GLA (2004i) *Guide to Preparing Open Space Strategies,* London: GLA, March.

GLA (2004j) *Industrial and Warehouse Land,* London: GLA, August.

GLA (2004k) *Comparison Goods Floorspace Need in London,* London: GLA, October.

GLA (2004l) *Sustainability Appraisal of the London Plan,* London: GLA, ENTEC, April.

GLA (2005a) *Reviewing the London Plan: Statement of Intent from the Mayor,* London: GLA, December.

GLA (2005b) *Housing Supplementary Planning Guidance* incorporating *GLA/Housing Corporation Joint Statement on Social Housing Grant and s106 Agreements.* London: GLA, November.

GLA (2005c) *2004 London Housing Capacity Study.* London: GLA, July.

GLA (2005d) *Draft Alterations to the London Plan: Housing Provision Targets, Waste and Minerals,* London: GLA, October.

GLA (2005e) *Growing Together: London and the UK Economy.* GLA Economics, January.

GLA (2005f) *Safeguarded Wharves on the River Thames,* London: GLA, January.

GLA (2005g) *Convenience Goods Floorspace Need in London,* London: GLA, June.

GLA (2005h) *Launch of Climate Change Agency: Statement by Mayor of London,* London: GLA, June.

GLA (2006a) *General Conformity with the London Plan: Principles and Procedures,* London: GLA, July.

GLA (2006b) *Delivering Increased Housing Output,* London: GLA, April.

GLA (2006c) *Early Alterations: Housing Provision, Waste and Minerals.* GLA, December.

GLA (2006d) *Housing Space Standards.* HACT, August.

GLA (2006e) *Draft Further Alterations to the London Plan,* London: GLA, September.

GLA (2006f) *Sustainable Design and Construction Supplementary Planning Guidance.* May.

GLA (2006g) *Tomorrow's Suburbs: Tools for Making London More Sustainable,* London: GLA, June.

GLA (2006h) *London's Urban Heat Island,* London: GLA, October.

GLA (2006i) *Early Alterations: Housing Provision, Waste and Minerals.* GLA, December.

GLA (2006j) *Strategic Parks Project Report*, London: GLA, May.

GLA (2006k) *Hotel Demand Study*, London: GLA, June.

GLA (2006l) *Equality Assessment of Further Alterations to the London Plan*, London: GLA.

GLA (2006m) *Response to DDPM Consultation Paper on the Powers of the Mayor and the Assembly*, London: GLA, February.

GLA (2006n) *Sustainability Appraisal of Draft Alterations to the London Plan*. Land Use Consultants, London: GLA, December.

GLA (2006o) *Alterations to London Plan: Sustainability Statement*, London: GLA, December.

GLA (2006p) *Providing for Children and Young People's Play and Informal Recreation: Draft Supplementary Guidance*, London: GLA, October.

GLA (2006q) *London Plan Density Matrix Review*. London: GLA, June.

GLA (2007a) *Climate Change Action Plan*, London: GLA, July.

GLA (2007b) *Draft Mayor's Housing Strategy*, London: GLA, September.

GLA (2007c) *London Office Policy Review 2007*, London: GLA, May.

GLA (2007d) *London-wide Town Centre Health Checks 2006 Analysis*, London: GLA, January.

GLA (2007e) *Outer London: Issues for the London Plan*, London: GLA, May.

GLA (2007f) *Land for Transport Functions*, London: GLA, March.

GLA (2007g) *Waste Apportionment Update*, London: GLA, April.

GLA (2007h) *Demand and Supply of Land for Logistics in London*, London: GLA, April.

GLA (2007i) *Assessment of Boatyard Facilities on the River Thames*, London: GLA, April.

GLA (2007j) *London Wholesale Markets Review*, London: GLA, June.

GLA (2007k) *Industrial Land Release Benchmarks*, London: GLA, April.

GLA (2007l) *Planning for Equality and Diversity in London: Supplementary Planning Guidance*, London: GLA, October.

GLA (2007m) *Action Today to Protect Tomorrow: The Mayor's Climate Change Action Plan*, London: GLA, February.

GLA (2007n) *Managing the Night Time Economy: Best Practice Guide*, London: GLA, March.

GLA (2007o) *Evidence Base: Climate Change in the Further Alterations to the London Plan*. ARUP, April.

GLA (2007p) *Sustainability Appraisal of the Draft Further Alterations to the London Plan*. Forum for the Future and Ben Cave Associates. Revised April.

GLA (2007q) *North East and South East London Industrial Land Baseline*, London: GLA, April.

GLA (2007r) *Housing in London*, London: GLA, August.

GLA (2007s) *Further Alterations to London Plan Examination in Public: Panel Report*. London: GLA, September.

GLA (2008a) *Focus on London 2008*, London: GLA.

GLA (2008b) *Monitoring the Implementation of Lifetime Homes in London*. Savills, August.

GLA (2008c) *Providing for Children and Young Peoples Play and Informal Recreation: Supplementary Planning Guidance*, London: GLA, March.

GLA (2008d) *Planning for a Better London*, London: GLA, July.

GLA (2008e) 'Mayor Moves to Reform Delivery of Affordable Housing'. Letter to boroughs (Mayor of London, 23 October).

GLA (2008f) *Bidding Prospectus: Regional Housing Pot: Targeted Funding Streams 2008–2011*, London: GLA, March.

GLA (2008g) *GLA Demography Update 3: 2008*, London: GLA, April.

GLA (2008h) *GLA Demography Briefing 2008: 10 London Borough Migration*, London, GLA, March.

GLA(2008i) *Affordable Housing Development Control Toolkit: Model, Benchmarks and Guidance Notes 2008/9 version* (version 5), London: GLA, November.

GLA (2008j) *Places of Worship in London*, London: GLA, May.

GLA (2008k) *Planning for a Better London: Mayor's Statement on Responses to Consultation*. GLA, December.

GLA (2008l) *Review of Intermediate Housing in London*. Steve Wilcox and Peter Williams. Completed April 2007 but published August 2008.

GLA (2008m) *The London Plan (consolidated with alterations since 2004)*, London: GLA, February.

GLRPC (1929) *Greater London Regional Planning Committee First Report*. London, GLRPC.

GLRPC (1933) *Greater London Regional Planning Committee Second Report*, London: GLRPC.

GOL (1996) *Strategic Guidance for London Planning Authorities*. London: GOL, May.

GOL (2000) *Circular 1/2000 Strategic Planning in London*. London: GOL, June.

GOL (2002) *Delivering Solutions: London Housing Statement*. London: GOL.

GOL (2003a) *Homes and Communities in London*. London: GOL.

GOL (2003b) Letter from Keith Hill MP, Minister for London, to GOL. 2 December. http://www.gos.gov.uk/497417/docs/202207/203154.

GOL (2004) *Housing Delivery Plan*. London: GOL, June.

GOL (2005) *Capital Homes: London Housing Strategy 2005–2016*. London: GOL.

Gordon, I. (2003) 'Capital Needs, Capital Growth and Global City Rhetoric in Mayor Livingstone's London Plan'. Paper to Association of American Geographers Annual Meeting, New Orleans, March.

Gordon, I. (2006) 'Future Growth in the Outer London Economy'. Report for the North London Srategic Alliance and Partners, LSE, October.

Gowling, D. and Penny, L. (1988) 'London', in van der Cammen, H. (ed.), *Four Metropolises in Western Europe*, Assen: Van Gorcum.

Graham, D. and Hibbert, M. (1999) 'Greater London', in Roberts, P., Thomas, K. and Williams, G. (eds), *Metropolitan Planning in Britain*, London: Jessica Kingsley for Regional Studies Association.

Greater London Council (1969a) *Greater London Development Plan Statement*, London: GLC, December.

Greater London Council (1969b) *Greater London Development Plan Report of Studies*, London: GLC.

Greater London Council (1976) *Greater London Development Plan as Approved by the Secretary of State*, London: GLC, July.

Greater London Council (1981) *Planning Policies for London: Appraisal*, London: GLC.

Greater London Council (1983) *Draft Alterations to the Greater London Development Plan*, London: GLC, November.

Greater London Council (1984) *Greater London Development Plan. Proposed Alterations*, September.

Hall, P. (1966) *The World Cities*, New York: McGraw-Hill.

Hall, P. (1969) *London 2000*, London: Faber and Faber.

Hall, P. (1988) *Cities in Civilisation*, London: Weidenfeld.

Hall, P. (1989) *London 2001*, London: Unwin.

Hall, P. (2006) 'London: a Millennium Long Battle, a Millennial Truce?', in Tewdwr-Jones, M. and Allmendinger, P. (eds), *Territory, Identity and Spatial Planning*, London: Routledge.

Hall, P. (2007) *London Voices, London Live*, Bristol: Policy Press.

Hall, T. (1991) *Planning and Urban Growth in Nordic Countries*, London: Routledge.

Hall, T. (2008) *Stockholm: Making of a Metropolis*, London: Routledge.

Halliday, S. (1999) *The Great Stink of London: Sir Joseph Bazalgette and the Cleansing of the Victorian Metropolis*, Stroud: Sutton Publishing.

Hambleton, R. and Gross, J. (2007) *Governing Cities in a Global Era*, Basingstoke: Palgrave.

Hamnett, C. (2003) *Unequal City: London in the Global Arena*, London: Routledge.

Hart, D. (1976) *Strategic Planning in London*, Oxford: Pergamon.

Harvey, D. (1973) *Social Justice and the City*, London: Verso.

Harvey, D. (2006) *Paris: Capital of Modernity*, London: Routledge.

Haughton, G. and Allmendinger, P. (2007) 'Growth and Social Infrastructure in Spatial Planning', in *Town and Country Planning*, 77(11): 388–91.

Hays, F. (1965) *Community Leadership: The Regional Plan Association of New York*, New York: Columbia University Press.

Healey, P. (1997) *Collaborative Planning*, Basingstoke: Palgrave.

Healey, P. (2007) *Urban Complexity and Spatial Strategies*, London: Routledge.

Healey, P., McDougall, G. and Thomas, M. (1982) *Planning Theory: Prospects for the 1980's*, Oxford: Pergamon.

Healey, P., Khakka, A. Motte, A. and Needham, B. (1997) *Making Strategic Spatial Plans: Innovation in Europe*, London: Routledge.

Hebbert, M. (1998) *London: More by Fortune than Design*, London: Wiley.

Herrschel, T. and Newman, P. (2002) *Governance of Europe's City Regions: Planning, Policy and Politics*, London: Routledge.

Hillman, J. (ed.) (1971) *Planning for London*, London: Penguin.

Home, R. (1997) *Of Planting and Planning: The Making of British Colonial Cities*, London: Spon.

Horden, C. H. and Holford, W. G. (1947) *City of London: A Record of Destruction and Survival*, London: City of London Corporation.

Hosken, A. (2008) *Ken: The Ups and Downs of Ken Livingstone*, London: Arcadia.

House Builders Federation (2005) Response to consultation on draft Housing Supplementary Planning Guidance.

Housing Corporation (2006) *London Factsheet*, London: Housing Corporation, September.

Housing Corporation (2007a) *Housing Quality Indicators (HQIs)* (April 2007 version). http://www.housingcorp.gov.uk/upload/pdf/HQIFormv4_Apr_2007.pdf.

Housing Corporation (2007b) *Design and Quality Standards*, London: Housing Corporation, April.

Housing Corporation (2007c) *A Cost Review of the Code for Sustainable Homes.* Report for Housing Corporation and English Partnerships, London: Housing Corporation, February.

Housing Corporation (2007d) *Housing Corporation Outturn Statement: London.* http://www.housingcorp.gov.uk/upload/doc/London_Outturn_Statement_2006–07.doc.

Housing Corporation (2008) *London Investment Statement 2008–2011*, London: Housing Corporation, April.

Jardine, L. (2004) *On a Grander Scale: The Outstanding Life and Tumultuous Times of Sir Christopher Wren*, London: Perennial.

Johnson, B. (2008) *Housing Manifesto: Building a Better London*, London: BackBoris Campaign, April.

Johnson, D. (1996) *Planning the Great Metropolis*, London: Spon.

Kochan, B. (ed.) (2006) *London: Bigger and Better?*, London: London School of Economics.

Livingstone, K. (1987) *If Voting Ever Changed Anything They'd Abolish It*, London: HarperCollins.

Livingstone, K. (2008) *Why London Needs a 50% Affordable Housing Policy: A Housing Manifesto for 21st Century London.* London: Livingstone 4 London election campaign.

London Assembly (2001) *Key Issues for Key Workers*, London: London Assembly.

London Assembly (2002a) *Scrutiny of Towards the London Plan*, London: London Assembly, January.

London Assembly (2002b) *Behind Closed Doors: Scrutiny of the Mayor's Planning Decisions*, London: London Assembly, June.

London Assembly (2002c) *Behind the London Plan: The Response of the London Assembly to the Mayor's Draft London Plan*, London: London Assembly, November.

London Assembly (2003) *Access to the Thames*, London: London Assembly, August.

London Assembly (2004a) *Designs on London*, London: London Assembly, April.

London Assembly (2004b) *London in its Regional Setting*, London: London Assembly, January.

London Assembly (2006a) *Mayoral Decisions on Strategic Planning Applications*, London: London Assembly, January.

London Assembly (2006b) *Response to Mayor's Consultation on Draft Further Alterations to the London Plan*, London: London Assembly, July.

London Assembly (2006c) *The Blue Ribbon Network*, London: London Assembly, January.

London Assembly (2006d) *Heathrow Expansion*, London: London Assembly, October.

London Assembly (2006e) *Size Matters: The Need for More Family Homes in London*, London: London Assembly, June.

London Assembly (2007a) *Semi-Detached: Reconnecting London's Suburbs*, London: London Assembly, June.

London Assembly (2007b) *Unintended Outcomes? Housing Corporation Grant and Affordable Housing in London*, London: London Assembly, June.

London Assembly (2007c) *Accommodating Change: Listed Buildings Serving London*, June.

London Assembly (2008a) *Scrutiny of Draft Mayor's Housing Strategy*, London: London Assembly, November.

London Assembly (2008b) *Response to the Mayor's Housing Strategy Consultation*, January.

London Assembly (2008c) *Who Gains? The Operation of Section 106 Planning Agreements in London*, London: London Assembly, March.

London Assembly (2008d) *Crunchtime for London's Affordable Housing*, London: London Assembly, November.

London County Council (1943) *County of London Plan*, London: LCC.

London County Council (1951) *Administrative County of London Development Plan*, London: LCC.

London County Council (1960) *London Plan. Administrative County of London Development Plan. First Review. County Planning Report Volume 1*, London: LCC

London County Council. (1962) *Administrative County of London Development Plan Statement*, London: LCC.

London Development Agency (LDA) with GLA (2004) *Thames Gateway Delivery and Investment Framework*, London: LDA, April.

London Housing Federation and London Councils (2006) *Think Big. Delivering Family Homes for London*, London: LHF, November.

LPAC (1988a) *Policy Issues and Choices*, London: LPAC, January.

LPAC (1988b) *Strategic Planning Advice for London: Policies for the 1990's*, London: LPAC, October.

LPAC (1994a) *London's Housing Capacity*, London: LPAC.

LPAC (1994b) *Advice on Strategic Planning for London*, London: LPAC.

LPAC (1996) *Offices to Other Uses*, London: LPAC.

LPAC (1997) *Sustainable Residential Quality: New Approaches to Urban Living*, London: LPAC.

LPAC (1998a) *Possible Future Sources of Large Housing Sites in London*, London: LPAC.

LPAC (1998b) *Dwellings Over and In Shops*, London: LPAC.

LPAC (1998c) *Cash in Lieu*, London: LPAC.

LPAC (1998d) *One Person Households and London's Housing Requirements*, London: LPAC.

LPAC (2000a) *LPAC's Endowment to the Mayor of London and the Boroughs*, London: LPAC.

LPAC (2000b) *Sustainable Residential Quality: Exploring the Potential of Large Sites*, London: LPAC, January.

LPAC and ALG (1997) *Affordable Housing, Regeneration and Sustainability in London*, September.

London Pride Partnership (1998) *Affordable Homes in London*, London: London Pride Partnership.

London Sustainable Development Commission (LSDC) (2003) *London's Sustainable Development Framework*, London: LSDC.

London Sustainable Development Commission (2005) *Making Your Plans Sustainable. A London Guide*, London: LSDC.

Loudon, J. C. (1829) *Hints on Breathing Spaces for the Metropolis and for Country Towns and Villages on Fixed Principles*.

LTGDC (2008) *Planning Obligations Community Benefit Strategy*, London: London Thames Gateway Development Corporation, March.

Mcgeehan, P. (2007) 'In Dueling Financial Studies, Fuel for New York–London Rivalry', *New York Times*, 19 March.

Marsh, C. and Marsh, G. (2001) *Planning Gain 2001*, London: London Residential Research.

Marquand, D. (2004) *Decline of the Public: The Hollowing Out of Citizenship*, London: Wiley.

Massey, D. (2007) *World City*, Cambridge: Polity.

Mayerson, M. and Banfield, E. C. (1955) *Planning, Politics and the Public Interest: The Case of Public Housing in Chicago*, New York: Free Press.

Ministry of Housing and Local Government (1947) *Memorandum on London Regional Planning*, London: MHLG.

Ministry of Housing and Local Government (1964) *The South East Study 1961–1981*, London: MHLG.

Ministry of Housing and Local Government(1967) *A Strategy for the South East*, London: MHLG.

Monk, S., Crook, T., Currie, J., Jackson, A., Rowley, S., Smith, K. and Whitehead, C. (2000) *Planning Gain and Affordable Housing: Making it Count*, York: Joseph Rowntree Foundation.

Monk, S., Whitehead, C., Crook, T., Lister, D., Rowley, S. and Short, C. (2005a) *Land and Finance for Affordable Housing*, York: Joseph Rowntree Foundation.

Monk, S., Whitehead, C., Crook, T., Henneberry, J., Rowley, S., Short, C. and Lister, D. (2005b) *The Value for Money of Delivering Affordable Housing through s106*, London: ODPM.

Monk, S., Crook, T., Lovatt, R., Lister, D., Whitehead, C., Rowley, S. and Ni Luanigh, A. (2006) *Delivering Affordable Housing through s106: Output and Outcomes*, York: Joseph Rowntree Foundation.

Montgomery, J. and Thornley, A. (1990) *Radical Planning Initiatives*, Aldershot: Gower.

National Health Service Healthy Urban Development Unit (HUDU) (2007) *Social Infrastructure Framework*, London: HUDU.

National Housing and Planning Advisory Unit (NHPAU) (2007) *Affordability Matters*, London: DCLG, June.

National Housing and Planning Advisory Unit (2008) *Affordability Still Matters*, London: DCLG, July.

Neill, W. (2004) *Urban Planning and Cultural Identity*, London: Routledge.

Newman, P. (1995) 'London Pride', *Local Economy*, 10 (2): 117–23.

Newman, P. and Thornley, A. (1996) *Urban Planning in Europe*, London: Routledge.

Newman, P. and Thornley, A. (1997) 'Fragmentation and Centralisation in the Governance of London: Influencing the Urban Policy and Planning Agenda', *Urban Studies*, 34 (7): 967–88.

Newman, P. and Thornley, A. (2005) *Planning World Cities:. Globalisation and Urban Politics*, Basingstoke: Palgrave.

Nicholson, G. (1990) 'Future Prospects', in Montgomery, J. and Thornley, A. (eds), *Radical Planning Initiatives*, Aldershot: Gower.

Nicholson, G. (1992) 'The Rebirth of Community Planning in London', in Thornley, A. (ed.), *The Crisis in London*, London: Routledge.

ODPM (2002) *Sustainable Communities: Delivering through Planning*, London: ODPM, July.

ODPM (2003) *Creating Sustainable Communities: Making it Happen in the Thames Gateway*, London: ODPM.

ODPM (2004) *Regional Spatial Strategies.* Planning Policy Statement 11, London: ODPM.

ODPM (2005a) *Affordability Targets: Implications for Housing Supply*, London: ODPM, December.

ODPM (2005b) *Planning Obligations.* Circular 5/05, London: ODPM, July.

Office for National Statistics (ONS) (2007) *Report on Short Term Migration*, London: ONS, November.

Olsen, D. (1964) *Town Planning in London in the Eighteenth and Nineteenth Centuries*, New Haven: Yale University Press.

Ormerod, P. and Rosewell, B. (2007) 'Innovation, Diffusion and Agglomeration'. Paper to Brisbane Club meeting, June. http://www.paulormerod.com/pdf/innovationmay07. pdf.

Owen, D. (1982) *The Government of Victorian London 1855–1889: The Metropolitan Board of Works, the Vestries and the City Corporation*, Cambridge, MA: The Belknap Press of Harvard University Press.

Papayanis, N. (2004) *Planning Paris before Haussmann*, Baltimore, MD: Johns Hopkins University Press.

Paris (2007) *Paris Plan Local d'Urbanisme*, Paris: Mairie de Paris, August. http://www. paris.fr/portail/urbanisme/portal.lut?page_id=6576.

Pimlott, B. and Rao, N. (2002) *Governing London*, Oxford: Oxford University Press.

Pinkney, D. (1953) *Napoleon III and the Rebuilding of Paris*, Princeton, NJ: Princeton University Press.

Planning Inspectorate (2006) *Development Plans Examination: A Guide to the Process of Assessing the Soundness of Development Plan Documents*, London: Planning Inspectorate, January.

PRP (2008) *Beyond Eco-Towns: Applying the Lessons from Europe*, London: PRP, October.

Power, A. and Houghton, J. (2007) *Jigsaw Cities: Big Spaces, Small Spaces*, Bristol: Policy Press.

Rasmussen, S. E (1967) *London: The Unique City*, Cambridge, MA: MIT Press.

Reddaway, T. F. (1940) *The Rebuilding of London after the Great Fire*, London: Edward Arnold.

Rhodes, G. (1970) *The Government of London: The Struggle for Reform*, Toronto: University of Toronto Press.

RIBA Greater London (1943) *Greater London Towards a Masterplan*, London: RIBA.

Roberts, P., Thomas, K. and Williams, G. (1999) *Metropolitan Planning in Britain*, London: Jessica Kingsley for Regional Studies Association.

Rogers, R. and Fisher, M. (1992) *A New London*, London: Penguin.

Rogers, R. (1997) *Cities for a Small Planet*. Reith Lectures. London: Faber and Faber.

Rogers, R. (1999) *Towards an Urban Renaissance*. Report of the Urban Taskforce, London: Routledge.

Rogers, R. (2005) *Towards a Stronger Urban Renaissance*, London: Routledge.

Rogers, R. and Power, A. (2000) *Cities for a Small Country*, London: Faber and Faber.

Rowe, P. and Sarkis, H. (1998) *Projecting Beirut*, Munich: Prestel.

Rydin, Y., Thornley, A., Scanlon, K. and West, K. (2004) 'The Greater London Authority – a Case of Conflict of Cultures? Evidence from the Planning and Environmental Policy Domains', *Environment and Planning C: Government and Policy*, 22: 55–76.

Saint, A. (ed.) (1989) *Politics and People in London: The LCC 1889–1965*, London: Hambledon Press.

Salet, W., Thornley, A. and Kreukels, A. (eds) (2003) *Metropolitan Governance and Spatial Planning*, London: Spon.

Salet, W. and Faludi, A. (2000) *The Revival of Strategic Spatial Planning*, Amsterdam: Royal Netherlands Academy of Arts and Sciences.

Sassen, S. (2001) *The Global City: New York, London and Tokyo*, Princeton, NJ: Princeton University Press.

Savitch, H. V. (1988) *Post-Industrial Cities*, Princeton, NJ: Princeton University Press.

Self, P. (1971) *Metropolitan Planning*, London: London School of Economics.

Simmie, J. (1974) *Citizens in Conflict: Sociology of Town Planning*, London: Hutchinson.

Simmie, J. (1981) *Power, Property and Corporatism: The Political Sociology of Planning*, London: Macmillan.

Simmie, J. (ed.) (1994) *Planning London*, London: Routledge.

Simmons, M. (2000) 'New London Government and its Spatial Development Strategy', in *Informationen zur Raumentwicklung*, Freiburg: University of Freiburg.

Simon, E. D. (1937) *Moscow in the Making*, London: Longmans.

South London Partnership (2005) *Town and District Centres Benchmarking Project Interim Report*, London: SOA Development and Kingston University for South London Partnership, October.

Summerson, J. (1949) *John Nash: Architect to George IV*, London: Allen and Unwin.

Sutcliffe, A. (1970) *The Autumn of Central Paris: The Defeat of Town Planning 1850–1970*, London: Edward Arnold.

Sutcliffe, A. (1981) *Towards the Planned City: Germany, Britain, the United States and France 1780–1914*, New York: St Martin's Press.

Tewdwr-Jones, M. (2002) *The Planning Polity*, London: Routledge.

Tewdwr-Jones, M. and Allmendinger, P. (2006) *Territory, Identity and Spatial Planning*, London: Routledge.

Thibault, C. (2000) 'Paris–Ile de France: For a Sustainable Environment', in *Informationen zur Raumentwicklung*, Freiburg: University of Freiburg.

Thomas, D. (1970) *London's Green Belt*, London: Faber.

Thornley, A. (ed.) (1992) *The Crisis of London*, London: Routledge.

Thornley, A. (1999) *Urban Planning and Competitive Advantage: London, Sydney and Singapore*. LSE London discussion paper 2, May.

Thornley, A. (2003) 'London: Institutional Turbulence but Enduring Nation-State Control', in Salet, W., Thornley, A. and Kreukels, A. (eds), *Metropolitan Governance and Spatial Planning*, London: Spon.

Thornley, A., Rydin, Y., Scanlon, K. and West, K. (2002) *The Greater London Authority: Interest Representation and the Strategic Agenda*. LSE London discussion paper 8, March.

Thornley, A., Rydin, Y., Scanlon, K. and West, K. (2005) 'Business Privilege in the Strategic Planning Agenda of the GLA', *Urban Studies*, 42 (11): 1947–68.

Travers, T. (2004) *The Politics of London*, London: Palgrave.

Travers, T., Jones, G., Hebbert, M. and Burnham, J. (1991) *The Government of London*, York: Joseph Rowntree Foundation.

Travers, T., Tunstall, R., Whitehead, C. and Provot, S. (2007) *Population Mobility and Service Provision*. Report to London Councils, LSE, February.

United Nations (1987) *Our Common Future: Report of the World Commission on Environment and Development*, Oxford: Oxford University Press.

URBED (2008) *Over the Edge: Town Centres and the London Economy*, London: URBED, October.

Vigar, J., Healey, P., Hull, A. and Davoudi, S. (2000) *Planning, Governance and Spatial Strategy in Britain: An Institutional Analysis*, London: Macmillan.

Walsh, A. H. (1968) *Urban Government in the Paris Region*, New York: Praeger.

Wannop, U. (1995) *The Regional Imperative: Regional Planning and Governance in Britain, Europe and the United States*, London: Jessica Kingsley for the Regional Studies Association.

Webb, A. (ed.) (1921) *London of the Future*, London: Dutton.

Whinney, M. (1971) *Christopher Wren*, London: Thames and Hudson.

West, K., Scanlon, K., Thornley, A. and Rydin, Y. (2002) *The Greater London Authority: Problems of Strategy Co-ordination*. LSE London discussion paper, 7 March.

Wynn, M. (ed.) (1984) *Planning and Urban Growth in Southern Europe*, London: Mansell.

Yaro, R. and Hiss, T. (1996) *A Region at Risk: The Third Regional Plan for the New York–New Jersey–Connecticut Metropolitan Area*, New York: Regional Plan Association.

Young, K. and Garside, P. (1982) *Metropolitan London: Politics and Urban Change 1837–1981*, London: Edward Arnold.

Young, K. and Kramer, J. (1978) *Strategy and Conflict in Metropolitan Housing*, London: Heinemann.

Index

Edwards, M. 221, 229
employment 171–3, 197
energy policy 117
Enfield 102, 153
English Heritage 199
English Partnerships 36–7, 124, 139, 144, 165, 218
Environment Agency 178, 245
equalities appraisal 201–2
ERM consultants 109
ethnic minority groups 200–8
European monetary union 137, 232
European Spatial Development Perspective 8, 11, 25, 207
Euston 193
Evelyn, J. 15
Evening Standard 243
Evenson, N. 13
Eversden, P. 118
evidence base 56
Examination in Public (EIP): 2003 56–60, 66–7; 2006: 116, 119, 122–3, 166; 2007 116

Faludi, A. 10, 222
Federation of Black Housing Organisations 36
fire of London 15
Fisher, M. 62
Fitzpatrick, J. 22
Fitzrovia 179
flooding 177–8
Foley, D. 10
Forshaw, J. H. 16
Future Housing Provision: Speeding up Delivery (2002) 46

Gallions Park 165
Gavron, N. 25, 38, 61, 69, 89, 123, 164, 167, 209, 210–11, 214–15, 217, 226
Geddes, P. 16
general conformity 86–8
geographic information system (GIS) 110
Germany 245
global city rhetoric 62
globalisation 246–7
Golland, A. 45
Gordon, I. 62–3
governance 209–19
Government Office for London (GOL) 7, 22, 32, 36–7, 58–60, 64–6, 68, 70, 87–8, 90 116, 125, 138–9, 153–4, 209, 225, 241
Greater London Authority Act (1999) 7, 24–9, 87, 225

Greater London Authority Act (2007) 24, 27, 120, 125, 127, 198, 217–19, 222, 238, 242
Greater London Council (GLC) 6, 18–20, 28–9, 200, 209, 221, 223
Greater London Development Plan (1969–76) 18–19, 61
Greater London Development Plan Review (1981–4) 19, 61
Greater London group (LSE) 69
Greater London Plan (1944) 16, 61
Greater London Regional Planning Committee 15–16
green belt 6, 16, 69, 110, 177, 198, 223, 238
Green Belt (London and Home Counties) Act (1938) 16
Green party 25, 214
Greenwich 87, 103, 113, 144, 179, 204, 213
Greenwich millennium village 235
Gross, J. 12
Growing Together (2005) 176
Gummer, J. 22

Hackney 153, 204
Hall, P. 12, 44, 67, 166, 229, 245–6
Hall, T. 13
Hambleton, R. 12
Hammersmith and Fulham 102, 179, 203–4
Hamwee, S. 21, 38
Haringey 109, 153, 170, 204, 213
Harloe, M. 12
Harris, T. 213–14, 226
Harrow 87, 102, 203–4
Hart, D. 11
Harvey, D. 8–9, 13, 221
Hawthorn, D. 231
Havering 88, 90, 99, 103, 143, 170, 204
Hays, F. 13
Healey, P. 9, 11
health facilities 148–52, 188, 197, 244
Heathrow airport 133, 221
Hebbert, M. 11
Herbert Commission 18
Herrschel, T. 13
Heseltine, M. 9
Higgins, D. 147
high-rise 99–100, 233
higher education 148–52
Hilditch, S. 25, 241
Hill, K. 22, 209
Hillier, M. 35
Hillingdon 102